NARRATIVES OF TRAVEL AND TOURISM

T0304298

Current Developments in the Geographies of Leisure and Tourism

Series Editors:

Jan Mosedale, University of Sunderland, UK and **Caroline Scarles**, University of Surrey, UK in association with the Geographies of Leisure and Tourism Research Group of the Royal Geographical Society (with the Institute of British Geographers).

Tourism and leisure exist within an inherently dynamic, fluid and complex world and are therefore inherently interdisciplinary. Recognising the role of tourism and leisure in advancing debates within the social sciences, this book series, is open to contributions from cognate social science disciplines that inform geographical thought about tourism and leisure. Produced in association with the Geographies of Leisure and Tourism Research Group of the Royal Geographical Society (with the Institute of British Geographers), this series highlights and promotes cutting-edge developments and research in this field. Contributions are of a high international standard and provide theoretically-informed empirical content to facilitate the development of new research agendas in the field of tourism and leisure research. In general, the series seeks to promote academic contributions that advance contemporary debates that challenge and stimulate further discussion and research both within the fields of tourism and leisure and the wider realms of the social sciences.

Narratives of Travel and Tourism

Edited by

JACQUELINE TIVERS

and

TIJANA RAKIĆ

Routledge
Taylor & Francis Group

LONDON AND NEW YORK

First published 2012 by Ashgate Publishing

2 Park Square, Milton Park, Abingdon, Oxon OX14 4RN
711 Third Avenue, New York, NY 10017, USA

Routledge is an imprint of the Taylor & Francis Group, an informa business

First issued in paperback 2016

British Library Cataloguing in Publication Data
Narratives of travel and tourism. – (Current developments in the geographies of leisure and tourism)
    1. Travelers' writings – History and criticism. 2. Voyages and travels – History – Sources. 3. Travel in literature. 4. Tourism in literature.
    I. Series II. Tivers, Jacqueline. III. Rakić, Tijana.
    910.4–dc23

Library of Congress Cataloging-in-Publication Data
Narratives of travel and tourism / edited by Jacqueline Tivers and Tijana Rakić .
    p. cm. – (Current developments in the geographies of leisure and tourism)
    Includes bibliographical references and index.
    ISBN 978–1–4094–3974–5 (hardback : alk. paper)
    1. Tourism – Philosophy. 2. Voyages and travels.
    I. Tivers, Jacqueline. II. Rakić, Tijana.
    G155.A1N36 2012
    910.401–dc23   2011046427

ISBN 978-1-4094-3974-5 (hbk)
ISBN 978-1-138-25020-8 (pbk)

The editors would like to dedicate this book to their families

Contents

List of Figures

List of Tables

Notes on Contributors

David Botterill is a Freelance Academic and Higher Education Consultant, Visiting Research Fellow at the Centre for Tourism at the University of Westminster and Professor Emeritus in the Welsh Centre for Tourism Research, University of Wales Institute Cardiff, UK. He has published extensively in the area of tourism and leisure studies.

Paul Cleave is a Freelance Researcher and Lecturer with academic interests in food and social history, tourism and hospitality education. He is currently investigating the evolving relationships between food and tourism in the twentieth century.

Sylvie Guichard-Anguis is a Researcher at the French National Centre of Scientific Research (CNRS) at the University Paris-Sorbonne whose academic research as a geographer and japonologist focuses on cultural heritage, travel, tourism and tea culture in Japan.

Lénia Marques is a Researcher at the CEMRI (Universidade Aberta), Lisbon, Portugal. Her current research focuses on Comparative Literature (Travel Writing and Arts) and on Cultural Tourism.

Chaim Noy is a Senior Lecturer at the Sapir College, Israel. His fields of interest include performance studies, narrative, discourse and semiotics, mobility, masculinity, and qualitative and experimental research methods.

Emmanuelle Peraldo is a Senior Lecturer in British eighteenth-century literature at the Université Jean-Monnet, Saint-Etienne, France. She is a member of the CELEC (Centre d'Etudes sur les Littératures Etrangères et Comparées) and has published a book titled *Defoe et l'écriture de l'histoire*.

Maria Sofia Pimentel Biscaia is a Researcher at the University of Aveiro, Portugal. At present she is working on the project *Terminological Dictionary of Postcolonial Literary Terms* in collaboration with the University of Roskilde.

Tijana Rakić is a Lecturer in Tourism and Events and Deputy Postgraduate Tourism Programmes Leader at Edinburgh Napier University, UK. Her research interests include visual research methodologies, ethnography, visual culture, world heritage, tourism and national identity.

Pamela Richardson is an Honorary Fellow of Exeter University, UK, where she was awarded her doctorate in 2007. She has published one book and several articles and her second book is scheduled for 2012.

Angharad Saunders is a Senior Lecturer in Human Geography at the University of Glamorgan, UK. Her research interests focus on the historical geographies of British literature in the period 1840–1940.

Jacqueline Tivers is an independent scholar, having retired from Nottingham Trent University, where she was formerly a Senior Lecturer in Human Geography. She was chair of the Geography of Leisure and Tourism Research Group of RGS-IBG from 2005 to 2009 and has contributed to research on tourism, gender, sport and cultural geography.

Kathryn Wilkins has recently completed her PhD in Geography at Durham University, UK. Her contribution is based on her postgraduate research.

Acknowledgments

The editors would like to thank the Royal Geographical Society with the Institute of British Geographers (RGS-IBG) for hosting the *Narrating the Stories of Travel and Tourism* conference session at the 2010 Annual Conference in London, which formed the basis of the proposal for this book, as well as the Geography of Leisure and Tourism Research Group (GLTRG) and the Historical Geography Research Group (HGRG) for sponsoring that session. We would also like to thank all those who have contributed in any way, both to the book itself and also to the conference session.

Chapter 1

Introducing the Narratives
of Travel and Tourism

Jacqueline Tivers and Tijana Rakić

Travel and tourism 'stories' have been told and recorded in almost every culture and period of oral and written history and across the breadth of the fact/fiction continuum; in fact, 'storytelling is an essential part of human nature' (McCabe and Foster 2006: 194) and narration, in its many forms, may be seen to lie at the very heart of both travel and tourism (Bendix 2002). Given the 'frightening vastness' (Fabian 2001: 3) of travel and tourism narratives, it is understandable that different scholars tend to approach this subject from different [inter] disciplinary perspectives and focus on a number of different thematic areas. Many researchers have studied 'travel writing', thus contributing to the development of a considerable body of knowledge about this particular element of tourism and travel narratives (for example, see Campbell 1988, Mills 1991, Holland and Huggan 2000, Smith 2001, Lisle 2006, Pratt 2008). Other scholars have focused on travel and tourism stories told during various stages of travel (for example, Elsrud 2001, Bruner 2005, Tucker 2005, McCabe and Foster 2006, Noy 2004, Noy 2007), while others have studied narratives of places, cultures, and travel and/or tourism contained in popular media such as guidebooks, online travel videos, and even operas (for example, Beck 2006, Tussyadiah and Fesenmaier 2009, Botterill this volume).

Existing research has indicated that narratives of travel and tourism are not only an essential ingredient in the construction of personal, collective and place identities but are also important in the process of contemplating, experiencing, remembering and disseminating travel and tourism experiences, both factual and fictional. Although written or spoken narratives tend to be the main focus within many existing studies, it was interesting to note that a number of the papers presented to the *Narrating the Stories of Travel and Tourism* conference session at the RGS-IBG Annual Conference in 2010 (see Tivers and Rakić 2010), many of which are included in an expanded form as chapters in this book, also mentioned the importance while 'away from home' both of collecting memorabilia and of image making (such as drawing, painting and photographing) in the recording, remembering, writing, telling and/or disseminating of stories about travel and tourism experiences.

However, the aim of this introductory chapter, and of the volume as a whole, is not to offer a comprehensive overview of existing, historical and contemporary, academic research about narratives of travel and tourism but, rather, to build on this research by contributing to scholarly discussions surrounding the narratives of travel and tourism (see, for example, Robertson et al. 1994; Meethan et al. 2006) by presenting papers that both include and move beyond the fascinating theme of travel writing, as well as addressing the subject through various relevant 'lenses' and in relation to different contexts. While the book is divided into two sections, inevitably there are some overlaps between the contents of chapters in these sections. In Part I, the principal focus is on travellers/tourists and their narratives, covering a range of different places, while the chapters in Part II focus on specific places and discuss how these have been presented through narratives of travel and tourism. Within each of the two parts the chapters are ordered, so far as this is possible, both thematically and chronologically. This being the case, the book may be read both cover-to-cover and also selectively, depending on the preferences and interests of its readers.

Part I begins with the chapter by Kathryn Wilkins. This introduces us, through a consideration of unpublished narrative accounts, to the 'London Season', the phenomenon that reached its height in the English Victorian period, comprising a series of events designed to enable social mixing and an opportunity for members of the British 'elite' to secure advantageous marriage alliances. She demonstrates how travel formed an integral and necessary part of the Season, both in terms of travel to and from the capital and in terms of the large amounts of daily travel, of a performative as well as of a functional nature, which took place within central London. The chapter provides a detailed reading of the diary kept by a certain Louisa Smythe, as well as reference to other diary accounts, emphasis being placed on Louisa's courtship and marriage settlement and the journeys made, by her and others, which contributed so importantly to her future life and status.

The next three chapters take as their starting point a number of unpublished holiday diaries, written by travellers from the late Victorian period to the second half of the twentieth century. In Chapter 3, Pamela Richardson presents the travel journals of the Fox family, which span the period 1895 to 1945, suggesting that such narratives add a different, more domestic dimension to the genre of travel writing. She tells us that the Foxes were a wealthy Quaker family, passionate travellers who recorded their journeys and experiences in fascinating detail, reflecting on the places visited, the people met and the modes of transport used. Richardson analyses the rich narrative contained in these journals, providing evidence for the motivations that lay behind the journeys made and for the use of varied transport technologies in different times and places. She also considers the ways in which pictorial images and memorabilia were used in the journals to supplement, or replace, written narrative.

In the following chapter Paul Cleave presents findings from a study of four contrasting personal travel records, written between 1936 and 1943. Like the narratives analysed by Richardson, these are unpublished journals of English origin, but not in this case written by members of the same family. They cover a broad spectrum of travel and tourism experience, from a pre-Second World War

'Grand Tour' of Asia and North America to a wartime holiday visiting friends in Devon, south-west England. Cleave demonstrates how the accounts reflect both the existing social structures of the period and the world as seen and recorded by the writers. He identifies five major themes from the diaries: travel routines; people encountered; food and drink; world events; and place experience and activities. Like Richardson, he notes the importance to the diarists of photographs and souvenirs, used to evoke memories of places and relationships. Cleave concludes that the analysis of personal narratives is invaluable in aiding the understanding of a specific period in the history of tourism.

Chapter 5, by Jacqueline Tivers, is also based on an analysis of unpublished, personal travel accounts, these being the 59 'holiday books' of one man (the author's father), written over a period of 60 years from 1937 to 1996 as records of 'ordinary English family' holidays. Tivers first outlines the detailed content of the books, their integration of words and images, the vital importance of the journeys themselves as part of the holidays, the focus on historic places, the author's need always to take independent control of activities and arrangements, the relationships within the travelling groups and the methodical approach taken to the recording of experiences. She then goes on to consider the contexts within which the narratives were written – the national, family and tourism contexts – and finally attempts to uncover the motivations that lay behind the assiduous documentation of tourism experiences by one man throughout his adult lifetime.

Moving away from analyses of unpublished narratives, Lenia Marques and Maria Sofia Pimentel Biscaia reflect in Chapter 6 on the links between tourism and travelling and the emotional framework that underlay the thoughts and impressions of Nicolas Bouvier, a Swiss travel writer and photographer, whose works cover the second half of the twentieth century. As a published travel writer, he based his narratives on correspondence, notes, observations and pictures, his best known works being *The Way of the World* and *Nomad*, which record his travels in 1953. Marques and Biscaia analyse Bouvier's work, not only as travel literature but also as illustrative of the relationship between tourism and travel. They portray Bouvier as, in essence, a 'traveller', but one who respected late twentieth century developments in cultural niche tourism and motivated others to be travellers and tourists through reading his narratives.

To conclude Part I of the book, David Botterill in his chapter opens up an unusual theme, as he considers the representations of tourism within twentieth-century opera. In the 38 operas selected for analysis, he identifies tropes that are consistent with, and supportive of, dominant narratives found within the tourism studies academy; those of exploration, wandering, opulence and spectacle. However, he also finds within the operas considerable evidence of counter-narratives, themes embodying transgression, inversion and vulnerability that challenge the dominant view of tourism. Botterill suggests that tourism studies should be at least as concerned as opera narratives with the emotional responses of travellers and tourists and with the potential for deception and chaos to be found within tourism.

The chapters in Part II of this book consider specific narratives of places in travel and tourism. First, in Chapter 8, Emmanuelle Peraldo looks at Daniel Defoe's representation of Britain in his *Tour thro' the whole island of Great-Britain (1724–26)*, which was presented in the form of 13 letters containing maps, tables, drawings and lists as well as written narrative. Peraldo shows how Defoe used his combined literary and geographical skills to rework space and produce an imaginative narrative of the nation in the early eighteenth century. She also indicates how his work exemplified the human and power relationships of the time, being produced with the ulterior motive of promoting trade and commerce through the creation of a positive national image.

Moving on to the nineteenth century and across the Irish Sea, Angharad Saunders next writes about Ireland, as seen and described by Anthony Trollope, the novelist and traveller who became part of Anglo-Irish society in the 1840s and 1850s. Saunders presents us with Trollope's dilemma; how to write a narrative that was true to the reality of place, but at the same time to produce a work of fiction that could be accepted for publication in England and depend on an English readership. She reminds us that novels are rarely considered as pieces of travel writing and yet they may depend for their veracity on a prior experience of extensive travelling and provide a descriptive narrative of place to be set alongside more traditional travel accounts.

In Chapter 10, Sylvie Guichard-Anguis moves us away from the world of Western travel and tourism narratives, to introduce the Kumano region of Japan and its ancient pilgrimage roads and sacred sites, set within the Kii mountain range. Her chapter speaks of the travelogues written about these roads for more than a thousand years that now provide insight into the nature of the environment at different periods in the past, the people who walked the routes and the activities they undertook as part of their journeys. She compares and contrasts the contents of these narratives, produced at various times since the tenth century and includes three dating from the twenty-first century. Her intention is to illustrate, through a consideration of these travel narratives, how memory is both created and preserved within Japanese travel culture.

From a consideration of pilgrim narratives in Japan, Chaim Noy takes us, in the next chapter, to a different type of 'pilgrimage' site; that of Ein Karem, a suburb of Jerusalem that was once a Palestinian village but is now occupied by Israeli residents. In contrast to the 'standard' tour of 'Mary's Spring' offered to overseas Christian pilgrims/tourists, Noy writes about two tours, provided primarily for liberal Israeli visitors during an event in 2009 instituted by a group of experimental artists; the first tour led by a Palestinian who used to live in the village and the second, by a Jewish environmentalist. Noy indicates how differently the place was narrated, depending on the perspective of the narrator, and identifies clearly that tourism narratives of place may have a strongly ideological, as well as an educational, function.

Finally, in Chapter 12, Tijana Rakić explores place narratives of the Athenian Acropolis, an important site believed to symbolise UNESCO's World Heritage idea and also to embody the Greek nation, within a selection of contemporary travel guidebooks. While relying on semiotic analyses of Acropolis-relevant texts and images, Rakić pays particular attention to the narratives of national versus 'universal' belonging that its World Heritage status intends to convey. She notes that only a few of these guidebooks have mentioned its World Heritage status and thus she reveals numerous tensions between the national and 'universal' belonging of the Acropolis. She concludes that in these guidebooks the narratives about the Acropolis have been marked primarily by their descriptions of the Acropolis as a global tourist attraction that both represents and belongs to Greece, rather than the world.

References

Beck, W. 2006. Narratives of World Heritage in Travel Guidebooks. *International Journal of Heritage Studies*, 12(6), 521–35.

Bendix, R. 2002. Capitalizing on Memories Past, Present, and Future: Observations on the Intertwining of Tourism and Narration. *Anthropological Theory*, 2(4), 469–87.

Blanton, C. 2002. *Travel Writing: The Self and the World*. London: Routledge.

Bruner, E.M. 2005. *The Role of Narrative in Tourism*. Conference paper presented at the On Voyage: New Directions in Tourism Theory Conference, Berkeley, October 7–8. Available at www.nyu.edu/classes/bkg/tourist/narrative.doc [accessed: 10 January 2010].

Campbell, M.B. 1988. *The Witness and the Other World: Exotic European Travel Writing, 400–1600*. Ithaca and London: Cornell University Press.

Elsrud, T. 2001. Risk Creation When Travelling: Backpacker Adventure Narration. *Annals of Tourism Research*, 28(3), 591–617.

Fabian, J. 2001. Time, Narration, and the Exploration of Central Africa. *Narrative*, 9(1), 3–20.

Holland, P. and Huggan, G. 2000. *Tourists with Typewriters: Critical Reflections on Contemporary Travel Writing*. USA: University of Michigan Press.

Leask, N. 2002. *Curiosity and the Aesthetics of Travel Writing 1770–1840*. Oxford: Oxford University Press.

Lisle, D. 2006. *The Global Politics of Contemporary Travel Writing*. Cambridge: Cambridge University Press.

McCabe, S. and Foster, C. 2006. The Role and Function of Narrative in Tourist Interaction, *Tourism and Cultural Change*, 4(3), 194–215.

Meethan, K., Anderson, A. and Miles, S. (eds). 2006. *Tourism, Consumption and Representation: Narratives of Place and Self*. Wallingford: CABI.

Mills, S. 1991. *Discourses of Difference: an Analysis of Women's Travel Writing and Colonialism*. London: Routledge.

Noy, C. 2004. This Trip Really Changed Me: Backpackers' Narratives of Self-Change *Annals of Tourism Research*, 31(1), 78–102.

Noy, C. 2007. *A Narrative Community: Voices of Israeli backpackers*. Detroit: Wayne State University.

Pratt, M.L. 2008. *Imperial Eyes: Travel Writing and Transculturation*. London: Routledge.

Robertson, G., Mash, M., Tickner, L., Bird, J., Curtis, B. and Putnam, T. (eds). 1994. *Traveller's Tales: Narratives of Home and Displacement*. London: Routledge.

Smith, S. 2001. *Moving Lives: Twentieth-Century Women's Travel Writing*. Minneapolis: University of Minnesota Press.

Tivers, J. and Rakić, T. 2010. *Narrating the Stories of Travel and Tourism Conference Session* at the Royal Geographical Society with Institute of British Geographers Annual Conference, London, 1–3 September.

Tucker, H. 2005. Narratives of Place and Self: Differing Experiences of Package Coach Tours in New Zealand. *Tourist Studies*, 5(3), 267–82.

Tussyadiah, I. and Fesenmaier, D. 2009. Mediating Tourist Experiences: Access to Places via Shared Videos. *Annals of Tourism Research*, 36(1), 24–40.

PART I
Travellers and their Narratives

Chapter 2

Travel Narratives of the Victorian Elite: The Case of the London Season

Kathryn Wilkins

Introduction

In May 1827 Mrs Walter Smythe, a widow aged forty-nine, arrived in London from her home in Brighton. She was accompanied by her two daughters, sixteen year old Louisa and twelve year old Georgina. Stepping onto the pavement of Great Cumberland Place, Mrs Smythe came face to face with the townhouse she had rented for their three month's stay in the capital. Renting in Great Cumberland Place, close to the 'bon air of the park', had stretched the family's dwindling financial resources. On 13th May, Louisa, chaperoned by her mother, travelled to a grand ball hosted by the 'formidable' Lady Salisbury, where she danced the Quadrille for the first time: she was officially 'out' in Society. For the three months that followed, Louisa was engaged in the whirl of socialising that characterised the West End during the period. She attended concerts and dinner parties, dressed in gowns designed to exude wealth, and danced with eligible suitors in crowded ballrooms. During the day, she rode along Rotten Row in Hyde Park in one of the family's two carriages accompanied by her aunt Maria Fitzherbert, the secret wife of King George IV (Irvine 2005). In the afternoon she gossiped with her aristocratic and titled friends, plotting the capture of a suitable husband at the next ball or private party.

Louisa's life in London was mirrored by thousands of other debutantes and their families, each a component part of the 'London Season'. In this chapter the Season is explored through an engagement with the travel practices occurring during the period. This marks a departure from much existing research in the field, in which the importance of travel is rarely discussed. In particular, the chapter discusses the way in which travel formed an integral and necessary part of the Season. Through the use of narrative accounts, written during the Season, it is possible to identify the appropriate means through which mobility was undertaken and consequently explore the use of travel by the elite as a means for the display of wealth and status during the period. Travel narratives are also used to shed light on the motivations behind participation in the Season, undertaken through a detailed reading of the narrative accounts of Louisa Smythe. Through these accounts, it is possible to uncover the often unwritten rules and activities of the Season, understanding in greater detail how the Season operated.

The London Season

The Season was an annual phenomenon, which saw elite[1] families in Society travel to the West End of London between May and July[2] to participate in a hectic round of social engagements. Whilst traces of the Season can be found in earlier decades, the period began in earnest in the eighteenth century, growing to greatest popularity during the reign of Queen Victoria (1837–1901). This increase in scale is attributable both to the loosening of the strict rules of social acceptability, which allowed wealthy industrialists also to participate during the latter part of the nineteenth century, and to the increased survival of members of the aristocracy, thanks to advances in medical care (Davidoff 1973, Beckett 1986).

The Season is difficult to summarise in its many forms and facets, Thompson (1963: 104) has, however, offered a useful description:

> This was the world of politics and high society, of attendance at the House and gaming in the clubs, the place where wagers were laid and race meetings arranged, the source of fashion in dress and taste in art, as well as being the world of drawing rooms and levees, glittering entertainments and extravaganzas, soirées, balls and operas.

Events such as balls, court presentations, concerts, dinner parties and appearances at artistic and cultural exhibitions were purposefully designed to allow for social mixing and congregation. Marriage, in particular, provided those at the apex of the social pyramid with the opportunity to renew social positions, to select a new member of their family based upon reputation, wealth and landholdings, and hence was the reason why the Season as a 'marriage market' became a useful tool for the elite. The importance of securing an advantageous marriage is demonstrated best by rumours circulating in 1876 that the American, William Vanderbilt, had spent $10,000,000 on securing his daughter Consuelo's marriage to the Marlborough dukedom (Abbott 1993). The expected standard of living for those participating in the Season was high; displays of wealth were seen to be crucial in forging alliances. Earl Fitzwilliam spent £3,000 on entertaining guests during the 1810

---

1   In this chapter, the term 'elite' is used to encompass all those participating in the Season. However, it is necessary to appreciate that there were differences in the wealth, title and land ownership of families in Britain and this was reflected in the varied experiences of the Season witnessed. It is possible to divide elite participants into three groups: those with landed wealth comprising the traditional aristocracy; those with money amassed from entrepreneurship and commerce whose wealth gradually led to their acceptance in elite circles; and the minor gentry comprising upwardly-mobile professional people.

2   The exact timing of the Season was never fixed, and fluctuated according to the timing of individual events occurring each year. As a rule, the months of May to July were typically the busiest in terms of both the number of participants and the number of organised events they were invited to attend.

Season alone, a figure dwarfed by the Duke of Northumberland in 1840, who spent over £20,000 (Sheppard 1971).

The majority of families attending would rent a townhouse in London's West End for the summer months. The urban spaces occupied by participants of the Season were relatively confined, bounded by Oxford Street to the north and Westminster in the south and from Kensington in the west to Piccadilly in the east (Evans and Evans 1976, Picard 2005). Participants resided, socialised, shopped, entertained and travelled within this area of the West End, only leaving it to attend infrequent events outside the capital.

Investigating Travel in the Context of the Season

Much existing literature regarding the Season describes the events which occurred in a general manner (Sproule 1978, Margetson 1980), using sources such as newspapers and periodicals, court directories, rate books and Census data. Whist these sources are useful in depicting long-term trends in the Season, it is possible to understand the period more comprehensively by drawing upon additional resources. Literature reviews tend to omit the importance of travel to the very existence of the Season but, without the ability to travel to London, participants could not have congregated in the capital. Likewise, the frenetic round of social networking for which the Season was designed could not have occurred without the means to travel quickly between events. To counter this gap in knowledge, this chapter responds to calls from within historical geography to utilise biographical sources to provide narrative accounts of the Season (Graham and Nash 2000). The turn to agency-centred research in this field has led to the increased utilisation of qualitative sources, which have significantly influenced the way in which knowledge is uncovered. The opinions and lived-experiences of those living in the past have been championed as a means by which marginalised aspects of history can be brought to the fore. In particular, scholars such as Blunt (2000), in relation to the domestic sphere during the Indian siege of the Lucknow Residency, and McDowell (2004), regarding Latvian women's experiences of war-time Europe, have suggested that broad historical situations can be approached at greater depth using biographical narratives.

In order to uncover information concerning the significance of travel during the Season, the narrative approach proposed by Blunt (2000) and others such as Ogborn (2002) has been adopted in this chapter. A selection of narratives has been chosen, based on the level of detail contained in the accounts. These range from the recollections of footman Frederick John Gorst to the daily accounts written by the debutante Louisa Smythe, niece of Maria Fitzherbert. In each case, information has been extracted in order to analyse the importance of travel to those taking part in the Season.

Frequency of Travel during the Season

As noted above, whilst literature regarding the Season has frequently discussed the importance of attendance at events during the period, the means by which such attendance was manifested has received far less attention. This travel must be contextualised. Whilst the growth of the British Empire signalled extensive transnational movements for some (see Magee and Thompson 2010), mobility for the majority during the early stages of the nineteenth century was limited to the local area. In London much travel was completed on foot and it was only with the advent of the horse-drawn tram in 1870 that travel became affordable for the majority of citizens (Pooley and Turnbull 1997, Jackson 2004). Within the context of this relative immobility, the journeys made by those participating in the Season are significant and uncharacteristic of society as a whole. Within this elite group, however, movement on this scale was treated as the norm, as can be witnessed through the use of narrative accounts.

The initial, and longest, journeys that occurred during the Season were those thousands undertaken by participants in migrating temporarily to London in April or May from their country estates in disparate localities across the country, or in some cases, abroad (Sproule 1978, Margetson 1980, Horn 1992). The Marchioness of Bath documented that when her family moved to their house in Berkeley Square for the Season, it was usual to require eleven horses to transport them with the help of seventeen servants (Thynne 1951). This migration would have required a great deal of planning with the family reliant upon domestic staff to facilitate the move. Davidoff (1973) noted that, in many cases, head servants were sent on ahead of the family group to make arrangements prior to travel and to assist in the mechanics of moving. Lady Carrington's diary supports this assertion, giving no hint of the effort involved but rather suggesting the ease with which movement occurred: 'the servants started for London by an early train and we followed' (11th May 1878). The task of migrating an entire family and staff from one region of the country to another must have been a significant one, yet the calm reflections of the narratives above reveal this to have been of little concern to those travelling.

Narrative accounts add further details of travel once a family had arrived in London and were participating in the Season. It is here that evidence of the full extent of this travel can be found. Using the diary of Mary Gladstone, who documented in detail the events of each day (Masterman 1930), it is possible to uncover the volume of journeys made during the Season. On 14th March 1883[3] Mary made sixteen separate journeys. Whilst several of these were made between her home in Downing Street (Mary's father was Prime Minister William Gladstone) and Parliament Square, or to visit her family in either Great George Street or Carlton House Terrace, both nearby streets, the vast majority of her daily travel was spread over larger distances. She paid a call in Grosvenor Square (2.5

---

3 Note that by 1883 the expansion of the Season had led to the stretching of the period. The events of the Season were already underway by the 14th March in that year.

km away), visited a friend in Portugal Street (1.8 km away) and was a member of the audience at the Royal Albert Hall (4.4 km away). In total, she travelled roughly 21 km on 14th March, with all journeys undertaken between addresses in west London. The level of movement displayed in Mary Gladstone's daily diary entries is mirrored regularly in accounts of the Season. Such narratives illustrate that the period was characterised by the continual movement of its participants. The analysis of narrative accounts reveals clearly the importance of travel in the daily lives of those taking part in the Season. It reveals that during the nineteenth century, this societal group relied upon the ability to travel frequently. Travel was an important and necessary component of the Season.

Importance of Appropriate Travel

The extensive movements made by those participating in the Season may, however, be further examined. During the Season, Society leaders dictated that the acceptable form of travel was via private carriage, pulled by horses (as recommended in etiquette books such as *Modern Etiquette in Public and Private* 1871). Even as technological developments signalled the rise in public transport, in the form of the horse tram, the underground railway and the extensions in omnibus routes, those participating in the Season maintained a reliance upon the private horse and carriage (Taylor 2001). Wildeblood, in a discussion of clothing, declared that: 'the lady's visiting-dress was synonymous with her carriage-dress, for no lady would entertain the notion of walking' (1965: 172). The ability to travel privately and independently was a marker of wealth and status during the period, as illustrated by Nicholson's interpretation of the diaries of Marion Sambourne: 'Owning a carriage was a definite step up in the social scale and Marion made a point of using it when she went to her grand dressmaker' (1988: 73–4). Constance Battersea recollected a similar use for the carriage, describing the drive to Court presentation as having taken place in the family's 'grand chariot' (Battersea 1922: 108–9). This use of a carriage as a marker of status can also be witnessed through the character of George Osborne in Vanity Fair, who remarked: 'My father's a gentleman, and keeps his carriage' (Thackeray 1848: 25). Those participating in the Season were not merely frequent travellers; they were frequent travellers in very specific ways. These narrative accounts illustrate the reliance upon one 'appropriate' method of travelling, further contextualising the period.

This desire to travel in a carriage during the Season is illustrated best through the example of traffic congestion. The road network in West London during the nineteenth century was not designed for the influx of many thousands of carriages which required access to them on a daily basis during the Season, as illustrated by Thomas Rowlandson's cartoon in Figure 2.1 below.

Biographical sources reveal the regular occurrence of traffic jams. Dowager Lady Leconfield recalled the difficulties in moving in *The Times:* 'Let no one suppose that our progress through the streets was unimpeded. When I read in

Figure 2.1   The Miseries of London by Thomas Rowlandson (Source: reproduced with permission from City of London, London Metropolitan Archives)

the papers now about the traffic problem, I remember the half hours we often spent in trying to get round Hyde Park Corner' (25th October 1930). What is most significant about narratives of traffic congestion, however, is that in no example do the passengers in the carriages continue their journey on foot. Such was the desire to arrive in the socially acceptable mode of transport that families would wait in the vehicle for hours, even when their desired location was just metres away. William Tayler, a footmen who rode aboard a family carriage (Wise 1998), recalled that a traffic jam was so extreme one evening that: 'Women was plentifull [*sic*], some screaming murder, others calling police, some fainting. There was such a kick up as never I saw in my life before. I went out at nine o'clock and got back at eleven. In that time I did not get more than half a mile' (24th May 1837). These accounts reveal that not only was the Season characterised by extensive travel but also that this travel had to conform to specific criteria, with movement used as a marker of social acceptability.

Travel as an Act of Display

Narrative accounts of travel also point to the specific use of travelling as an act of display during the Season. The carriages used throughout the period were ordered by families to specific and individual specifications. Many were emblazoned with the family crest which acted as a mobile advertising board during the Season (Sidney 1873). The horses which pulled the carriages were also subject to scrutiny. Huggett (1979) declared that one grey haired lady, who favoured grey clothing, requested a horse of exactly the same shade of grey as her hair so that, not only would she match the horse but any hairs blown back onto her whilst the animal was moving would blend in with her appearance unnoticed. Narrative accounts reveal the footmen who travelled on the carriages with family members were subject to similar scrutiny whilst on duty. Frederick John Gorst recollected his preparations for a new post as Lady Howard's travelling footman:

> The next morning I had my first lesson in powdering my hair. It began with a shampoo and when I had soaped my hair thoroughly, instead of rinsing the soap away, I felt it on my scalp and parted my hair neatly on the side. Then Trowbridge took a big, thick, powder puff and doused my hair with the 'violet powder' until it formed a pasty coating. After it had dried, my head seemed to be covered in a white wig. I found it a bit of a shock to look at myself in the glass and see how I had aged in ten minutes! Of course the purpose of the headdress was to have all the footmen look as much alike as possible and to create a picture of uniformity when we served together.
>
> (Gorst and Andrews 1956: 88)

Whilst these accounts clearly reveal the desire for travelling vehicles and staff to display the correct image required by the family, the display potential of travel reached its greatest prominence along Rotten Row in Hyde Park. It was here that carriage rides took place three times daily during the Season, a spectacle of promenading carriages and horses, whose occupants attended in the hope of spotting an advantageous connection and being 'seen' participating in the elite activity. The art of movement was used by those in Rotten Row as a form of social dance, a scripted act of travel performed by all those present in the hope of meeting the gaze of a potential contact. The display potential of these movements was witnessed by Percy Colson, a social commentator in the late nineteenth century:

> In the afternoon it was de rigueur to drive on the Knightsbridge side of the Park. There the carriageway would present an almost solid phalanx of victorias, barouches and landaus, all with coachmen and footmen, many of them powdered. In them sat elaborately dressed and coiffured women and their daughters, les jeunes filles á marier. Up and down they drove for the regulation number of turns, bowing to their friends and trying to look as if they were enjoying themselves.

Women not quite in the swim trying to look as if they were; in the seventh
heaven if someone belonging to the inner circle gave them a careless half-bow.

(Colson 1945: 22)

This recollection confirms clearly the importance of travel in this particular space
during the Season as part of an act of performance, a display of attendance designed
to advertise the family to potential suitors or powerful connections. This is an
important facet of the period, positioning Hyde Park as central in the activities
of the Season for much of the nineteenth century, and once again confirming the
central position of travel during the Season.

The Travel Narratives of Louisa Smythe

Narrative accounts of travel during the Season have an additional value. As well
as illuminating the amount and type of travel occurring during the period, they
also help to explain the reasons behind travel to specific events. The analysis
and comparison of the different experiences reveals differences in the enjoyment
of, and motivation for, travel. They show that the period was not experienced
in a uniform manner, but must instead be appreciated as a complex process.
Different participants were clearly engaged in travel for different reasons and with
contrasting experiences.

Thus far, travel narratives have been shown to be useful in documenting the
micro-scale activities of the period, providing details often lacking in previous
accounts (Davidoff 1973, Horn 1992). One specific 'story of the Season' will
now be used to illustrate the multi-dimensional nature of the period, a story told
through the experience of Louisa Smythe, the debutante introduced at the start of
this chapter. Louisa's family was a small one and, following her father's death, also
one which suffered from financial insecurity. Outside the Season, the family lived
in Brighton close to their Aunt, Maria Fitzherbert, the secret wife of George IV
and their late father's sister. Whilst immensely popular in Brighton and powerful
there as a hostess at the Brighton Almacks, at a time when the city was a popular
winter destination for aristocratic families (Irvine 2005), Maria's reputation was
not favourable in London. Her affair with the King had spanned decades and,
although their marriage was largely kept secret from Society to protect his royal
position,[4] many were still distrustful of her and embarrassed by the problems she
had caused (Irvine 2005). Reputation was vitally important to those participating
in the Season and upholding Society etiquette and morals was normally essential
for social acceptability. Despite this negative reputation, Aunt Fitz (as the Smythes

---

4   The marriage between the Prince of Wales and Maria Fitzherbert was kept secret
owing to Maria's situation in life; she held no title, but more significantly she was a
Catholic, so a public declaration of the marriage would have led to a constitutional crisis
(Irvine 2005).

Figure 2.2　Louisa Smythe by James Holmes (Source: originally published in Buckle 1958, reproduced with permission)

called her) was financially secure; she was still receiving an allowance from the King of £10,000 per year (Buckle 1958), money she invested, in part, in the Seasons of her nieces. This colourful family connection was balanced by Louisa's cousin Minney, known to them as Aunt Minney. Adopted by Maria Fitzherbert as a baby, when her mother, a mutual friend of both Maria and George IV, died, she had maintained close links to royalty throughout her childhood and into adulthood, granting her invitations to the most exclusive events of the Season. Minney was influential in the lives of the Smythe girls, a useful chaperone and a popular lady. This connection would have been useful to them, for it is evident in the diaries of both sisters that they were distrustful of their mother, who was said to have been socially 'pushy' and often drunk (Buckle 1958).

Louisa's early experiences of the Season point to the existence of a tiered Society with popular and well-connected families, participating in the traditional manner depicted by Worsely-Gough (1952), accompanied by families on the fringes who found the experience more challenging. It is clear that Louisa struggled to receive invitations to events, as travel to entertainments is rarely documented by her ('we took the trouble of travelling for a disagreeable, hot and crowded ball, where I knew three people': 11th May 1827), and she was left feeling delighted when a network she deemed appropriate requested her inclusion ('I was much delighted at Lady Londonderry asking to be introduced to us': 28th May 1827). Louisa was clearly aware of the necessity of forging advantageous alliances in order to increase her popularity and position in Society. By the end of her first Season her persistence had paid off for she had seven suitors who regularly travelled to pay calls, although none of these had made any serious intentions known to her. This situation did not please her mother, however, who scolded her for 'having no heart' (14th August 1827), clearly suggesting that, had Louisa been more forthcoming with her emotions, one of these men might have proposed. Her mother's desperation regarding the situation indicates the importance placed upon Louisa to marry well and to do so at the first possible opportunity.

Louisa's first major suitor was Thomas Hyde Villiers, a 27 year old second son and MP for Hedon, Yorkshire, whose travels to visit Louisa during her first Season were documented frequently and whose intentions became clear during subsequent regular visits to her home in Brighton, presumably to the delight of her mother (Courtney 2004). This potential liaison was curtailed, however, by the appearance and subsequent interference of her Aunt, Maria Fitzherbert, who warned Louisa of the dangers of the network ('She ... put me on my guard as to not showing him any particular preference, because I would not wish to give him my encouragement': 2nd February 1828). It was clear that Aunt Fitz differed from Mrs Smythe in the appropriate course of action for Louisa and advocated holding out for a better option.

This came in the form of Sir Frederick Hervey Bathurst, twenty years old in 1828, an officer in the Grenadier Guards and a baronet with a property in Wiltshire (Buckle 1858). During the 1828 Season the pair regularly danced together and Louisa talked of her wish to marry him ('He is certainly the only one of my acquaintances or intimate friends who I would accept instantly': 12th July 1828). However, a month later, when Sir Frederick is noted to have travelled to her mother's home in Brighton to ask for her permission to propose, upon her mother replying with a provisional 'yes', it was Louisa herself who declined the match. Whilst Louisa's diary indicates that this was an incidence of 'cold feet', Buckle (1958) has suggested that it was likely Aunt Fitzherbert had once again travelled to warn Louisa against the match, for she made no attempt to hide her hatred for his lack of manners.

It was not until the Season of 1830 that Louisa found herself networking with a suitor whom she definitely wished to marry. Lord Ossulton was the son and heir of the Fifth Earl of Tankerville and, as such, a highly advantageous connection for Louisa. Again the pair went through the scripted performances of dancing and travelling regularly to visit one another, with Louisa noting that she was travelling so frequently specifically to maintain the connection (Cass et al. 2005). This led to an invitation for the Smythes to visit the Tankerville country estate at Chillingham in Northumberland over the winter months. It was here that all hopes for a match between the two young people ended, largely due to Lord Ossulton's mother, who disliked Mrs Smythe. It became apparent to Louisa that, whilst the Tankervilles may have found appropriate and desirable characteristics in her, they had found none in her mother, so it was her family connections that ended the possibility of marriage ('Lady Tankerville proposed Mama's going on to Edinburgh and leaving me at Chillingham until her return, that I was thoroughly pressed to do; but Mama declined for me': 1st October 1830).

Following this further failed attempt at marriage, Maria Fitzherbert once again entered the scene. Enjoying new found social acceptability following the death of her husband, George IV, and the invitation to use royal livery by his successor, Louisa's Aunt had finished a period of mourning, and was once again 'out' in Society (Irvine 2005), as illustrated by her frequent travel to events. Within a month Louisa had decided she loved Sir Frederick Hervey Bathurst once more, no doubt after persuasions by Maria Fitzherbert to do so for the latter had also changed her opinion of him ('I am half in love with Fred Bathurst myself': December 1831). The renewed connection between Louisa and Frederick appears to have been achieved during a series of documented visits between members of their respective families to each other's country estates. It was not until 28th March 1831 that Louisa finally met Frederick, himself, four months after she had decided that she did, after all, want to marry him. Fortunately, both this meeting and subsequent meetings were successful, ultimately leading to a proposal and acceptance of marriage during the autumn of 1831. The complete reversal in the apparent feelings of both Louisa and Aunt Fitzherbert towards a connection they had both previously wished to reject perhaps signals Louisa's change in position. Aged now 21 and with a series of failed opportunities behind her it is possible that both felt that securing a husband was now a priority. It was fortunate that Sir Frederick Hervey Bathurst, the provider of a relatively advantageous alliance, was in a similar position himself.

The story of Louisa's experiences of the Season is important because it adds relevant detail to the broad research previously undertaken. The finding that a Season was clearly fraught with anxiety refutes the happy and sociable image portrayed in the accounts of Worsely-Gough (1952). The calculated approach with which Louisa managed connections is also revealed, as is the impact that family opinion and selection had on the overall outcome and the choice of marriage partner. Whilst biographical material in general is useful in providing detailed accounts, it is, nevertheless, the accounts of travel during the Season which provide the most insight, as shown in the example above. The calculated nature of the Season ensured that travel was always purposeful, designed specifically to attract or secure a particular network. Such intentions during the Season can be understood through an analysis of the journeys made. Likewise, opinions can be gauged through the details of travel reported; for example, Louisa would not have written of her mother's unpopularity directly, yet by documenting that Mrs Smythe had been encouraged to travel on to Edinburgh from Chillingham, this information can be inferred. Concerning the eventual marriage between Louisa and Sir Frederick, it is the accounts of frequent visits to the family, undertaken by Maria Fitzherbert, which signal who actually secured the match. Both examples highlight the importance of family to the outcome of a Season and thus add to previous research by Davidoff (1973), Sproule (1978) and Margetson (1980).

Conclusions

Travel narratives of the London Season have been used in this chapter to highlight four important facets of the period. First, travel was essential to the operation of the Season, and prompted a level of movement which was at odds with the relative immobility of vast swathes of the capital's population at the time. Second, this travel was required to be appropriately undertaken, using a specific mode of transport, the carriage, which clearly distinguished the elite from less wealthy members of society. Third, the importance of travel as a means of display has been highlighted, with Hyde Park noted as being the focus of a fashionable promenade during the period. Finally, the importance of travel narratives in illuminating the lives of individuals during the Season has been revealed through the story of Louisa Smythe whose accounts of her various travels and meetings chart her journey from debutante to bride.

By using travel narratives it is possible to delve more deeply into the processes of the Season and to highlight the importance of movement to those taking part. The narratives may also be used, not just as a record of journeys undertaken, but also as a tool through which to decipher the often unwritten rules of the period. Travel is a means through which to understand how the Season operated, and illuminates the varied experiences of those taking part.

References

Abbott, M. 1993. *Family Ties: English Families*, 1540–1920. London: Routledge.

Anon. 1871. *Modern Etiquette in Public and Private*. London: Frederick Warne.

Battersea, C. 1922. *Reminiscences*. London: Macmillan.

Beckett, J. 1986. *The Aristocracy in England 1660–1914*. Oxford: Blackwell.

Blunt, A. 2000. Embodying War: British Women and Domestic Defilement in the Indian 'Mutiny' 1857–8. *Journal of Historical Geography*, 26(3), 403–28.

Buckle, R. 1958. *The Prettiest Girl in England*. London: John Murray.

Cass, N., Shove, E. and Urry, J. 2005. Social Exclusion, Mobility and Access. *Sociological Review*, 53(3), 539–55.

Colson, P. 1945. *Close of an Era*. London: Hutchinson.

Courtney, W. 2004. Villiers, Thomas Hyde 1801–1832, in *Dictionary of National Biography*, edited by H.C.G. Matthew and B.H. Harrison. Oxford: Oxford University Press.

Davidoff, L. 1973. *The Best Circles: Society Etiquette and the Season*. London: The Cresset Library.

Evans, H. and Evans, M. 1976. *The Party that Lasted 100 Days: The Late Victorian Season*. London: Macdonald and Jane's.

Gorst, F. and Andrews, B. 1956. *Of Carriages and Kings*. London: W.H. Allen.

Graham, B. and Nash, C. 2000. *Modern Historical Geographies*. London: Longman.

Horn, P. 1992. *High Society: The English Social Elite 1880–1914*. Phoenix Mill: Alan Sutton.

Huggett, F. 1979. *Carriages at Eight*. Guildford: Lutterworth Press.

Irvine, V. 2005. *The King's Wife: George IV and Mrs Fitzherbert*. London: Hambledon.

Jackson, L. 2004. *Victorian London*. London: New Holland.

Leconfield, C. 1930. Correspondence Page. *The Times*, 24 October, 7.

Magee, G. and Thompson, A. 2010. *Empire and Globalisation*. Cambridge: Cambridge University Press.

Margetson, S. 1980. *Victorian* High *Society*. London: Batsford.

Masterman, L. 1930. *Mary Gladstone: her Diaries and Letters*. London: Methuen.

McDowell, L. 2004. Cultural Memory, Gender and Age: Young Latvian Women's Narrative Memories of War-time Europe 1944–1947. *Journal of Historical Geography*, 30(4), 701–28.

Nicholson, S. 1988. *A Victorian Household*. London: Sutton Publishing.

Ogborn, M. 2002. Writing Travels: Power, Knowledge and Ritual on the English East India Company's Early Voyages. *Transactions of the Institute of British Geographers,* 27(4), 155–71.

Picard, L. 2005. *Victorian London: The Life of a City 1840–1870*. London: Weidenfeld and Nicolson.

Pooley, C. and Turnbull, J. 1997. Changing Home and Workplace in Victorian London: the Life of Henry Jaques, Shirtmaker. *Urban History*, 24(2), 148–78.

Sheppard, F. 1971. *London, 1808–1870: the Infernal Wen*. London: Secker and Warburg.

Sidney, S. 1873. *The Book of the Horse*. London: Cassell and Petter.

Sproule, A. 1978. *The Social Calendar*. Poole: Blandford Press.

Taylor, S. 2001. *The Moving Metropolis: a History of London's Transport Since 1800*. London: Laurence King.

Thackeray, W. 1848. *Vanity Fair*. London: Bradbury and Evans.

Thompson, F.M.L. 1963. *The Rise of Respectable Society*. Cambridge, MA: Harvard University Press.

Thynne, D. 1951. *Before the Sunset Fades*. Longleat: Longleat Estate Company.

Wildeblood, J. 1965. *The Polite World*. London: Davis Poynter.

Wise, D. 1998. *The Diary of William Tayler, Footmen 1837*. London: Westminster City Archives.

Worsely-Gough, B. 1952. *Fashions in London*. London: Alan Wingate.

Chapter 3

A Family of Travellers

Pamela Richardson

Introduction

This chapter focuses on the travels, between 1895 and 1945, of one wealthy Quaker family – the Foxes. This family comprised Charles (1848–1929) and Gulielma Fox (1848–1931) and their six surviving children. From left to right of the photograph (see Figure 3.1 below) we see Father Charles, the eldest son Reginald (Rex) (1877–1962), Harold (1884–1961), Gladys (1888–1950), Mother Gulielma, Maude (1882–1976) and Bonvile (Bonnie) (1886–1961). Violet (Vi), the sixth child, is not in this photograph. Charles and Gulielma married in 1874 and the family lived in South Devon. It was a typical middle-class family of the time, of liberal politics and with great respect for Royalty. Inter-marriage and close Quaker ties gave them wide contacts that were useful on their travels, in a similar way in which Celia Fiennes, a well-known English traveller in the seventeenth century, had also found family and friends useful during her extensive travelling throughout England (Fiennes 1888). In some respects, Celia Fiennes' travels are comparable to the travels of the Fox family in that her travelling began for health reasons and her accounts were intended initially only for close relatives. Family and friends were a part of travels undertaken in this period, as seeing off travellers and welcoming them home echoed both the perceived and the actual danger of travelling in these times.

The Foxes admitted two extravagances: a thirst for new technology, especially in transport, and a passion for travel. This was shared with their wider kinship group, whose travel journals were sometimes circulated privately among family. The extensive textual and visual travel narratives of the Fox family are sometimes contained within general family journals and sometimes in separate ones. Although these were not published, the Fox family journals do bear similarities with professional travel writing. For example, these include chorographic descriptions in the style of Celia Fiennes (1888) and Tobias Smollett (1721), and a light touch of economic comment reminiscent of Daniel Defoe (1724–26), all of which are from an earlier era and which have undoubtedly informed the style used in Fox family journals. In a similar way the Fox family accounts also show the enjoyment of sharing the reactions of a cultivated person to an interesting place, comparisons of cultures or religions, as well as reflections on history or human conditions.

This chapter presents an analysis of three key themes contained in the Fox family travel narratives: first, the different reasons for travelling and for visiting

Figure 3.1   The Fox Family *c.* 1905 (Source: author's archive)

particular places, second, the influence of transport technology on their travels, and third, pictorial images and memorabilia used either alongside or replacing the written narrative to enrich the impressions of spaces, places and people. In addition to the three key themes, the influence of different viewpoints, relating to gender, age and family status, also becomes evident.

Reasons for Travelling

When the Fox family travelled together destinations were a parental choice, while it was only when individual family members travelled on their own, that they had the opportunity to choose where they went. Harold, for example, spent six weeks in South America in 1907 and in 1908 Rex travelled to Tenerife and Tangiers and Bonnie visited Scotland. In addition to visiting many places in England, between 1911 and 1914 members of the family visited Switzerland, Portugal, Norway, Madeira and Italy. In the spring of 1914 the family toured Italy for five weeks (where Bonnie had been in 1913), while electricity was installed in their Devon home. All these journeys were recorded, some with matching albums. Whatever the reasons for their travelling, the Fox family travels were done in leisurely comfort and the family members enjoyed both the travelling and the destinations.

Certain factors, beyond the simple pursuit of holidaying, stand out from their travel narratives as important reasons for travelling.

Education

The girls were educated at home, mainly by their mother, and as was usual with middle class girls of that period, there was a strong emphasis on social accomplishments like singing and painting. In 1845, Lady Elizabeth Eastlake emphasised that:

> It may be objected that the inferiority of a woman's education is, or ought to be.
> a formidable barrier; but without stopping to question whether the education of
> a really well-educated English woman be on the whole inferior to her brother's,
> we decidedly think that in the instance of travelling the difference between is
> greatly in her favour
>
> (Robinson 1994: xiii)

For the Fox girls, going away from home was an extension of their education, taking the contours of the school atlas to real continents, broadening experience, improving language, powers of observation and reporting and developing the ability to sketch, paint and use a camera. They describe different types of transport, details of places, buildings and people, dress and culture with great enthusiasm and an imaginative use of language, demonstrating their great enjoyment of travelling.

A good example is the development of Gladys's narrative style and her use of grammar, vocabulary and images in her journals throughout the period. Familiarisation with other lands and cultures and the practicalities of travelling encouraged confidence and made young ladies less willing to accept the prescribed life role of women. This was important in an era when women were gaining greater freedom though it was often frowned upon, as Robinson (1994: 1) indicates with the example of contemporary humour from Punch magazine. Foster (1990: 173) could be describing the Fox girls when she writes of the eagerness of early women travellers to move from the commonplace into the unknown and their interest in small details as well as in the grand sights. In contrast, the Fox boys were accustomed to living away from home at boarding school so education through travel was a less important motive for them. Harold sought adventurous travelling with friends while Bonnie was happy to chaperone his unmarried sisters, showing concern for practicalities such as costs, travel arrangements and the comfort of his travelling companions.

Health

Health sometimes dictated, or was an excuse for, travel. For example, in 1907 Violet was taken to the South of France to recuperate after major surgery. -A nurse travelled with her and a local doctor was always on hand. The descriptive narrative of the trip in Gladys's journal is accompanied by an album of postcards, photographs and memorabilia. The text provides a vivid description of the start of such a journey and the luggage deemed necessary for an invalid

> And now a great undertaking is on foot no less than a flight to Cannes, to try and cheat the winter and give Violet a good change as she has come to standstill in her recovery. So off we go ... by the 'Omrah' a steamer of some 8,000 tons – Orient. ... After lunch at the Millbay station where Uncle Reynolds and Aunt Fanny, Aunt Jane and Aunt Kate met us ... Rex in his new motor brought Vi ... and we all went on board the tender ... which conveyed us out to the breakwater to go on board the Omrah. We got all our parcels and luggage only 22 or so safely on board (except for a case of umbrellas which must have met with a watery grave ...).We were going as far as Marseilles in this steamer and found it so full we had difficulty in getting seats at table for so many, 6 in number namely Father, Mother, Violet, Bonnie, myself [Gladys] and Nurse Stephenson and all our bags and baggage deck chairs, chair bed cushions and pillows etc.etc. besides personal luggage ...

The account continues, but with less emphasis on the health of the invalid and more on the activities of the family members who accompanied her! This extract comes from a later section of this journal:

> We all went together one day to Monte Carlo. Oh what a beautiful wicked place!!!! ... the Casino; here I very nearly missed getting in by reason of my tender years, as you may not enter under 22 [Gladys was then 19] and they are *most* particular ... However they were fussing over another girl and I slipped in with the rest and we saw the big tables crowded by people all busily intent on the game. ... we visited *Monaco* ... We got back to tea at Monte in a very grand place and rather expensive but we had by this time got regardless of expenditure (perhaps something in the air of the place caused it). It is quite something to have seen!!!! Mentone we also spent a day at and visited Francie Tuke's [a cousin to Gulielma] grave high up in a sweet spot with the everlasting hills looking down upon it. ... [They watched a Tennis Tournament at Nice and through the good offices of a fellow guest (named Fox but no relation) got into the beautiful Chateau Thorence, the home of Lord Rendell. At the end of March parents, Bonnie and Gladys left for Paris en-route for home, Violet and Nurse remained in Cannes and Bruce and Maude went to Mentone] ... we travelled up by the Rhone Valley ... very comfortable in our drawing-room car ... Neither B nor myself had been in Paris before and everything was very impressive and interesting! ... how hot it was, but we greatly enjoyed seeing everything ... but longing for a cup tea rather took off the edge (as our poor toes began to hurt etc). ... Next morning we left Paris ... had a very foggy crossing. ... glad to be safely home again and feeling, in the words of an ancient poet 'There was no place like home'!!!!

In October 1908 the parents, with Violet and Gladys, accompanied Harold to Switzerland to consult a specialist about his deafness. They travelled from Plymouth to Cherbourg on the steamer 'Amerika', and then by train to Paris, 'a long and tiring journey' according to Gladys's narrative. At Lausanne, finding that treatment would be delayed, they decided to join Aunt Fanny and Uncle Reynolds (Charles's brother) at The Grande Hotel located in the nearby lakeside town of Vevey. The journal entry describes the hotel, the evening and the scenery:

> A charming place, once the home of the Count of Paris and lovely gardens down to the Lake where are the boats and landing place of the Hotel and steamers on the lake which made it very convenient for us when going on Lake Geneva ... a lovely evening it was with the sunset and long orange poplars against the pearly tints of the lake and mountains (the Jura) opposite and a flaming scarlet bed of dwarf salvias and red geraniums on the lawn.

During the same journey they also stayed four days at Les Avants, a village in the same region, at which time they experienced early snow in Switzerland, which prompted Gladys to write more colourful descriptive prose. Returning to Lausanne, the parents went home and Violet and Gladys remained for the duration of Harold's treatment. They enjoyed hotel life, sight-seeing and shopping for six weeks and were mischievous when describing fellow guests. Of one, Gladys wrote: 'we call him the spider he is always abt [about] when not wanted'.

In 1909 Violet and her nurse, were accompanied by Gladys and Bonnie on a three-week cruise from Tilbury to the Mediterranean and the Azores. Again, although the apparent motivation for the trip was Violet's health, Gladys concentrates mainly on chronicling their adventures and includes photographs from this cruise in a general family album. Three days at Lisbon were followed by a visit to Cintra: 'What a lovely place it was. The Cathedral, the most wonderful carving. 800 little boys in blue aprons at the orphanage who tried to speak English.' In Funchal, Madeira, they travelled in a bullock cart and had tea at the Reids Hotel. They arrived at Ponta Del Garda, Azores, in rain and found it Italian-looking but dull; the women wearing long hooded cloaks were viewed as 'rather comical'. The journey home was full of enjoyable on-board entertainment, enthusiastically described. Harold greeted them at Plymouth which was: 'looking very pretty' and they 'felt it compared favourably with foreign ports'.

Business

Father went to America in 1895 on a five week business trip. Rex followed him in 1906, using his father's connections and travel experience to business advantage and for his own comfort. In 1910 Harold sailed to Canada to look for work. Father and Bonnie had business to conduct in Hamburg and Berlin in the same year and Gulielma and Violet accompanied them. Gulielma's account describes the people and places: 'Father's business friend was very kind and took us about – one night to the Opera to hear Lohengrin.' The family enjoyed the cities and urban culture and it is interesting to learn something of the Germany of that period from the travel accounts. In 1912, Bonnie went to America with his father on business, and later took extensive business related trips to Belgium, Holland and Germany.

Living Away From Home

Living away from home presents rather a different narrative to that of the other travels. In 1910 Gladys spent a month in Ireland with a friend whom she had met in Lausanne and who lived in Waringstown, near Belfast. She describes this as a different experience from general holiday-making, although she still managed to meet relatives while there, which bears some resemblance with other travels. Gladys' writing style is similar to that of her mother, but less formal. Her enjoyment of the Irish and their lifestyle comes out of these pages, from her wealthy hosts and their friends, with polo ponies and a footman, to the outworkers in their cottages weaving linen and the peat-cutters in the bogs.

During World War One (1914–19) Harold and Bonnie sent home regular accounts of their travelling. Harold, a soldier, wrote from the Middle East and Bonnie, in the Friends Ambulance Unit, from Belgium and France. Interesting comparisons were made in the accounts with their earlier peacetime holiday and business travels. At the beginning of World War Two, at the age of fifty-one, Gladys undertook her first independent journey abroad. Although the most travelled of the Fox girls she would not risk flying and preferred to travel across wartime France and the Mediterranean to join her husband, posted by the Royal Navy to Alexandria in Egypt. It was a nightmarish journey, uprooting her from all that was familiar, and in Marseilles she confessed herself to be: 'rather desolate, no-one knew where she was at home and no-one in Marseilles cared'. She was relieved to be reunited with her husband. Her three year stay in Egypt was chronicled for their four children; the writing is vivid and humorous, supported by sketches, photographs, and postcards, newspaper cuttings of local people and news. She writes of the trials and triumphs of daily life, learning Arabic, doing charity work, the naval social life and travelling in the desert with her husband. Like her mother in 1895 on her trip to America (discussed later in this chapter), she saw cotton workers and bales awaiting shipment, in this case Egyptian-style, and took an interest in artisans at work. She wore trousers for the very first time in Alexandria, since they made it easier to go on board ships and to get up and dress in a hurry during night bombing raids. She provides a fascinating, detailed account of travelling and living in a foreign country that is as graphic as her mother's visual narrative of the 1895 trip to America, though in other ways her narrative is totally different.

The Technology of Travel

In everyday life the Fox family members were accustomed to walking. Whenever they moved house there was new countryside to explore, paint and write about. They often walked up to twelve miles in a day in Victorian dress with hats, and such stamina proved useful, for when abroad little was left unexplored. Both parents rode regularly and went further afield on horseback, Gulielma riding side-saddle. The family transport was a carriage and pair, and Gulielma also had a donkey cart for local travel. The children had bicycles as soon as they became available. Cycling was particularly liberating for Gladys, especially in the clothes and hats she was permitted to wear (see also Davidson 1889 in Robinson 1994 who offers advice on this subject). Train travel was commonplace, although Gladys did not travel alone on a train until she was over twenty-one. Steamships were familiar, used frequently, recorded and compared.

In 1905 Rex became the first car owner in the family, and took family members on excursions. Throughout his life he kept meticulous motoring records; the state of roads, car and tyre repairs, petrol availability and consumption, distances travelled and amenities en route. The first family car, a Humber Landaulette, was bought in 1907 and the groom retrained as chauffeur. This widened their local travel though early motoring was often unreliable. In the early twentieth century Gulielma's brother wrote and illustrated a poem titled *'Of Motors and Oss'es'*, one of which verses says 'All changed the scene, the horse and chaise too slow it seemed to be, and nothing but a motor car will satisfactory be.' The poem concludes: 'They reached the Hall and sat down sore, upon the nearest seat and vowed they'd not forsake the oss for any motor cheat ... Henceforward may their path be peace wherein they proceed and may the lucre of smelly grease no more their soul impede' (Kirkland and Roberts 2005: 30–31). A series of misadventures befell this poetic traveller, which echoed some of those recorded by the family. Nonetheless, the Fox family took to motoring and felt liberated: '[we] find our fine motor a great and vast comfort'.

Developing forms of transport spawned associations to facilitate travel. The Cycle Touring Club (CTC) was founded in 1878 and the Royal Automobile Club (RAC) in 1897, followed by the Automobile Association (AA) in 1905; Rex was a founder member of the Devon and Cornwall branch of the AA. These clubs pioneered the introduction of road signs and safety measures and their membership manuals recommended routes, hotels and boarding houses. The CTC, in particular, stimulated the growth of places where young ladies could enjoy the freedom of cycling and where they could safely eat and stay (see also CTC 2011). Such organisations undoubtedly promoted tourism by publicising destinations and offering discounts to their members.

It is apparent from their journals that the Fox family took advantage of all forms of transport and extended their field of travel as transport technology developed, with the exception of Gladys who, as mentioned earlier, refused to fly in an aeroplane when travelling towards Egypt to be reunited with her husband. An interesting comparison may be drawn between the modes of transport employed during the family trip to America in 1895, discussed later in this chapter, and those of their Quaker cousin sixty six years earlier who had used horses and a sulky and riverboats, while they travelled by train and river steamer. The cycling trip that Gladys and Bonnie took in 1910 combined bicycles, steamers and trains. Two female friends joined them and they all left by steamer for St. Malo where, with Bonnie monitoring the cost of travel, they put their bicycles on the train for Mont St. Michel. They cycled up to thirty miles a day and at Pontarson Bonnie records:

> Madame of the Poulard Aimé was ready to take us in (in more ways than one). She wanted me to pay 3fr more than my CTC book allowed for. G and I with our best French and signals etc., at last got her to understand and we got quite reasonable prices all round.

They also met three elderly relatives of Aunt Fanny en route, also on a cycling holiday, proving age was no barrier to the new cycling craze.

Visual Narratives

The 1910 cycling holiday, referred to above, illustrates the use of narrative imagery in the Fox family journals. Bonnie and Gladys both described the trip in detail and an album, with a map to show their route and a collection of postcards of places, buildings and people in strange costumes, enriched their written accounts.

The earliest of all the visually rich narratives concerns the five week trip to America in 1895 undertaken by Charles and Gulielma and her sister, Priscilla Richardson. While Charles was on business in Florida the ladies travelled and their graphic record charts their journey through the eastern part of America relying only on pictorial images with few captions – a style seen by some as an 'ideal' form of travel narrative since it may be viewed as neither biased nor judgemental (Robertson et al. 1994). The inequality of southern American life, with its wealth, poverty and hardship is explicit in the grand photographs and simple sketches. Colourful American Indians seem proud in contrast to the poorly dressed cotton field workers. The grandeur of landscape, vast distances, modes of transport and man-made monuments tell their own stories of space and difference. The ladies' experience was of the 'other' (Robertson et al. 1994), far from their sheltered life in the smallness of West Country England. Through this well-constructed visual narrative one gets to know these lady travellers, their religious faith and their catholic interests; their interest in history and literature, as well as their great love and admiration of flowers and landscapes, people and customs.

The journal relies on a map, publicity literature, sketches and photographs to convey to the reader details of the crossing of the Atlantic aboard the steam ship 'RMS Lucania'; the Captain, crew and other passengers are depicted as well as the ship itself. One sketch illustrates a short stop in Queenstown, Ireland for mail and passengers, another, coloured, sketch depicts the Statue of Liberty on their arrival in New York, while the 1895 street map of New York is used to locate their hotel on Fifth Avenue. The visit to New York is illustrated by the inclusion of postcards, including one of spacious Central Park. They strolled down Broadway on Easter Sunday and attended a service to commemorate the fiftieth anniversary of the founding of Temple Emanu-El, the occasion being marked by the inclusion of the service sheet.

After New York the ladies travelled down to Savannah, Georgia by train in a drawing room 'car' which they represent through a sketch and an inclusion of a large map. En route, they depict sunrise in the Allegheney Mountains, peach trees in bloom and eagles and a black woman and child feeding chickens through a painting and a caption. Photographs depict the countryside, where there are ox-carts, young boys sucking sugar cane, workers in their homes and in cotton fields, cotton bales awaiting shipment and areas of dismal swamp land.

At the De Soto hotel, a telegram included in the journal advises the ladies that all is well with Charles in Florida. The ladies then made a call on Mrs Hull at Bonneventure, from which visit they include pressed flowers as a reminder. Mrs Hull took them sightseeing before a visit to the beautiful colonial home of the McAlpine family, which is depicted in a photograph alongside more painted and pressed flowers – a stark contrast to the old slave huts on the plantation depicted in an earlier sketch. The ladies also explored Florida and the Suwanee River and use the New Florida Short Line railway map and detailed timetable to describe their journey. Visiting cards are also included, as a reminder of people they met and their extended kindnesses. After this they went north to Arlington, with its impressive Garfield monument, Washington, Philadelphia, Chesapeake Bay and Baltimore; the visual narratives reveal their travel through the pages of line drawings and paintings and the newspaper cuttings that provide local colour. In Philadelphia, a shrine for all Quakers, they commemorated William Penn as well as attending a Missionary Rally to celebrate the 25th anniversary of the Women's Foreign Missionary Society.

The Niagara Falls Short Line carried them to Niagara Falls and a souvenir brochure offering a variety of sightseeing excursions is also included in the journal. They then stayed at The Prospect House Hotel on the American side of the Falls at which time they explored this spectacular place, with tumbling and roaring water where one feels damp with spray and dazzled by rainbows.[1] They made paintings of golden orioles and humming birds and picked hypaticas beside the water for pressing, all of which are included in the journal. Leaving for Boston, the Hudson River Railroad took them along this lovely river through Buffalo, Rochester, Athens, Rome and Attica. The journal describes the founding of Harvard University at Cambridge, Boston in 1653 and quotes poetry that

---

1   As Frances Kemble had similarly found in 1835 and 1878 (see Foster and Miles 2002), it is impossible to capture in words the glory of Niagara. Photographs do not do it justice and the paintings are far more evocative.

chronicles the Boston Tea Party, once again enriched with sketches and pictures cut from brochures. The ladies were also impressed by the home of the American poet Henry Longfellow (1807–82) and the birthplaces of Oliver Wendell Holmes (1809–94), doctor and author, and James R. Lowell (1819–91), poet and diplomat and record their visits to their homes through an inclusion of photographs and pressed flowers.

In nearby Concord, the ladies visited the home where the novelist Nathaniel Hawthorne (1804–64) had lived and once again use photographs and pressed flowers to record their visit. They also visited the Old North Bridge at Bunker Hill, Concord, where fighting began in the American War of Independence on 19 April 1775. The battle lasted less than an hour and in the journal they mention the words of a Concord resident, Ralph Waldo Emerson (1803–82), who called this event 'the shot heard round the world'. They copied into the journal the inscription from a granite block dedicated to the memory of two British soldiers killed in the battle; this was clearly an emotionally moving site for these peace loving Quakers.

Following their visit to Concord, the steamer 'Priscilla' transported the ladies back to New York. They describe the steamer as 'a floating palace–6 decks, 300 staterooms, grand Saloons 275ft long 21ft high panelled with choicest wood' and they also include an on-board menu, and a pen and ink sketch of the steamer, in the journal. Plymouth Harbour, where the 'Mayflower' had set down the first settlers in 1620, merits a whole page in the journal. A painting of the ship is contrasted with photographs depicting the 1895 America's Cup sailing competition when England's 'Valkyrie' lost the series against America's 'Defender'. As the steamer 'Priscilla' took them back into New York and passed under Brooklyn Bridge this part of the journey is depicted through pen and ink sketches, accompanied by a newspaper article detailing the philanthropic work of the 'Shut-In' Society, formed to keep housebound sick people in touch with the outside world. This newspaper article must have touched a chord with these ladies travellers, free to wander wherever they chose. They left America on 4th of May 1895, on the steamship 'Campania' and the journal includes sketches of the receding coastline, a list of saloon passengers, a saved dinner menu and a painting of icebergs looming en route.

Similar imagery is used, although this time accompanied by more descriptive text, in an intimate account of a family excursion attended by Father, Mother, Violet, Maude, Harold, Bonnie and Gladys, which took place on the 3rd of September 1899 to mark the silver wedding anniversary of the parents' marriage. The journal was written and illustrated by Violet who titled it *The Silver Wedding Trip*. The carriage took the parents and four of the children to Kingsbridge, where Charles had been born in 1848, while Harold rode his bicycle. The family continued by steamer to Salcombe; a sketch of three nuns in black habits who were fellow travellers on the steamer is included in the journal. She describes their excursion as a joyful journey of reminiscence, meeting old friends of their father and hearing of past adventures. During this excursion the family also built sandcastles, recited Tennyson's 'Crossing the Bar', sketched, took photographs and walked to Bolt Head. They stayed the night at the Marine Hotel, where Gladys saw her first

English bishop, attired in gaiters and frock coat. On the homeward journey from Kingsbridge, they enjoyed tea in a cottager's garden, a common practice before the advent of tea rooms. It was a happy and relaxed excursion, which is reflected in Violet's writing style and the illustrations she included in the journal. The photographs were taken by the children, more familiar with that technology than their parents. The finished record was quite probably an anniversary present for the parents and also allowed Rex, who was working at the time and was unable to join them, to share the experience. Six years later, on a Saturday afternoon, Rex took his parents on the same journey in his new car and his mother was astonished that they could travel all that way and still be home in time for dinner.

In 1905 the family took a nineteen day Mediterranean cruise in 'S.Y. Vectis'. The visual narrative is similar to that of the 1895 America trip. A map of the route begins the journal: out from London to Barcelona and home again, calling at Lisbon, Tangier, Algiers, Palma, Barcelona, Malaga and Gibraltar. This is followed by a series of postcards, photographs and well executed paintings of places and people as the journey progressed. Being ardent royalists, the family also included foreign Royalty in their records thus, pasted to the page recording Lisbon, there is a newspaper cutting dated 1 February 1908 reporting the assassination of the King and Queen of Portugal in the Praca do Commercio where the family had walked. This journal also portrays an obvious fascination with the way people dressed, from a road sweeper in Tangier to businessmen in snowy white robes and colourful turbans, while the crowds of people on foot and the fact that horses, and horse and ox-drawn carts, were the only forms of transport are also mentioned. The journal includes photographs of landscapes and seascapes, imposing buildings complemented by towering palms, botanical gardens and the bullring at Malaga and photographs taken on board ship, as well as a copy of a Costume Concert programme of light-hearted music, piano and banjo playing, singing and short stories. Unlike the 1895 America visual narrative that includes only one sketch of family members, the 1905 travel narrative features some photographs in which family members appear although, interestingly, the pictures are not posed and the actual emphasis is placed on the objects of their gaze.

Conclusion

Travelling from the end of the nineteenth century to the mid-twentieth century was usually the privilege of the wealthy, who had the money and time to travel, to visit and enjoy different places. It was a confidence builder for the young of both genders as well as an occupation for young ladies who at that time were not expected to work. The Fox family journals constitute an impressive record of family travelling over a fifty-year period (1895–1945). Members of the family embraced other cultures for varying periods of time and in so doing added a new dimension to their lives. Their travel narratives include itinerary travelogues, specific motoring records and chorographic writing, while a wealth of images and text creates a kaleidoscope of spaces, places and people. The difference and development in narrative form and style between genders and generations and across types of family status is also evident, while the easy transition between describing places and using a paintbrush and colour to tell a story is enviable. This analysis of the Fox family travel journals lends support to the view that pictorial records, in their perceived lack of bias or opinion (see Robertson et al. 1994), allow the reader to create their own interpretation of the journeys depicted. In fact, it can be argued that the value of this type of family record lies not only in the spread of enthusiasm for travel, outwards from relatives and like-minded friends, but also in the historic record itself, in the images of places, buildings, people, fashion and transport, and the written detail of the journeys taken. The rich diversity of these textual and visual travel narratives, vividly recorded, adds a different, domestic dimension to the early genre of travel writing.

References

CTC 2011. *About CTC*. Available at: http://www.ctc.org.uk/DesktopDefault. aspx?TabID=3327 [accessed: 18 May 2011]

Defoe, D. 1971 [1724–27]. *A Tour Through the Whole Island of Great Britain*. London: Penguin.

Fiennes, C. 2010 [1888]. *Through England on a Side Saddle: In the Time of William and Mary*. Cambridge: Cambridge University Press.

Foster, S. 1990. *Across New Worlds Nineteenth Century Women Travellers and Their Writings*. New York: Harvester Wheatsheaf.

Foster S, and Miles, S. (eds.). 2002. *An Anthology of Women's Travel Writing*. Manchester: Manchester University Press.

Kirkland, J., and Roberts, R. 2005. *A Week on Wheels: Extracts from the Journals of Samuel Tuke Richardson*.

Robertson, G., Mash, M., Tickner, L., Bird, J., Curtis, B., and Putnam, T. (eds). 1994. *Traveller's Tales: Narratives of Home and Displacement*. London: Routledge.

Robinson, J. 1994. *Unsuitable for Ladies: An Anthology of Women Travellers* Oxford: Oxford University Press.

Smollett, T. 1919 [1766]. *Travels Through Florence and Italy*. London: The World's Classics.

Chapter 4

Narrating Travel and Tourism in Peace and Wartime, Home and Abroad

Paul Cleave

Introduction

The period of the 1930s and 1940s is significant in terms of travel and tourism. Stevenson (1984: 381) suggests that between 1914 and 1945 the growth in leisure and recreation was one of the most important developments in twentieth-century society, contributing to the development of a 'more uniform and homogenous society, partaking of an increasingly common culture'. Numerous travellers wrote accounts of their experiences and adventures. Popular publications of the period include Priestley's (1934) *English Journey*, Gibbs's (1934), *European Journey*, and Grey-Turner's (1934) *The Casting of a Pebble*. These tend to focus on the prevailing social and political conditions as observed by the traveller-author. The foreword to Gibbs's *European Journey* describes it as: 'Being the narrative of a journey in France, Switzerland, Italy, Austria, Hungary and Germany in the spring and summer of 1934 with an authentic record of the ideas, hopes and fears moving in the minds of common folk and expressed in wayside conversations' (Gibbs 1934b). However, as valuable as these published records and commentaries are, they lack the informative spontaneity and insight often found in confidential and personal accounts of travel and tourism within private, unpublished works. It is the latter that are the focus of this chapter.

Personal narratives refer to stories told about specific individuals or small groups (Caldiero 2007) and tourists' accounts represent stories told in the context of travel and tourism and of encounters with fellow travellers, hosts or the indigenous population. Murray (1991: 67–9) suggests that we are autobiographical in the way we write and that our writing reflects the way we look at the world, the way we select detail and use language to communicate what is seen. Unpublished records of travel and tourism are important in that they provide the reader with a personal snapshot in time and a glimpse into the private world of the narrator. Wall (2006: 148) affirms the significance of the personal narrative in autoethnographic qualitative research as it draws on 'experience to extend understanding about a societal phenomenon'. Ousby (1990) considers tourism as a state of mind as much as an industry, and that narratives of tourism reflect the individual's thoughts and impressions of the experience. Hutto (2007: 1) asserts that our world is 'replete with narratives' and that we are essentially narrative or story telling animals. Human narratives are described as complex representations that relate to and describe 'the course of some unique series of events, however humble, in a coherent but selective arrangement' (ibid.: 1). This is significant as travel narratives range from accounts of grand tours to those of a day excursion, each important in developing our understanding of travel and tourism.

The research discussed in this chapter investigates holidays and travel in the 1930s and 1940s, an era of economic depression followed by the restrictions of wartime and austerity. It was a period of considerable change in travel and leisure, but Middleton (2005) indicates that the interest and demand for holidays was not diminished by general economic conditions; indeed, holidays, leisure and travel increased in popularity and consumption. Pimlott (1976: 238) asserts that holidays became a cult in the twentieth century and that for many 'they are one of the principal objects of life'. Surviving contemporary accounts provide an insight into the evolution of twentieth-century travel and tourism, indicating a growing interest in tourism and in the consumption of leisure by all sectors of society. Graves and Hodge (1941), for example, suggest that the 1930s was a period characterised by domestic tourism for the masses and new forms of leisure consumption, which included the holiday camp and an interest in keeping fit. European tours, and cruises were popular with the middle classes but 'most working class families spent their short annual holiday at seaside resorts at home' (ibid.: 381) although some may have aspired to one of the day trips across the channel to Calais or Dieppe.

Four Unpublished Narratives

This chapter explores four accounts of travel and tourism (see Table 4.1).These are personal records from my own collection, which were not written for publication and which represent a genre of travel writing that encapsulates twentieth-century tourism and leisure. Two show Devon (in south-west England) as a wartime destination for domestic tourism, while the other two describe holidays and travel abroad. Three are identified by name and one is anonymous. Edward's diary contrasts with the others in that it is a daily record covering a lengthy period; January to October 1936. His chronicles encompass extensive travels in Egypt, India, upper Assam, Burma, Siam, Malaya, Java, Bali, China, Japan, America and Canada. Edward writes approximately 150 words each day, with the exception of 7th July when four words are used to describe the monotony of his journey; 'uneventful day at sea' (see Figure 4.1).

Edward's diary of some 30,000 words in length contrasts with Marguerite's, which contains minimal text but is enriched by the addition of travel related ephemera. Both Annie's diary and the anonymous wartime journal are written as descriptive accounts recalling daily activities and holiday routine. Towner (1995: 339–42) suggests that much of tourism's recorded history is concerned with the activities of the affluent and a leisured elite and that 'tourist's diaries, letters and journals tend to be concerned with the more remarkable travel events in people's

Table 4.1   The four travel records

Edward 1936 **Diary, 1936**	**Marguerite 1939** **June 23rd – July 6th 1939, Italy**
'Grand Tour' Egypt -Canada Hand written, daily account in the form of a diary	Hand written with postcards, mementos and ephemera
10 months	2 weeks
Anonymous 1940 – 1942 **Holidays in England and Wales**	**Annie 1943** **Holiday in Devonshire**
A few recollections of a pleasant *holiday spent in North Devon –* *Ilfracombe, August 1941*	Record of an independent wartime holiday
Typed with additional postcards, photographs and ephemera	Typed and carbon copied
1 week	3 weeks

TUESDAY, JULY 7.

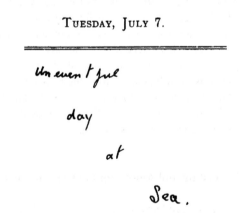

Figure 4.1   Edward's diary

lives'. Consequently the Grand Tour has been much researched (Black 1992), while more routine forms of travel and tourism have tended to be overlooked. The four contrasting records discussed in this chapter provide examples of the exceptional and the routine, demonstrating that each is significant in tourism research.

Little is known about the backgrounds of the authors and, with the exception of Annie's account, the diaries were acquired as commodities, discarded curiosities and mementos of an earlier era. However, the surviving travel records tell us much about the writers themselves, their interests and the times in which they travelled. Further research indicated that Edward was the eldest son of wealthy landowners in Devon and that he later served as Engineering Lieutenant Commander on HMS Ajax. He was killed in action on 3rd April 1945, at the age of 32. His twentieth-century diary is remarkable in that it is written in the tradition of a Grand Tour, in which, as Urry (1990: 3–4) notes, 'travel was expected to play a key role in the cognitive and perceptual education of the English upper class' and was regarded as an opportunity for discourse, eyewitness observation, and the private and the 'passionate experience of beauty and the sublime'. However, this is a twentieth-century version of the Tour with little rigidity of itinerary, as described by Black (1992: xi).

Each of the four records describes features of landscape and townscape separated from the everyday experience of the observer. Urry (1990) suggests that people linger over such a gaze, which is then captured through film, photograph or postcard, which together with the accompanying narrative enable the gaze to be reproduced and recaptured. The other three diaries present a European tour, an example of Voluntary Organisation (Worker's Travel Association) travel, and an independent holiday visiting friends in Devon. They reflect the comments of Graves and Hodge (1941) in that some tourists, such as the example provided by Marguerite of her first visit to Italy, enjoyed a European tour but that for many this would have been an aspiration only. Edward's extensive travels were exceptional, reaching destinations that for many would only have been accessible vicariously. The wartime examples show how, during a period of austerity, tourists made the best use of domestic tourism and limited resources and were still able to enjoy their holidays in the countryside. Brunner (1945: 59) states that Devon is for many people 'first and foremost a place to go to for a holiday' and that even during the war 'crowds of holiday makers moreover have managed to go to Devon every year'.

Travellers' Tales: Recording and Analysing the Experience of Travel

Each account tells a story that reflects social structures and the world as observed by the narrator. McCabe and Stokoe (2004: 602) indicate that place and identity are fundamental to understanding the 'dynamic character of destinations and meanings attached to places by tourists'. They suggest that accounts of travel and tourism are formulated as stories containing biographical detail, temporal formulations and the activities of others. The four accounts document a period of twentieth-century social history and emphasise the importance of the travel narrative in providing evidence of the experience of travel and tourism for another, earlier, generation at a particular point in time; in these examples, the pre-Second World War and wartime era. The accounts reflect that era, in which they were written, showing how travel may encapsulate a period in time.

Content analysis is an appropriate method to employ with these narratives, since it can provide knowledge and understanding of the phenomenon under study (Downe-Wamboldt 1992) and it is regarded as a flexible method for analysing qualitative texts, documents or speech to see what themes will emerge. It is based on reading the documents and returning to the focus of the research, the personal narrative (Veal 2006). Extending beyond counting and classifying words, it provides the researcher with personal insights into a particular era and activity. Manual analysis was considered appropriate (as there were only four records) and traditional, as interpretation remains with the researcher. The content analysis reveals something of the language and literary style of the time; Edward's and Marguerite's narratives are succinct and contrast with the longer, more descriptive narratives of Annie and that of the anonymous author. Table 4.2 below presents the five major themes to emerge from the four narratives; each writer referred to their routine of travel, their modes of transport, the weather and the season, observations of people (whether fellow travellers, friends or the local population), food, drink and culinary customs and, finally, world events and experiences associated with the places they visited.

Analysis of Travel Narratives

Travel Routines and Schedules

The routines of travel, and various forms of transport used, are noted in each record; for example, all travel by train, often supplemented with motor coach and bus. In contrast Edward's tour extends to travel in a cruise ship, a private yacht, by car and aeroplane. His journey starts on 1st January 1936 and he records that: 'the tourist end of the Peninsular & Oriental Steamship Navigation Co. passenger liner "Cathay" is like a cork in a storm – even in the waters of the canal!' There are occasional references in each of the four accounts to season and weather, typically: 'rain'.

The schedule of holidays in Anonymous – *Holidays in England and Wales from 1940*, arranged through the International Friendship League, Co-Operative Holidays Association and the Workers Travel Association, includes travel arrangements. The pattern of travel from London to each destination is noted with train times; for example, Ilfracombe, August 1941: '… independent travel was made, leaving Waterloo Station at 10–36 a.m. and Ilfracombe was reached at 5 p.m. after a rather long drawn out journey', while *Diary of a week's holiday spent in Wales, October 1940* opens with: 'it was a welcome break to spend a week's leave out of "blitzy" London and get the 12.20 p.m. train from Paddington to Pencader.'

Table 4.2   Emerging themes from the four travel records

Themes/ records	Edward	Marguerite	Annie	Anonymous
Routine/travel	Itinerary Boat, train, January – October 1936	Tour Ferry, train June – July 1939	Independent Train, bus August 1943	Pre-arranged Train, bus August 1941
People	Indigenous Fellow passengers	Indigenous American voices	Hosts 'Locals'	Friends
Food and drink	Tea houses Hotels Self-service	Spaghetti Cassata	Farmhouse food, British restaurant	Cider *Real* Devonshire tea
World events 1936–43	Death of King George V Sino-Japanese war	Spanish republican	Wartime damage Coast defence	Bomb damage (Damage tourism)
Experience	Cook's tours Fishing Hollywood tour	Art & Architecture Gondola ride	Rural customs Countryside	Factory visit – Brannam's Pottery Concerts Landscape

Marguerite's account of her trip to Italy contains her travel warrant, which is included in her list of memories. It cost £2 18s 0d (valued at £500 in 2010) and is noted as: 'worth its weight in gold'.

People

All four of the narratives contain detailed observations of people encountered during the holiday; for example, Marguerite's account demonstrates a strong impression of the new and exciting tourist experience through this means:

> ... eyes of the Italian passport officer at frontier, facial expression of policeman in Firenze when asked about hotel, expressive gestures of Italian hands, Madonna like hand maiden at Assisi pensione, American voice on entering train to Rome, republican Spaniard, and conversation with Frenchman on train to Paris.

Edward's diary tends to focus on his fellow travellers, Cook's tour guides and the indigenous population; for example the Cook's guide in Kobe, Japan on 16th July is recorded in this way:

> I had one of Thomas Cook's 'stranger' guides; he should be given a chair in a minor University. This bald old man was 70 but thrilled with life. He talked – not 'on the left is a temple and on the right a mission school' but in philosophy. He talked freely and I was glad of this for in many countries even Cook's guides have to hold their tongues.

Later on 23rd June in Singapore he notes:

> Sultan of what not has breakfast at next table in Raffles and later while buying films in market Prince of Siam the brilliant amateur photographer. Do Cook's tour around Singapore. Most struck by the Botanical gardens and cleanliness of the streets. Also the Malayan quarter which brings the jungle into Singapore.

Having crossed the equator Edward flies to Bali (25/26th June) observing that:

> … the pilot is a grand fellow and flies dead low to show me the coast. First impression of Bali most favourable. You can't escape the fact that the island (is) happy – very happy. I drove about 100 miles through this beautiful country nominally to visit tombs etc. But Bali is a country of living, vitally alive yet with a calmness beneath the warmth of friendship. I stopped and took many photos. This place is a paradise for artists. Whatever they are doing the people assume perfect balance of pose. Moreover they totally lack self consciousness so that a photo can be taken of the eager concentrating face of a man ploughing or the relaxed smile of a maiden washing with equal ease.

Conversely the wartime accounts tend to refer to the friends the narrators encountered. Annie's sketches of baking day, farmers, children, and animals appear bucolic and evocative. Her Devonshire holiday depicts a rural community and way of life, one associated with the rituals of the Plymouth Brethren and almost untouched by the war. It is redolent of Spender's (1945: 13) commentary that for some the war was 'something which had happened abroad'. The anonymous wartime holiday journal refers to friends met in North Devon and fellow travellers. Both wartime holidays indicate that visiting friends and relatives was a motivation for visiting Devon.

The Attraction of Food

Each account narrates the food consumed as an experience, speciality and attraction of the location visited. Annie's narrative includes descriptions of domestic hospitality, but each of them identifies the commercial provision they experienced. Edward provides details of a tea house in Shanghai (12th July) and later whilst in America he comments on the novelty of a self service restaurant in San Francisco (2nd September):

> Walked through China town making purchases here and there. The tea house was very interesting. Of picturesque shape it was built on pilons and approached by wooden bridges over sea green water. Turtles were about and there were fish.

> ... a visit to Dinah's Shack, an unusual type of road house. A variety of some 30 types of salads and hors d'oeuvre were assorted on a large table and guests could take all they wanted of all they liked. The result was a plate mountainously high.

Marguerite's observations reflect that whilst in Italy she also tried the local food, 'eating spaghetti', Cassata (a type of ice cream) and Bel Paese (cheese). On a restaurant card from Sienna is noted, 'Good supper, good service, good company.'

These descriptions are contrasted with those of the food consumed in the wartime accounts of Devon holidays. During a period of rationing, scarcity and shortages, food assumes a greater significance. This is reflected in Annie's descriptions of domestic hospitality, alluding to the pre-war cream tea ('a good Devonshire tea'), in addition to descriptions of visiting cafes for afternoon teas and lunch at a 'British Restaurant' (a wartime innovation introduced to provide communal meals at a set price) where 'we had quite a good meal'. During the Second World War clotted cream was not available commercially and in the anonymous record the writer alludes to the luxury of having a cream tea during a visit to Clovelly in 1941: 'A stop was made for tea and I was able to join friends who were on holiday in the town, and came in for a *real Devonshire tea* despite war restrictions.'

World Events: The Bigger Picture

Each of the narratives is indicative of a period in time, demonstrating that travellers were aware of external events, impending dangers and portents, for example, the era of the Second World War. Edward's diary records on 21st January 1936: 'The king is dead, long live the King, the day fittingly is dismal and rainy, causing me to put off my tour of New Delhi till afternoon.' Later, on 12th July 1936 his diary provides a foretaste of the Sino-Japanese war of 1937–45 as he observes: 'Three Japanese war ships in harbour. Considerable tension reminder of Japanese subject' and on 13th July: 'in the afternoon we approach the Japanese (Nagasaki) shores. The whole country seems to be a fortified zone.' Marguerite's record notes 'Spanish republican' making a fleeting, but significant reference to the recent Spanish Civil War 1936–39.

The accounts written during the Second World War provide interesting examples of holidays obviously affected and restricted by events, but show that domestic tourism was still highly valued. Rural Devon and its coastlines provided a welcome refuge from the cities. Both accounts indicate that the visitors had travelled from London, motivated to escape from danger and destruction. Although each refers to seeing the effects of blitz and bomb damage during their holidays, this was certainly not the object of the visits. The holidays could not be described as examples of dark tourism, unlike the incidence of damage tourism reported by Mass Observation File Report 626 (1941: 5) which noted that, following the Plymouth blitz, 'there was very extensive damage tourism on Sunday 23rd March when people came into the town from miles around'. Annie's references to wartime conditions include a note that most of the windows in Exeter Cathedral had been damaged in air raids and that: 'we saw many parts outside in the city with gaps telling the sad tale that the enemy had been at work in destroying buildings and business premises'. She enjoyed a visit to the popular seaside resort of Exmouth:

> ... altho' War Defence prevented our getting very near (the sea) the sun shone over the water, and had it not been for the shore protection we should have thought how peaceful it all was, for the country hill sides all round spoke of rest and quiet as far as we were concerned.

The anonymous account also refers to travel in wartime Britain (13th June 1942): Leaving Paddington promptly at 1.15 p.m. there followed a very comfortable journey to Weston via Bath (showing much evidence of the May 'blitz').

Place Experiences and Activities

It is important to note that all the accounts emphasise elements of experience and education in their observations of another way of life and culture. They all provide examples of contemporary experiential activity, perhaps typical of the time and type of holiday (and a foretaste of Pine and Gilmore's (1998) experience economy). The anonymous journal, for example, demonstrates a routine of planned activities and events; these include the Co-operative Holidays visit to a blanket factory and the Workers Travel Association excursion to Brannam's Barnstaple Pottery where each stage of production is described. The writer also includes descriptions of the area visited, for example in this entry:

> ... this was my first visit to the beauty spot and from which there will remain many pleasant recollections! We had cider and lunch at the New Inn, and then followed the cobbled slopes to the bottom of the village. If one has been to Lake Como in Italy, one cannot but associate the tremendous similarity to some of the Italian lakeside villages with their cobbled steps leading down to the waterside, and we were fortunate in picking a particularly bright day, the recollection was vivid! The visit was all too short and we joined the coach to continue to Westward Ho!

Annie's observations of country life provide the reader with nostalgic and timeless descriptions of the Devonshire countryside, its lanes and views of Dartmoor; for example, on Tuesday 10th August:

> ... in the evening we called at a lovely farmhouse called Pollards, the ladies who reside there belong to our own assembly at the Gospel Hall. In the hall is an old oak carved chest with the date 1752 carved on the lid, on this chest stands among other things a very large copper kettle as bright as it can be kept, then we were taken into the large farm kitchen and saw a very long kitchen table which would possibly seat around 20 people.

Later, whilst on a visit to a neighbouring village, Annie observes:

> We saw a woman drawing water from a well by the side of the road, she was just coming away with her two pails filled and with the rope she had used for drawing in her hand.

> The old home "Poleford" is a picturesque cottage, with whitewashed walls outside and neatly thatched roof, with a large garden and orchard. The house was very interesting for there is a large open fireplace hearth in the kitchen. The fire was kindled into flame by a blow from the bellows (bellowses in Devon) and on a hook hung the large black iron kettle and three legged crock and we were told they bake on the fire by hanging up a Baking Kettle.

These descriptions are redolent of Cummings's (1944) *This England,* a nostalgic account of the English love of the countryside. The England of 'thatched houses with the little rose gardens, the warm deep set lanes of Devon and Surrey' (ibid.: 28) was something that was especially valued during wartime. He concludes:

> ... farm labourers or mine workers, university professors or commercial travellers the English love the soil. Though they don't read Macauley anymore and don't speak in his idiom it is true to them an acre in Middlesex (or Devon) is better than a principality in Utopia.

In contrast, the account of Marguerite's Italian tour refers to numerous visits to museums, churches and art galleries, during a full itinerary that includes the cultural sights of Florence, Rome, Assisi, and Venice. Each city is recorded in the journal using postcard imagery. She writes of 'gondola ride at Venice, Harry's bar (Venice), blueness of (lake) Garda, and Castello by moonlight' and lists 'Some memories', a diverse compilation of 44 concise descriptions of holiday activities; for example, 'drinking 'Bordeaux out of a tooth mug, first glimpse of snow capped mountains, and smell of limes'.

Edward proudly documents his successful catches when salmon fishing in Canada, recording the weights of each fish. Concerning his visit to Hollywood, on 5th September he notes that he: '... took the Hollywood, Beverly Hills, Santa Monica bus tour' and on 12th September writes these comments: 'ring Warner Bros. Gain admittance to studios. In the evening the Hollywood Bowl, stage setting and lighting superb.'

Photographic Keepsakes, Mementoes and Souvenirs

A personal account of travel and a holiday may be regarded as a form of keepsake and reminder of the holiday for the author. Ballengee-Morris (2002) suggests that other souvenirs may take many forms, enabling tourists to capture memories of their experiences. The four narratives demonstrate the significance and diversity of tourist souvenirs as touchstones of memory, evoking memories of places and relationships (e.g. see also discussion in Morgan and Pritchard, 2005).

Three of the narratives include references to postcards; for example Annie records: 'At the post office we were able to buy some very nice post cards of Yeoford and district'. The postcard as a mass-produced resource is associated with the rise of mass tourism from the late nineteenth century onwards. Postcards provide an important source of information for tourism researchers as they not only convey images of the resorts but are greatly enhanced by the senders' messages inscribed on to them. Prochaska (2000) emphasises the significance of postcard messages, in that the message puts the card into circulation, appropriating it from the producer, but notes that the message often does not refer to the postcard image. Albers and James (1988: 138–9) suggest that, since their introduction and mass production: 'postcards have functioned quintessentially as souvenirs for tourists and maybe as a means of validating the holiday to family and friends'. Stevens (1995) states that, both individually and collectively, postcard messages reveal a great deal about individual or societal values, as well as being valuable for their display of visual images. Ephemeral items, made to be used and often discarded, postcards: 'offer a window into the world as viewed by the society of its time' (ibid.: 1–3) and are subsequently viewed as historical records by researchers. Kneafsey (2000) also supports the use of postcards by researchers as an important form of supplementary secondary data.

Photographic postcards are important visual records of place and time. Batchen (1999: 212) asserts that photography and the photographic image are often held to be 'a proof of that thing's being'. The postcards identified in the narratives are used to enhance the descriptions of places visited and also serve as souvenirs and mementos. Marguerite has utilised the postcards sent home to her mother in Exeter within her notebook. The messages confirm the busy holiday schedule, for example: 'We liked Florence so much we stayed an extra night', or 'it [Rome] is really wonderful here we are continually re-arranging our days. It is so difficult to fit it all in.' Her tour includes some of the major tourist attractions and is recorded with the aid of postcards: 'Had two nights in Assisi that has been the most wonderful place so far'. Architecture and scenery create a strong impression:

'In the train from Como to Milan, have been to Como (simply gorgeous lake) set off for Paris tomorrow.' The card showing the Piazza Venezia is captioned thus: 'Our first sight of Rome really.'

Two of the narratives are supplemented by travel related ephemera. The anonymous account of holidays in England and Wales in 1940 is augmented by the inclusion of postcards, and photographs of holiday companions. References to the Workers Travel Association, documents from the International Friendship League (Bradford Branch) and the Co-operative Holidays Association Summer Holidays at Llangollen, provide period detail. These details enhance the narrative, with advice regarding food rationing, morning prayers, the 11 p.m. recommended 'retiring hour' and stating that 'NO INTOXICANTS are allowed in the guest house'. Such details, which might otherwise have been overlooked, add value to personal accounts, telling the reader about the organisation and the traveller. Snape (2004) suggests that the Co-operative Holidays Association established the practice of providing simple affordable accommodation and access to the countryside as an alternative to the commercial seaside resorts. Pimlott (1976) refers to the positive approach of these organisations in encouraging leisure and tourism consumption and suggests that this is illustrated by the objectives of the Holiday Fellowship – 'to provide for the healthy enjoyment of leisure, to encourage love of the open air; to promote social and international friendship; and to organise holidaymaking and other activities with these objects' (ibid.: 239).

Edward's diary contains no photographs or postcards, only a diagram of an opium pipe. However, he refers frequently to the *subjects* of the photographs and cine films (home movies) that he has taken and also notes when he has written home, for example: 'write Devon'. Photography was popular with tourists; snapshots were described in the Kodak handbook (Kodak Limited, 1920: 21–2) as being 'instantaneous exposures popular with amateurs' that visually enhance the narrative.

Conclusions

The four records utilised in this chapter represent different interests within the context of travel and tourism; for example, whereas Edward's diary keenly observes his travelling companions, the indigenous population and their characteristics, Marguerite's demonstrates an interest in the people she observes during her Italian tour. These accounts of overseas holiday trips may be contrasted with the wartime records of holidays in Devon, which are inclined to focus on the peaceful appealing landscape and domestic details of the period. Although a private record, not at all intended for the public domain, Annie concludes the account of her holiday rather prophetically in this way:

> When the winter evenings come we shall be able to go over these notes and remind ourselves of the August sunny days and our doings away in Devonshire.

I think anyone who may read these notes will agree we covered some ground during our holiday, and altogether, one day with the other, Sundays as well, have had a very happy time.

Nearly three quarters of a century later, such narratives are important survivors, valuable records of social history in a particular era and an important archival resource to be used in developing our understanding of tourism's evolution in the twentieth century. They are important records of place, time and experience. Sethi (2005) suggests that much of what we know and think about the evolution of tourism is conditioned by particular historical perspectives and by activities such as the Grand Tour. The focus in tourism history tends to be placed on the exclusive and prestigious, overshadowing the relevance of the commonplace and the significance of tourism in people's lives. The records utilised in this chapter not only demonstrate the importance of the seemingly ordinary, as well as the exclusive, in tourism but also emphasise the importance of the holiday to the tourist.

This chapter has demonstrated that the personal narrative is an invaluable resource in tourism research, providing access to original and unique records of travel and tourism and evoking a specific period in tourism's history. In addition, it has been argued that the private narrative has added value over published works, emanating from the inclusion of ephemera, photographs, postcards and mementos, which contribute to our understanding of tourism in the context of the narrator and their era. Individuals' reflections of experience are important contributors to the evolving historiography of travel and tourism.

References

Albers, C.P. and James, W.R. 1988. Travel Photography: a Methodological Approach. *Annals of Tourism Research,* 15(1), 134–58.

Ballengee-Morris, C. 2002. Tourist Souvenirs. *Visual Arts Research,* 2(56), 102–8.

Batchen, G. 1999. *Burning with Desire: the Conception of Photography.* Massachusetts: Massachusetts Institute of Technology.

Black, J. 1992. *The British Abroad: the Grand Tour in the Eighteenth Century.* Stroud: Sutton Publishing.

Brunner, E. 1945. *Holiday Making and the Holiday Trades.* London: Oxford University Press/Humphrey Milford.

Caldiero, C.T. 2007. Crisis Storytelling: Fisher's Narrative Paradigm and News Reporting. *American Communication Journal,* 9(1), online.

Cummings, A.J. 1944. *This England: an Appreciation by A.J. Cummings.* London: Gawthorn.

Downe-Wamboldt, B. 1992. Content Analysis: Method application and issues. *Health Care for Women International,* 13(2), 313–21.

Gibbs, P. 1934a. *European Journey.* London: Heinemann/Gollancz.

Gibbs, P. 1934b. *European Journey.* Foreword. London: Heinemann/Gollacz.

Graves, R., and Hodge, A. 1941. *The Long Weekend: A Social History of Britain 1918–1939*. London: Readers Union/Faber and Faber.

Grey-Turner, E. 1934. *The Casting of a Pebble*. Newcastle: Andrew Reid.

Hendry, P.M. 2007. The Future of Narrative. *Qualitative Inquiry*, 13(4), 487–98.

Hutto, D.D. 2007. *Narrative and Understanding Persons*. Cambridge: Cambridge University Press.

Kneafsey, M. 2000. Tourism and Place Identities and Social Relations in the European Rural Periphery. *European Urban and Rural Studies*, 1(7), 35–50.

Kodak Limited 1920. *How to Make Good Pictures*. London: Kodak Limited.

Lucaites, J.L. and Condit, M.C. 1985. Re-constructing Narrative Theory: a Functional Perspective. *Journal of Communication*, 35(4), 90–108.

Mass Observation File Report 626, 1941. *Second Report on Plymouth*. Mass Observation Archive, Special Collections, University of Sussex.

McCabe, S., and Stokoe, E.H. 2004. Place Identity in Tourists' Accounts. *Annals of Tourism Research*, 31(5), 601–22.

Middleton, V.C. 2005. *British Tourism: the Remarkable Story of Growth*. Oxford: Butterworth-Heinemann.

Morgan, N., and Pritchard, A. 2005. On Souvenirs and Metonymy: Narratives of Memory, Metaphor and Materiality. *Tourist Studies*, 5(29), 29–53.

Murray, D.M. 1991. All Writing is Autobiography. *College Composition and Communication*, 42(1), 66–74.

Ousby, I. 1990. *The Englishman's England: Taste, Travel and the Rise of Tourism*. Cambridge: Cambridge University Press.

Pimlott, J.A.R. 1976. *The Englishman's Holiday: A Social History*. Hassocks: The Harvester Press.

Pine, B.J. and Gilmore, J.H. 1998. Welcome to the Experience Economy. *Harvard Business Review*. July-August, 97–105.

Prochaska, D. 2000. Exhibiting the Museum. *Journal of Historical Sociology*, 13(4), 391–438.

Priestly, J.B.P. 1934. *English Journey*. London: Heinemann/Gollancz.

Sethi, P. 2005. *Tourism: Today and Tomorrow*. New Delhi: Anmol Publications.

Snape, R. 2004. The Co-operative Holidays Association and the Cultural Formation of Countryside Leisure Practice. *Leisure Studies*, 23(2), 143–58.

Spender, S. 1945. *Citizens in War, and After*. London: Harrap and Co.

Stevens, N.D. 1995. *Postcards in the Library, Invaluable Visual Resources*. New York: Haworth Press.

Stevenson, J. 1984. *British Society, 1914–45*. Harmondsworth: Penguin.

Towner, J. 1995. What is Tourism's History? *Tourism Management*, 16(5), 339–43.

Urry, J. 1990. *The Tourist Gaze*. Sage. London.

Veal, A.J. 2006. *Research Methods for Leisure and Tourism*. Harlow: Pearson.

Wall, S. 2006. An Autoethnography on Learning about Autoethnography. *International Journal of Qualitative Methods*, 5(2), 146–60.

Chapter 5

'Keeping the Holiday Book': Travel Stories of a Twentieth-Century English Family

Jacqueline Tivers

Introduction

Much has been written about twentieth-century tourism, including descriptions of tourist practices and considerations of the relationship between tourism and identity construction. However, in the vast majority of cases, this material has not been based on personally written narratives. There are, of course, numerous studies of 'travel writing' but these refer to published works that are, at least in part, *fictional*. Unpublished narratives, written as factual accounts in 'holiday books' or travel diaries, have received little attention from researchers, although the personal, everyday diaries of research subjects have often been 'mined' for information by historians and biographers and, in a rather different context, Driver and Martins (2002: 59) examine 'relationships between travelling, seeing and knowing, as articulated in the field and keeping a log' in the case of a nineteenth-century midshipman. Lorimer (2003) and Lorimer and Spedding (2005) discuss the construction of 'small stories' of personal knowledge acquisition and geographical practice, through the analysis of field diaries, expedition logbooks, letters and oral recollection. Similarly, this chapter seeks to tell the 'small story' of the travels and activities of an 'ordinary' twentieth-century English family by presenting an analysis of one man's 'holiday books', written over a period of 60 years between 1937 and 1996.

The writer of the 'holiday books' was my father, John Edward (always known as Jack) Tivers (1910–97). He was the 10th surviving child of a working class, south London family. He won a grammar school scholarship but his family could not afford to keep him in education beyond School Certificate level. As a young adult he moved with his family to Islington, north London, when my grandfather became the caretaker of the National Insurance building. Here, while working as a bookkeeper in a millinery establishment and taking evening classes in accountancy, he spent most of his free time in the Scout Movement and it was through this body that he met my mother, Jean (1911–2010), a local Cub Scout leader. They were married in 1937. My sister, Jennifer (1939–89), I myself (1946–) and my brother John (1952–2011) completed the family. After the Second World War my father trained as a Further Education teacher and he finally retired in 1975 as Deputy Head of the Business Studies department at (what was then) Kingston Technical

College. He retained a life-long commitment to the Scouts, receiving the highest award of the Movement from the Queen, and finishing his formal scouting career in 1980 as head of leader training in south London.

I mention all this detail because it is relevant to the narrative that I am seeking to analyse. The Scout Movement provided my father with the 'character' and 'citizenship' training (Warren 1986) that directed his whole life, as well as teaching him to camp out in a tent, to be inquisitive about his surroundings, and to keep expedition logs. As a working class boy from a poor family with no opportunity for higher education, he used his (considerable) intelligence in the compiling of these logs, and of the 'holiday books' which followed a similar pattern, as well as in pursuing his professional accountancy qualifications. He was an active explorer and compiler of facts. Without fail, and despite being registered blind for the last ten years of his life, he would sit down with his 'holiday book' and make an entry each evening of every holiday, detailing the day's journeys and places visited and noting down the content of meals taken, the changing weather and precise information about overnight accommodation. When I was young, and when my own children were young, we were also required/encouraged to keep our own 'holiday books'. Everywhere my father (and my mother) travelled he collected postcards, leaflets and tickets, and these he inserted into his 'holiday books', together with maps (especially maps on postcards) and photographs (up to 1964).

My father stored the books in two, rather dusty, cupboards and there they remained after his death in 1997, until my mother agreed to pass them on to me in December 2009 shortly before her own death at the age of 98. There are 59 books in total, each book and its contents carefully dated and generally covering the holidays of one calendar year between 1937 and 1996. However, in some years there is more than one book, while, occasionally, a book covers more than one year. There are no books at all from six particular years (1939, 1940, 1941, 1952, 1955 and 1960). I suggest likely reasons for this later in the chapter, although it is also possible that certain books were loaned to individuals and not returned and hence are now lost. In the early years a range of book styles was employed but from 1964 to 1990, after which failing sight meant that a much larger scale was required, my father always bought identical books; small, black, hard-covered books with narrow ruled lines, which would be held together by thick rubber bands.

The 'holiday books' now constitute a unique and substantial archive of twentieth-century English family tourism practice. Their analysis is not, however, unproblematic. Questions arise concerning both the *content* and the *context* of the narrative presented by the books, as well as the *motivations* for the assiduous completion of the books by their compiler, my father. These questions are explored in the following sections of the chapter, referring not only to the contents of the books themselves, but also to personal and collective memories of the different holidays.

Content of the Narrative

In terms of the described holiday journeys, my father and mother lived at the same house in Wimbledon, south London, from their marriage in 1937 to their deaths, in 1997 and 2010, respectively, so all holidays started from there. Considering the record contained in the 'holiday books' my parents' holidays may broadly be categorised as follows:

- 1937–38, walking holidays in south-east England (travel by train)
- 1942–67, holidays in England and Wales, mainly at seaside locations (travel by train up to 1956 and by car thereafter)
- 1968–82, car touring holidays 'on the Continent' via Dover car ferry
- 1983–84, car touring holidays in the UK
- 1985–96, holidays mainly in England (travel by train or coach, unless accompanying one of their children in their car).

The contents of the 'holiday books' were compiled in great detail. There are the precise addresses and names of 'bed and breakfast' hosts and 'bungalow' owners with sketch maps and directions for reaching their establishments and other sketch maps of walks taken. Extremely precise directions are provided for the latter, for example 'going N by E' (Pilgrim's Way 1937). Weather conditions are minutely recorded with variations noted throughout each day. At the end of some books (particularly those from the earlier years) there is a comprehensive list of costs of different aspects of the holiday, set out in a business-like way, as befitted the hand of a bookkeeper (later, accountant and teacher of accountancy). Nevertheless, the writing style is not always terse and to-the-point; factual details are often inter-mixed with more flowing, descriptive passages, as in these examples:

> We visited Rhodes House and were shown round by the hallkeeper. This building is very new, but quite in keeping with its surroundings. And the domed entrance hall, in South African marble, is a very fine monument to Rhodes himself (Oxford, 1942).

> Jennifer [my sister] and I again spent the morning in the sand pit. The martins are very busy in and out of their nests in the face of the pits – it seems amazing that of all the holes showing each one can find its own nest. It was beautifully hot and sunny again today (Salisbury, 1943).

> As we have TV we were able to see Perry Mason as well as making up log books before having an early night The site looks quite nice – it is in a lovely position – but the caravan is somewhat smaller than we are used to, and we are finding some difficulty in getting settled in (Keswick, 1964).

Figure 5.1   Example of a 'holiday book' entry, illustrating the integration of text and images (Source: author's own photograph)

One interesting aspect of the content of the 'holiday books' is the integration of words and images. The books, as they appear today, contain postcards, leaflets, maps (both printed and hand-drawn) and some photographs, as well as written entries, precisely dated and located (see Figure 5.1). Each day's entry is carefully laid out with text and images organised sequentially. There is a conscious effort to cross-reference the material, for example:

> They [Belsay Gardens] are fully described in the leaflet on the next page, but one important fact is worth noting.. (Warkworth, Northumberland, 1986).

In some early books there are blank pages with a pencilled note indicating the later presence of a particular photograph that for some reason was never actually included, perhaps because it was poorly developed. In many of the later books the amount of space to be left for illustrations has been under-estimated and extra leaflets and postcards are pushed in between the already-bulging pages. There are many personal photographs in the early books, both of people and places, but there are no photographs after 1964, the last year in which I, as a child, accompanied my parents on a family holiday (and in that year the photographs were taken by me with my camera under instruction from my father, who wrote the annotations in the book). Subsequently, my father preferred to purchase pictures of places visited for the 'holiday books', sometimes as commercial photographs but more often as postcards; he made the point verbally on many occasions that this was an easier way to collect 'suitable' images. However, this meant that no photographs of himself, my mother and brother were taken on holidays after this date (until I accompanied my parents again with my own children after 1975, but these later photographs were not included in *his* books).

Analysis of the content of the 'holiday books' reveals certain elements standing out very strongly. In the first place, unlike many tourists, for my father the *journeys* were as important as the ultimate locations and he always describes them very explicitly. In relation to wartime train journeys he notes when they 'managed to get corner seats' (1943) and when the train 'was already full before we arrived' (1944). As Sladen (2002: 68) notes: 'Travelling by rail in wartime could certainly be slow and uncomfortable' and strenuous efforts were made by the government to persuade people to 'holiday at home', but this did not seem to have deterred my parents from undertaking recreational journeys. As early as 1938 he began his long love affair with car-based holidays, as a passenger in a richer friend's car. He records his first holiday car trip in immense detail:

> We had started with one window open. At Staines the second one opened, and at Basingstoke the hood was put down so that we could have a good blow across the plains ahead ... Leaving Barnstaple we climbed steadily uphill for two or three miles on the road to Ilfracombe. At one point we were confronted with fork roads and in stopping the car to discover which way we ought to go we found the petrol tank to be empty and had to turn round (quite a job on a steep hill with no engine to help) and coast back to Barnstaple for petrol (Friday 15th April).

As soon as he was able to acquire a car himself, touring, to visit places or just to drive through towns, villages and the countryside as an activity in itself, became his principal holiday interest, and completely dominant once my parents were able to go away on their own again.

Secondly, my father was always fascinated by places and their history. He had a real and lasting interest in both geography and history, particularly in relation to the built environment of towns and cities. (It was, of course, his avid pursuit of these disciplines 'in the field' which acted as a significant, formative influence on my own academic studies and career.) His passion for visiting 'places of interest' lasted his whole life; the very last book entry he ever made, on Sunday 14th July 2006 in Oxford, reads:

> We went to lunch at the Crown in Cornmarket, where Shakespeare apparently stayed. On the way back we looked into the Ashmolean Museum.

My father never saw himself as a 'normal tourist'. Beach-oriented holidays may have been a necessity when his family were young but the accounts speak of bathing (in all weathers and at any time of the year between April and October), 'French' cricket, sandcastle building, boat trips, children's playgrounds and long walks, rather than simple relaxation, and all the time there was an emphasis on visiting historic sites, village churches, local towns and bus trips away from the holiday location. Unlike many holiday-makers, he was never interested in any sort of 'night life', apart from occasional visits to the theatre, when available; evenings were spent quietly 'at home', eating a simple meal ('fish and chip suppers' occur frequently in the narrative), playing cards, doing crosswords and, of course, writing down the day's events in the 'holiday book'.

Thirdly, the importance of *independent control* emerges strongly from the narrative of the books, as may be seen from this 1943 extract:

> I must say we got worried about it all – first, we found out that we were not expected, then Sid [my uncle] did not appear to know the way, then when we arrived nobody was at home. However, everything turned out alright *[sic]* (Saturday 17th July).

My father hated not being fully in charge of arrangements and always tried to organise the entire holiday himself (a less common occurrence in an era before the availability of the internet); bookings, accommodation, routes to be travelled, food to be purchased for self-catering and places en route to stop for coffee and lunch. There was little that he delegated to my mother on these occasions; perhaps, cooking meals, the packing of suitcases and the provision of necessities for the children, although he took an equal share in child care and house cleaning. He was a fluent linguist, speaking both French and German at a high level and also a little Italian and Spanish, so he always took the role of 'negotiator' during their continental European holidays. When, in later life, he was forced to rely on me for transport, and condemned to occupy his holiday time at the behest of my children, he complained forcibly about sitting around on beaches for too long and not being able to get about as once he had done; in fact, about not being in control. Of a 1988 holiday in Gower, South Wales, for example, he commented: 'A very nice break, but I had too much beach for my liking'!

Fourthly, the books reveal a high level of social interaction during holidays, primarily with family and/or friends and neighbours from home, but also with the owners of 'bungalows' and 'bed and breakfast' accommodation; several times my father mentions leaving my sister in the care of the latter while he and my mother went out for walks together. When I was young, not only were holidays taken with specific family members (various uncles, aunts and cousins of mine), but a constant stream of day and weekend visitors was apparently also entertained, including my godparents, next-door neighbours and friends from Scouting. This was possible because we nearly always rented cottages or bungalows a relatively short distance from home and invariably went away for a two-week period. Much of the narrative in the 'holiday books' of this era is occupied by people arriving, taking part in holiday activities and then leaving, to be shortly replaced by others. From primary school age, we children were each allowed to take a friend away with us on holiday as well. The high level of sociability evident in the early books was clearly, at least in part, due to the fact that many of our friends and relatives could not afford to go away on holiday separately at that time. After 1961 matters appear to have changed dramatically in this respect and we (my immediate family) went away without other people for the last few years before my parents started their long car touring holidays alone in 1965. In the late 1970s family holidays were re-introduced, only this time variously with me and/or my siblings and our children.

Finally, the content of the books illustrates very clearly the importance to my father of a methodical approach to the recording of experiences. In this respect he fulfilled the 'stylized accountant stereotype', undertaking 'painstaking and eye-for-detail work' (Bougen 1994: 319, 321), as well as the stereotype of observant Scout (Matless 1998: 75). Specific books were purchased prior to holidays and specific pens were used in making records. My father refers in the books to his own bodily engagement with the discipline of writing, whether this took place at the kitchen table or on a folding camp table. It was essential to him that the record was complete and, apart from in a very few exceptional cases, the last days of holidays and the journey home were completed after his return, as previous days had been. Just once, in 1956, my father was forced to leave the family on holiday, while he went home so he could go away the next day to Rome with his Scout group (he was a Group Scout Leader at this time and this was an important exchange programme with an Italian troop, whose members were due to visit the UK the following year to take part in the International Scout Jamboree marking the 50th birthday of the Scout Movement). However, the 'holiday book' was not neglected at this point. The writing changes as the page is turned, but the nature of the content does not; my older sister, Jennifer (aged 17), continued the required narrative in my father's absence.

Context of the Narrative

In order to understand the narrative presented in the 'holiday books' it is necessary to consider the *context* within which the books were written, as well as their overt *content*. This is particularly important when what has *not* been written is being considered; that is, omissions from the narrative. Thus, a hermeneutical approach is required to explain features which otherwise might appear incongruous. In the first place, I will consider the *national* context of the holidays taken and the records about them, secondly I will review the *family* context, and finally I will consider my father's holiday experiences in the light of what we know of normative twentieth-century English family tourism practices, in other words the *tourism* context.

National Context

There are no 'holiday books' from the years 1939, 1940 or 1941, the first years of the Second World War. This is, perhaps, unsurprising. What is possibly more surprising is that my father and the family took holidays in 1942, 1943 and 1944, which were also War years, although Sladen (2005) does contradict the generally held idea that people did not take holidays during the War, using evidence drawn from railway company statistics. My father worked in civil defence as a firefighter, so he was not living away from home or fighting on the European mainland, as many other men were at that time. However, most surprisingly of all, he never specifically mentions the War in any of his holiday narratives. There are oblique references to the *results* of war; a visit to a relative at a 'camp', the conversion of the Oxford University Examination Schools into a military hospital and the use of a church crypt as an air raid shelter, the removal of stained glass from church windows, the need to use ration coupons for food, and this entry from a 1943 day trip (from the holiday location in Salisbury, Wiltshire) to Bournemouth:

> We sat on the little bit of front still available and had lunch. Afterwards, Jennifer played on about two square yards of sand, all mixed up with barbed wire (Friday 23rd July).

However, the word 'war' never actually occurs in the text of any of these 'holiday books', nor indeed in any of the immediately post-War books, despite the importance of the War in framing the lives of the British population for a decade. The only conclusion that I can reach about this omission is that, as a registered conscientious objector, he studiously avoided thinking and writing about the War, especially when he was away on holiday (but, indeed, the War was never mentioned in our house at all during my childhood).

Similarly, there are no references in the 'holiday books' to other national political events or to economic changes during the period. My parents' holidays are not overtly set within any over-arching narrative of national or international situations or change, despite the detailed references to places, journeys, weather conditions, theatrical and musical performances, church services and inter-personal relationships, any of which could be 'read' in terms of a wider national or international context. However, one item of national sporting history does creep into the text; staying at a caravan park with a 'TV hut' in North Wales in July 1966, my father records that 'John [my brother] and I watched England beat Portugal on TV (Tuesday 26th) and later, on Saturday 30th, that 'John and I watched the World Cup Final during the afternoon while Jean [my mother] straightened the van'. (Interestingly, he does not go on to note that England won the Final!)

Family Context

The pattern of holidays described in the 'holiday books', and outlined earlier in the chapter, clearly reflects life cycle stages. My sister, Jennifer, was born in 1939, after which specific walking holidays were removed from the agenda, although a considerable amount of walking was clearly undertaken on holidays until well into the 1970s. In 1942 the family went to Oxford (described by Sladen (2005: 229) as 'an inland holiday resort' for those who were unable to get to the seaside during the War), but after this there was a shift to beach-oriented family holidays as children's needs were accommodated. After the War, my father entered Further Education teaching from the world of business and this enabled him to enjoy extended holidays, notably during the summer months. My brother, John, was born in August 1952, one of the years in which no holiday was recorded. In 1957 my father acquired a car for the first time and from then, until his sight began to fail in 1984, travelling by car became the focus of holidays. In 1960 my sister's wedding took place and there was no recorded holiday that summer. In 1965 my parents took their first holiday alone since 1938, a fact which is specifically mentioned by my father at the beginning of that year's book. They chose a touring, camping holiday, the first of many holidays of this type, reflecting their new 'solo' status and 'adjusting to a new life situation' by 'experimenting with different holiday forms to (re)discover their personal interests' (Therkelsen and Gram 2008: 276).

The number of holidays taken each year increased markedly after my parents both retired from work in 1975 (although this change is never referred to specifically). In some years they took five or six holidays, certainly at my father's insistence, but also reflecting his generosity in contributing financial and personal support to holidays taken by his three children and their families. In 1986, for example, my parents were away from home for nine weeks altogether, on six different holidays, despite being by no means wealthy people. My mother had never learned to drive, always joking that she had never even ridden a bicycle, so, in the later years when my father was no longer able to drive, they visited cities that they could reach by coach or train and from which they could take coach trips into the surrounding areas, in addition to going on car-based holidays with their children's families. Finally, in the last three years (1994–96), it became necessary for me to drive them to and from their holiday locations because they could no longer manage public transport. Nevertheless, going on holiday was still an essential part of the year's activities for my father. Clearly, throughout his life, he vested a great deal of importance in travelling and this is reflected in the diaries that he kept for 60 years. His last recorded holiday took place in 1996, only seven months before his death, but the 'holiday book' for that year is as full of postcards and accounts of visits as any earlier book. As a footnote, it should be added that, after my father's death, my mother was very happy to stop going away so much!

As well as the omissions from the narrative noted above in relation to the national context, there are also significant omissions in relation to the family context. I have already mentioned my parents' retirement in this respect. I have also inferred that there was no holiday in 1952 because my brother was born that summer (and, in fact, my mother nearly died in childbirth), but this is not actually recorded anywhere. In 1988 my sister was suffering from cancer at the time of her holiday with my parents, but the 'end note' to that holiday simply states 'A very nice break, and Jennifer especially enjoyed it'. In the following year (1989) my father notes that on 23rd June my sister 'arrived 8.45 p.m. for convalescence' and that she left two days later; she was seriously ill at this time and died five months later, but her illness is not referred to specifically. After 1984 my father's sight deteriorated rapidly and he was soon 'registered blind', but the main way this can be inferred is by consideration of his physical writing style. There are few specific references in the text to his situation; on 2nd August 1984 he records that he 'tried to buy a new magnifying glass' and on a later holiday that year he notes that 'This will be scrappy as I now cannot see very well', but after this he says nothing about his disability in any other books, merely noting at the end of the following year's summer holiday that 'We have had an enjoyable fortnight, for the first time without a car, and it has been an experience' (Saturday 13th July 1985).

One aspect of the 'holiday book' narrative and its family context should be specifically noted; the fact that it was my *father* who wrote the books and never my mother, not even in 1956 when, as previously mentioned, he left the completion of the 'holiday book' to my sister, or after 1984 when he could barely see the page he was writing on, let alone write on the printed lines. I have argued, previously, that my father's background in the Scout Movement was significant in encouraging him to keep logs of his travels, but my mother came from the *same* background; it will be recalled that my parents met through Scouting. In addition, my mother was a primary, and later a nursery, school teacher for most of her working life, having specialised in English language at college. I can only hypothesise the reason why it was my father who always 'kept the books'; perhaps, because he *was* a 'bookkeeper' by profession and saw the 'holiday books' as records, in the same way as one might keep the records of financial income and expenditure, while that sort of writing was of less interest to my mother, or perhaps because he took the role of family 'organiser' and this type of record was part of the 'organisation' of a holiday. In fact, my mother *did* write whilst on holiday; she wrote all the postcards, sent home to family and friends. She was also the collector of the souvenir tea-towels, of places on maps, which covered the walls of the hall, stairs and upstairs landing as well as acting as chair back covers in their house. In many ways these souvenirs were a much more physically 'present' record of all the holidays taken, than were the 'holiday books' stored away in a cupboard.

Tourism Context

I have described our family as an 'ordinary twentieth-century English family', but it is interesting to question how 'ordinary' or typical of mid-twentieth century tourism were the experiences that my father recorded. My father eschewed 'mass' tourism, packaged tours and hotel accommodation, he never flew in an aeroplane in his life and he hated crowds. Whenever possible, he travelled in his own car and used a tent for the night, or rented a 'bungalow' for the week. As previously mentioned, he hated sitting for too long on beaches and soon became bored with 'watching the world go by'. He spent most time on holiday exploring historic sites or just 'touring' in the car. When abroad, he did not seek out specifically 'English' experiences (food and drink, or signs written in English, for example); unlike so many post-war British tourists, he not only was a competent linguist, but actively sought to use and develop his foreign language skills. One could argue, therefore, that twentieth-century mass tourism developments had little influence on his holiday behaviour. In many ways, my father was ahead of his time, his type of tourism representing the more nuanced and individualistic, self-determined tourism practices which are evident at the present time; cultural tourism and city 'breaks', heritage tourism, individually booked holidays, visiting friends and relatives, and so on (although all of the latter clearly have much older roots). Like Harrison's sample of twenty-first century Canadian 'travel enthusiasts', for my father:

> There is always a new journey to take, a new place to explore, or something exciting to experience in some place far from home ... there is always another trip to be contemplated, planned, imagined, or organized (Harrison 2003: 3).

Motivations for Writing the Books

Why did my father keep 'holiday books' all his adult life, in such detail and with such dedication? There are several possible answers to this question, mainly inferred from his life in general, rather than from the text of the books. I never thought to ask him why he wrote holiday records; it was so much a part of holiday expectations, so 'normal' to me as to be unexceptional. It is only very recently and, in particular, since acquiring the archive that I have begun to question his motivations for this activity.

My parents' walking holidays, undertaken in 1937 and 1938 along the 'Pilgrim's Way' (between Winchester and Canterbury) in southern England, were recorded for a clearly-stated reason, as noted in the following extracts; the first from the (named) 'Prologue' of the 1937 book, the second from the last page of that book, and the third from the 'Prologue' to the 1938 book:

> All good Pilgrim stories start with a prologue, whether necessary or not, but it is essential that this log has one for this reason – until we had walked for nearly two days we did not decide to keep a record ... The log is written that it may prove of interest to us and possible help to others in the future. We have tried to keep to the Way as shown by Ordnance Survey maps and 'The Pilgrim's Way in Kent' by Donald Maxwell – where these vary we have followed the latter. On the other hand, we have, for various reasons, deliberately left the Way at times.

NB. We have given no mileages, as we spent so much time on winding paths and
fields as to make it impossible to calculate any distance.

So ended the pilgrimage. We were lucky with weather, digs, food and everything
else. There was a deal of pure road walking (where the Way is made up for
modern use) but there were also miles of paths and tracks in the wilds. For hours
we would see no one and not until Canterbury did we see a crowd.

This [the Prologue] is most necessary, as we have worked backwards with
this journey, doing the second half first and the first half a year later. Since
last year we have acquired a marvellous book "The Pilgrim's Road" by J.C.
Elliston Erwood, and this is going to be very useful on a stretch of country that
is practically unmapped as far as the Pilgrim's Way is concerned.

It is clear from the extracts given above that guidance for later travels, either by my
father, himself, or, more likely, by other travellers, was the principal motivation
for setting down details of these two holidays, including sketch maps of the
route taken and notes on accommodation. Although my father refers his reader
to two published guide books, which are in my possession now and which make
fascinating reading in themselves, it seems that what he was actually trying to do
was compile an alternative guide for walkers on the Pilgrim's Way (see Figure
5.2). It is interesting that the inter-War period has been described by many authors
(e.g. see Korte 2000) as the 'golden age' of travel literature and this may well have
encouraged my father to write his own, personalised accounts. Whether the books
were ever used in this way by later travellers, I do not know, although the rapid
on-set of War in the following year possibly put paid to the likelihood of their use
until such time as they would have been substantially out of date.

Nevertheless, these two 'holiday books' and all the later ones *were* 'used'
subsequently to some extent. Each Christmas, during the gathering that always
took place in my parents' home on Christmas Eve, the book compiled that year
would be produced and pored over by family and friends. In addition the books
were often consulted in the years following their completion when someone was
visiting a specific place and wanted to know what there was to see there. I often
used the books myself in this way, but I am unsure whether my father ever referred
back to his own previously written books. In his writing he occasionally notes
having visited places before, for example in this entry from 1992:

Our 55th wedding anniversary, so we thought we would renew acquaintances
with Winchester, where we spent a night in 1938 before starting on a walk along
the Pilgrim's Way to Canterbury' (12th June).

However, he had clearly forgotten that they had not actually walked as far as
Canterbury in that year. Later in 1992, on another holiday, he writes:

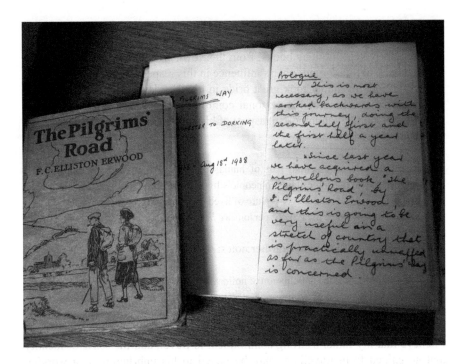

Figure 5.2   A 'Pilgrim's Way' holiday book (Source: author's own photograph)

I feel certain that we have been there [Wallington House] before, but I cannot remember when' (11th July).

These two examples also illustrate the fact that the 'holiday books' were always written in full at the time, rather than in draft for later correction, as would have been the case had they been intended for 'publication' in any sense. The 'holiday books' were certainly not written for a wider audience, outside the circle of family and friends, so I am unsure whether my father would have wanted me to analyse the books in the way I have done here (although my mother, before her death, did give her permission for them to be used in the current project).

Apart from establishing a permanent record for possible later use, there were clearly other motivations behind my father's keeping of 'holiday books'. I believe that he used the activity as a form of habitual mental discipline, which is why he persisted in it as he aged and after he was 'registered blind', despite the fact that the entries made often recorded little beyond trips to the shops, lunches eaten and evenings spent playing cards. Other examples of this mental trait were his need to read or hear the national news, and also to complete the Daily Telegraph cryptic crossword (when he was blind, from clues read out to him) on a daily basis, all his life. He tried (largely unsuccessfully as far as I personally am concerned) to instil this mental discipline into his children and grandchildren; two of my children have regularly kept 'holiday books' from their own world travels and have often referred back to their grandfather's influence in this respect.

In addition, my father took great pride in his 'holiday books', not as literary works but as evidence of his personal commitment to holidays and travelling, which provided such an important aspect of his personal identity. As McCabe and Foster (2006: 194) note:

> Storytelling is an essential part of human nature .. Experiences of tourism achieve a type of iconic status in people's lives, as they communicate the story of their worlds into the bigger picture of lived identities created through actions, attitudes and values, the type of person *'we like to think we are'*.

And as Desforges (2000: 930) further notes:

> The full process of the anticipation of holidays, the act of travel, and the narration of holiday stories on return are all tied into an imagination and performance which enables tourists to think of themselves as particular sorts of person.

I believe that my father's strong commitment to travel, and the sense of identity that he gained from travelling, may be linked to his upbringing as a working class child and his lack of opportunity to take holidays until he had established himself in a middle class profession as an adult. It is interesting that he recorded no holidays, apart from Scout camping trips, until after he was married. By contrast, my mother came from a (newly) middle class family and her experiences of month-long family summer holidays, which were occasionally mentioned to me over the years, went back to early childhood and were continued with college friends in her twenties, so she was much more relaxed about the whole business of holidays away from home (and, indeed, about life in general). Therefore, it is probable she did not feel the same personal need as my father to record the holidays in detail, either for posterity, or in order to establish a sense of identity through travelling.

Conclusion

This chapter has attempted a preliminary analysis of the archive of 'holiday books' left by my father, Jack Tivers, dating from the years 1937 to 1996. I have tried to show that significant themes arise from a consideration of the contents of the books and also that the specific *contexts* within which the books were compiled need to be taken into account in order to understand and interpret the contents. In addition I have attempted to tease out the chief underlying motivations that may have led to the construction of the archive. There is much material not as yet analysed in detail; in particular, there is the potential for a more thorough investigation of the narrative itself, and of the mode of narration, as well as an opportunity to enliven parts of the narrative by attempting to reconstruct certain holidays in the present, in order to make comparisons of places and their representations at different times. Furthermore the scope of the archive would enable useful, longitudinal studies to be made within a number of areas; for example, time use on holidays, spatial mapping of travels, postcard and place imagery, and holiday costs and expenditure, amongst other potential subjects in the study of twentieth-century tourism.

References

Bougen, P.D. 1994. Joking Apart: The Serious Side to the Accountant Stereotype, *Accounting Organizations and Society*, 19(3), 319–35.

Desforges, L. 2000. Traveling the World: Identity and Travel Biography, *Annals of Tourism Research*, 27(4), 926–45.

Driver, F. and Martins, L. 2002, John Septimus Roe and the Art of Navigation, c. 1815–1830, *History Workshop Journal*, 54(1), 145–62.

Harrison, J. 2003. *Being a Tourist: Finding Meaning in Pleasure Travel*. *Vancouver:* UBC Press.

Korte, B. 2000. *English Travel Writing: From Pilgrimage to Postcolonial Explorations*. Basingstoke: Palgrave.

Lorimer, H. 2003. Telling Small Stories: Spaces of Knowledge and the Practice of Geography, *Transactions of the Institute of British Geography*, 28(2), 197–217.

Lorimer H. and Spedding N. 2005. Locating Field Science: a Geographical Family Expedition to Glen Roy, Scotland, *British Journal of the History of Science*, 38 (1), 13–33.

Matless, D. 1998. *Landscape and Englishness*. London: Reaktion.

McCabe, S. and Foster, C. 2006. The Role and Function of Narrative in Tourist Interaction, *Journal of Tourism and Cultural Change*, 4(3), 194–215.

Sladen, C. 2002. Holidays at Home in the Second World War, *Journal of Contemporary History*, 37(1), 67–89.

Sladen, C. 2005. Wartime Holidays and the 'Myth of the Blitz', *Cultural and Social History*, 2(2), 215–46.

Therkelsen, A. and Gram, M. 2008. The Meaning of Holiday Consumption: Construction of Self Among Mature Couples, *Journal of Consumer Culture*, 8(2), 269–92.

Warren, A. 1986. Sir Robert Baden-Powell, the Scout Movement and Citizen Training in Great Britain, 1900–1920, *English Historical Review*, 101(399), 376–98.

Chapter 6

Stories and (E)Motions: Travelling in Nicolas Bouvier's Narratives

Lénia Marques and Maria Sofia Pimentel Biscaia

Even if your night's shelter is uncertain
and your goal still far away
know that there doesn't exist
a road without an end -
don't be sad

Hafiz

Introduction

In this chapter we will focus on the work of the Swiss traveller, Nicolas Bouvier (1929–98) seeking to understand how motivations and, in particular, emotions, feelings, sensations and impressions experienced along the journey are artistically expressed. This study will focus firstly on the interrelationship between travelling/tourism and emotions in the work of one of the landmark writers of travel literature from the second half of the twentieth century, and secondly on how this work has encouraged others to travel, write and express themselves by artistic means in the context of an interpretation of this emotional framework. Indeed, Bouvier's works recreate imaginaries beyond psychic and physical exoticised landscapes. Bouvier's writings have acquired an increasing importance in contemporary configurations of social and geographic travel imaginaries. In this context the anthropologist Jean–Didier Urbain (2001), among other scholars such as Erik Cohen (1979), Dean MacCannell (1976) and John Urry (1990), provides an interesting perspective for dialogue between the social sciences and the humanities. The artistic works by Bouvier will therefore serve as a departure point for a discussion that aims to provide new perspectives for research about emotions, artistic expression, travel and tourism at the intersection of social sciences, literature and other arts.

The Beginning of the Story

Nicolas Bouvier was a traveller, a writer, a photographer and an iconographer. He made his first long trip from Geneva, his hometown, to northern Europe when he was a teenager. He went to Lapland on his own and his father's sole request was that he wrote about what he saw. This is the story's starting point. For Nicolas Bouvier correspondence was central in defining himself and his relationships. He saved all letters and he asked others to do the same. He also gathered notes, observations, pictures and, through an exercise of concentration and evocation of memory, he started a very precise and careful writing. His best known journey is the one he made in 1953 with his friend, the painter Thierry Vernet, to Afghanistan. This journey was the origin of *L'Usage du monde [The Way of the World]* (1963), a book written by Bouvier and illustrated by Vernet. In Kabul, Bouvier and Vernet went their separate ways and this book's narrative ended there. However, Bouvier continued his journey for a further three years; after Afghanistan he went to India, Ceylon (Sri Lanka) and Japan, returning to the latter some years afterwards with his wife. After *The Way of the World*, Bouvier wrote *Le Poisson-Scorpion [The Scorpion-Fish]* (1981), a dark narrative approaching the fantastic and illustrating his painful experience in Ceylon. Though this book was only published in 1981 (more than 20 years after his visit), in the interim Bouvier also published *Japon [Japan]* (1967), which later became *Chronique japonaise [The Japanese Chronicle]* (1975). During his travels Bouvier was always using a camera but it was only in Japan that he began to practice professional photography. Behind the travelling, pieces of both writing and photography build and recreate Bouvier's story. In these artistic works emotion and motion go hand-in-hand, which is why this artist's, and traveller's, works provide an interesting field of reflection about tourism and travelling, on the one hand, and the emotional scope implied in motion, on the other.

Between Nomadism and Sedentarism

Bouvier's thoughts and impressions proffer interesting new ways of looking into the act of travelling and the motivations implied in the motion of people. During his life Bouvier travelled in many different ways, driven by a large variety of motivations and factors. As well as the places already mentioned, he also wrote about and photographed other places that he visited at different periods in his life, such as the Isle of Aran in Ireland, China and Korea. Meanwhile, Geneva, his hometown, remained his safe harbour: 'I always had long sedentary periods in this house: every boat needs a dry hold and a port of registry, whose name is engraved on the stem' (Bouvier 2004: 1380).[1] It seems then that, at certain points, the 'nomad' became sedentary.

Haunted (and pushed) all his life by an internal need for motion, Bouvier was a nomad who brought back home emotions, objects and experiences to be carried on

---

1   Please note that while all other quotes from Bouvier's writings included in this chapter are sourced from English translations included in the list of references, the quotes from Bouvier's (2004) *Routes et déroutes* are authors' own translations.

in his day-to-day life. As Urbain (2002: 328) notes, when speaking of the tourist (and one could conflate 'tourist' with 'traveller' at this point): 'Does the tourist cease to exist once back at home?'.[2] Urbain makes the point that, not only is he [*sic*] still – maybe always! – a tourist, but he should probably also be considered 'a temporarily settled nomad' (2002: 329). This seemingly simple statement has greater implications when space itself is described as 'nomad' or 'sedentary': 'sedentary space is striated, by walls, enclosures, and roads between enclosures, while nomad space is smooth, marked only by "'traits" that are effaced and displacd in the trajectory' (Deleuze and Guattari 2004: 420). According to Deleuze and Guattari, it is not movement that makes the nomad; it is a concurrence of aspects, but mainly the appropriation of a smooth space. In nomad space, deterritorialisation is permanent and is never replaced with reterritorialisation (Deleuze and Guattari 2004: 420). Nomad and sedentary spaces may exist solely in their mutual and complex relations (Deleuze and Guattari 2004: 524). Whether in a physical or a psychological way, the tourist and the traveller are more than the simple exporters of influence; they are importers as well (Urbain 2002: 330). Therefore, in this sense, one is offered two different perspectives on the same reality; detachment and appropriation, deterritorialisation and reterritorialisation, input and output. The familiar place transfigures itself into the unfamiliar; it becomes the 'ailleurs'. Urbain explains how this occurs: 'He [the nomad] achieves it through these transfers from the "ailleurs": clothing, gastronomy, photography or others; these traces, images, gestures, flavours, perfumes, all the memory of "hereafter". ... *He fuses the worlds...*' (Urbain 2002: 331). Reterritorialisation happens in this case, though in the familiar (and striated) space that will be reorganised and restructured according to the new and unfamiliar experiences made possible by travel. Furthermore, not only do tangible objects and experiences become part of the traveller's world, but they also become an integral part of the subject's own psychological and sociological construction. Chains of emotions (Collins 2004) are built, not only among subjects, but also related to elements (for example, objects and symbols) that represent other cultures, and 'otherness' in general.

   Misunderstandings between traveller/tourist and locals do sometimes take place but, in spite of potential cultural confusion, this process of appropriation does have a fundamental impact, both in helping the memory and in perpetuating the trip. Like most travellers Bouvier is a 'collector', despite what he asserts in the following:

> I am certainly not a collector, but every important trip has its own gris–gris. ... You
> obviously do not exhibit it all, since this is not the museum of Man. But everything
> that is on the wall recalls important things. When I am writing a book, the walls
> of the room where I am writing are covered with scribbles, photos or documents
> regarding this text. Once the book is finished, and this is the graphic framing of

---

2   Similar to the quotes from Bouvier's (2004) *Routes et déroutes*, all the quotes from Urbain's (2002) *L'Idiot du Voyage* included in this chapter are authors' own translations.

an intellectual project, everything disappears in a big envelope ... and the walls
become bare once more.

(Bouvier 2004: 1380)

Here Bouvier describes the 're-experience' of travelling. His re-creation of
experiences is, however, not permanent, since the walls must become bare again
so that new items can be attached to them temporarily. He understands that the
items he has collected were parts of the experience of only one man and he does
not wish to carry the weight of representing a 'museum of Man'. The objects
and notes that Bouvier collected are voices that have something to tell him about
his journeys, about the cultures he came across and, most particularly, about the
people he met. That is why, more than mere physical and tangible objects, they
evoke the spirit of travelling and of the encounters he experienced.

Encounters: Revivification and Disenchantment

Despite the recurrent fatigue during his journeys, humour, irony and an insightful
look at the *outside* permeate Bouvier's work. *The Way of the World* and *The
Scorpion–Fish* constitute two complementary parts of the same journey before
Bouvier had arrived in Japan. The first is characterised by a cheerful tone, even if
human misery, pain, poverty and death are often evoked. The joy of the encounter
resides in simple gestures and, as in many other places, Bouvier and Vernet make
friends in Turkey:

> He was a large, cordial man, waiting for us in his pyjamas ... between a basket
> of apples and a red-hot stove. He didn't have a word of German, English or
> French. We knew scarcely twenty words of Turkish and were too tired to launch
> into gesticulations and sketches, so we all sat eating apples and smiling at each
> other. Then he showed us the skin of a bear he'd killed the previous week, and
> a silver fox. When we admired it, he offered it to us, holding out the fur with
> trembling hands while his brown eyes pleaded to keep it. We firmly declined it.
> (Bouvier 2007: 87–8)

This episode, a simple anecdote, offers much food for thought. The description
of the man does not tell us much about his physical characteristics. It is his
psychology that is crucial; the man appears as 'cordial'. His eyes are brown but
they express an imploring attitude; he wants to give away something that he
values and he smiles. In the context described, the possibilities of communication
are considerably reduced. The subjects involved do not have any language in
common and the fatigue is too encumbering either for gestures or drawings to
be attempted. However, mutual observation, sharing and smiling seem to be
sufficient to establish a successful relationship between native and foreigner; as
he says in another work: 'There is no better communication than laughing; no

better passport' (Bouvier 2004: 1358). As a writer, Bouvier is careful to provide cultural details explaining things that could appear strange to most of his readers. Thus, for example, he writes in one footnote: 'in Turkey, as in Persia, as soon as the day's business was done men put on pyjamas' (Bouvier 2007: 87). His writing becomes a bridge, not only between individuals, but also between cultures. Ultimately, his priority is to communicate and to avoid tensions, especially those of a cultural or linguistic nature.

Nevertheless, not every encounter and experience that he has is positive. As a traveller he can see, feel and in a certain way express the concurrence of misery and beauty. Bouvier writes the following in Persia, for example:

> Despite the poverty on the one hand and the baseness on the other, it remains the most consistently refined nation in the world, and also the most resigned. Why would a peasant, deprived of everything, have a taste for traditional poetry, which is not at all a rustic form of expression ... ?
>
> (Bouvier 2007: 207)

He sees misery, turpitude, resignation and a delight in poetry; a complex texture of feelings. He views the great encounters that he has as enriching and healthy, no matter in what conditions the traveller has found himself, and therefore creates *The Way of the World* as an outstanding and powerful piece of writing. Rather than presenting his own feelings and emotions, in his works Bouvier tries to observe and capture those of others.

Bouvier supported his written work with his photography. At the time of his travelling to Afghanistan photography was merely a hobby, a means of helping memory and providing a more immediate approach to the world, since he considered that writing took him too much time.[3] However, a few months later in Japan, the camera became his means of livelihood. In Bouvier's photographs, we see landscapes and people, details of everyday life, everyday gestures, as well as numerous faces expressing indifference, curiosity, rebellion, joy, and many other feelings and emotions. His photographs represent space and time; they arise in that exact moment where the subjectivity of the Other and of the Self (the one behind the camera) are brought together in a single movement. In a similar way to the largely unknown photographs that he left, the texts by Bouvier, and *The Way of the World* in particular, bring to life the different encounters, people and episodes that he experienced. Some comments are simple, direct, honest and beautiful; for example, 'The Baluchi kept me happy' (Bouvier 2007: 241).

Harmony and joy are constant echoes in *The Way of the World*. Conversely, in *The Scorpion-Fish*, pain, disease, suffering and a sort of disenchantment are experienced in the 'enchanted island', where one loses a sense of conscience and identity fades away; body and mind seem to fuse with the surroundings. Here,

---

3   The photographs taken prior to his arrival to Japan remained unseen for many years. A set of photographs was later published with the title *L'Œil du voyageur* (Bouvier 2001).

encounters are difficult and people indifferent: 'Our relations are thus reduced to a reciprocal tolerance, hesitant and shy. ... But it's fine as it is: ... this place unlike any I've known, a lair where I take the double pulse of the town, that of the men and that of the insects' (Bouvier 1987: 42). There is mutual tolerance, even if the outsider is seen as an invader, a tolerance that is characteristic of a neighbourhood where people of several different castes live. Despite the relationship tensions, Bouvier is sensitive to the beauty and the particularities of the island. After all, it is the latter that Bouvier constantly seeks and, indeed, also what he expects the traveller in general to search for; the particularities of places, cultures, and communities. The unfamiliarity of a place, made up of specific features that make it unique, is what makes that place special, completely different from the rest and 'authentic'.[44] He sees the challenge as being to gain entrance to an unfamiliar world and, once there, gradually to achieve a balance between positive and negative aspects through personal experience. Therefore, in summary, encounters may be reviving and give a sense of harmony and peace with the world, the Other and the Self, but they can be also a source of disenchantment.

Boundaries in Motion

Reading Bouvier's verbal and visual works, cross-referencing these readings with other works, notably Jean-Didier Urbain's (2002) *L'Idiot du voyage*, and simultaneously considering the general field of tourism studies, a question arises about the actual difference between two traditionally opposing concepts, 'travel' and 'tourism', and what exactly 'travelling' means in the late twentieth and early twenty-first centuries. Bouvier was clearly a traveller more than a tourist, even though Urbain (2002: 328) says that this status can be questioned, since there are some 'problematic travellers: heroes with undefined status'. The difficulties in delimiting a traveller from a tourist also arise from the fact that, nowadays, tourists can go (almost) anywhere and see (almost) everything.

It is interesting to note that, when talking about some organised circuits, Bouvier considers tourists simply as 'travellers' (Bouvier 2004). His choice of terminology might be explained by the negative connotation that the concept of 'tourist' still has today, as Jean-Didier Urbain suggests in his works. However, it

---

4   Authenticity' is a subject long discussed but about which there is little consensus. We consider that authenticity should nevertheless be taken into account because, on the one hand, cultural tourists still stress 'authenticity' as one of the main reasons for travelling to certain destinations, while on the other hand, and maybe as a reaction to this, some destinations are promoting themselves as *authentic* (for example, in the tourism campaigns: 'Mali – Une Afrique authentique' and 'Auténtica Cuba'). Simultaneously, it is also important to bear in mind that globalisation clearly influences the ways in which authenticity is perceived and studied.

is possible that Bouvier uses the word simply because being a tourist is, after all, also to perform a certain kind of travelling.

For a period of time Nicolas Bouvier worked as a guide for a travel agency that organised cultural trips; the lonely traveller (even if he sometimes travelled with a friend or his wife) became the leader of organised tour groups. At first he doubted himself, even if everything went well. He recounts his experience of this new positionality: 'Harmony must prevail in a group of travellers who have different characters, different rhythms, but who also want to see as much as possible, since it is so expensive. It is exhausting; we are running all the time' (Bouvier 2004: 1357–8).

These travellers belong to a 'tribe' of tourists that are looking for culture, monuments and places but also want to interact with people. They head off, they walk, they get tired, they take public transport, they eat and they are open-minded. Their expressed need is tremendous, not only in the sense of getting 'value for money', but also insofar as the travellers want to get the most out of their trip, within a limited time, in terms of culture. Nevertheless, he focuses on observing and capturing the surroundings: 'I did not make many comments while we were looking at things, because I believe that you have to let them strike the eye, the ear, the nose without enclosing them in gloss' (Bouvier 2004: 1359). This is the philosophy of a traveller – of the traveller, Nicolas Bouvier. As a traveller, an explorer or a tourist, in a distant land or just around the corner, one should focus on observing and receiving what can be apprehended with all the senses. The gloss comes afterwards, at a specific moment. The concepts 'traveller' and 'tourist' are difficult to define especially given the rapid changes in tourism experiences. If there is a significant difference between the two concepts it might lie in the differences of attitude and time. Differences in attitude have been considered in the example above while differences relating to time will be considered in the next section.

The Christmas Tree: Appropriation and Intangibility

It would seem that the main difference between the *homo viator* and the *homo touristicus* (Urbain 2002: 175) is, in essence, time; for the *homo viator*, there is no set date for the return. In contrast, according to the World Tourism Organization (UNWTO), the notion of tourism 'comprises the activities of persons travelling to and staying in places outside their usual environment for not more than one consecutive year for leisure, business and other purposes not related to the exercise of an activity remunerated from within the place visited' (UNWTO 2001: 13). In Bouvier's case, the longer a journey lasted, the harder it became to support himself (teaching French, lecturing, writing newspaper pieces or taking photographs). Today, a traveller has to go further and further, unperturbed by danger, to find new unexplored spaces (like the desert, the jungle, and so on). However, Bouvier's wish was to find for himself what others had already discovered. Writing and photography relieved tensions as well as serving as an exercise against oblivion and as a way of creating memories. He was not a wandering pilgrim; he was a nomadic traveller, with fairly accurate maps. His great journey to Asia was planned largely with Thierry Vernet. They were limited in money but not in time; thus, both stayed as long as they wanted. Their car, a Fiat Topolino, also marked the rhythm; for instance, they stayed all winter in Tabriz because it was impossible to continue until spring. The length of Bouvier's stay in Ceylon was another example; seven months (nine in the novel *The Scorpion-Fish*), during which he had to wait until he gained sufficient psychological and physical strength to leave the island. From there, he went to Japan, where he found a culture that would inspire him until his death.

The attitude of a traveller towards time has an immense influence on space, since space has to be perceived differently. More time allows a better appropriation of the new experiences; other spaces, a greater variety of cultural constructions, wider sets of experiences different from the ones proffered by their own culture, a vast range of impressions and memories, and new acquaintances. Coming across new peoples and cultures presupposes being confronted by 'otherness'. Thus the encounter brings about emotional reactions; identification, confrontation, differentiation. A structured identity is confronted with an unfamiliar world that challenges it. Possession becomes important and new experiences give way to seizing what is happening.[55] Afterwards a process of adaptation is initiated, during which each traveller integrates the experience of space and of culture. It is in this respect that Bouvier's works are unique in the history of travel writing. The charm of his writing and photographs lies in the way he expresses his point of view in order to set off a wide range of emotions. The strength of this emotional universe might seem contradictory when thinking of the poetics of disappearance, which are characteristic of his works (Hambursin 1997, Ridon 2002). However, a delicate balance is maintained. Despite his appropriation of the outside world, Nicolas Bouvier attempts to focus human beings on their more humble needs; in the end, travel is not only about them, it is about perceiving and understanding human nature. Bouvier's works depict the human condition.

Although time can create a distinction between the 'traveller' and 'this innumerable little traveller' (Urbain 2002: 27) – the tourist –, it is the attitude the two have regarding seizing new experiences that is often the substantially different element. For his part, Bouvier believes that '[y]ou don't travel in order to deck yourself with exoticism and anecdotes like a Christmas tree, but so that the route plucks you, rinses you, wrings you out, makes you like one of those towels threadbare with washing that are handed out with slivers of soap in brothels' (Bouvier 1987: 38). Hence, travelling acts more as a purge than as a way of having a string of experiences. For Bouvier, the experiences of travelling are the means to become a more humble and selfless human being; the Christmas tree experience is empty of signification. A sort of detachment has to be learned during the process:

---

5   Henri Michaux, another writer, traveller and painter, also emphasises this in his works. One of his last works is entitled *Saisir* (1979).

> Like water, the world ripples across you and for a while you take on its colours.
> Then it recedes, and leaves you face to face with the void you carry inside yourself,
> confronting that central inadequacy of soul which you must learn to rub shoulders
> with and to combat, and which, paradoxically, may be our surest impetus.
>
> (Bouvier 2007: 317).

Travel serves the purpose of purifying the Self; it is, indeed, motion that makes everything possible. It is not the result that is primary, but the process, that is, the travel itself: 'Travelling outgrows its motives. It soon proves sufficient in itself. You think you are making a trip, but soon it is making you – or unmaking you' (Bouvier 2007: 13).

However, despite the differences outlined above, it could be argued that boundaries between 'traveller' and 'tourist' remain blurred. In fact, '[t]oday's tourist is more and more committed to this movement of exploration of spaces *and men*. The present development of international, cultural, ethnic or even participating tourism, like "holiday on the farm", shows this' (Urbain 2002: 35). Agrotourism, ecotourism and cultural tourism are evidence of evolution, in the sense that they contribute to the intersection of fields that previously stood apart. A cultural tourist can go on a journey alone or in the company of a few friends, to visit monuments and landscapes as well as seeking to understand local cultures, to meet local people, to savour local gastronomy, and so on. This type of tourist may often straightforwardly recognise the boundary between real local practices and those which are set up for tourists in order to meet their expectations. However, in the case of the latter, an interesting phenomenon sometimes occurs. The actions that are constantly repeated are in fact incorporated into the community's everyday life; these acts, which are *performances* of authenticity, become habitual. In this situation, the concept of authenticity is subject to an ongoing process of re-evaluation and reconstruction as change is motivated by attitudes to social cohesion and by economic convenience. With regard to boundaries, another aspect has to be considered. In Western culture and thought, the traveller appears as the first one to get somewhere or the one who accomplishes a certain kind of travel that no one has done before. Therefore s/he is unique, or at least the first in the line of other travellers. Bouvier's experiences of travel are situated on quite a different level, thus challenging this paradigm. Nicolas Bouvier was certainly not the first to take the route to Asia. He was, in fact, inspired by many previous accounts of travel.

Bouvier wrote extensively about his travels, these taking place alone, with his friend or his wife, or, as already mentioned, with a group. Occasionally, he lectured at various universities around the world and also considered this to be a form of travelling, since he always took the time to explore beyond the campuses. He wrote books, gave talks on the radio, participated in exhibitions and was the central character in a documentary (*Le Hibou et la baleine*, 1993). Other documentaries and tributes followed: *Nicolas Bouvier, le vent des mots* (1999 [2008]); *Nicolas Bouvier – 22 Hospital Street* (2005); *Nomad's land: Sur les traces de Nicolas Bouvier* (2008); *Usure du monde: Hommage à Nicolas Bouvier* (2008).

In the preface to the last of these documentaries, Nicolas Bouvier's widow, Éliane Bouvier, states that Frédéric Lecloux (the director) is one of 'Nicolas's children'. In fact, all those who are inspired by his work may in some respects be considered his 'children'. It is interesting to speculate how many more there are to be found around the world; the many travellers who are motivated by Nicolas Bouvier's writings and photographs or by the documentaries about him, made by others. Should these travellers, who have also testified to their travels with a documentary or a book, be thought of as part of the same model? A more poignant question might involve considering those who will follow Lecloux, who followed Bouvier who, himself, to some extent, followed Ella Maillart; who shared her travelling experience with Bouvier prior to his long journey. Perhaps 'follow' is not the best word to use; perhaps the term 'be inspired by' or 'follow in the footsteps of' would be better. It is interesting to ponder whether 'followers' should be considered 'tourists', pursuing literary tourism or, possibly, film tourism. There is no doubt however that they are also travellers. Objects that inspire others, such as a book, a photograph, a documentary or a fiction film, cease to be mere objects, and turn into an integral part of a given culture, in this case, the intangible culture of travel.

Conclusions

As an observer and anthropologist, Jean-Didier Urbain (2002) refers to the changes brought about by tourism. For his part, he avoids taking a stand on the differences between a traveller and a tourist. However, this attitude may involve risks, in that it overlooks potentially damaging consequences, both cultural and economic, which may result from tourism. Urbain (2002: 65) asks: 'could cultural underestimation of tourism, since its origins are deeply rooted in mentalities, have determined the ensuing economic underestimation?' Places may benefit from tourism, and not only from an economic point of view. However, if tourism is harming part of what makes up the distinct sense of a place, a better solution should be sought. Tourism can be both a constructive and a destructive phenomenon, as is well known,. We should turn to the example of Bouvier's attitude and works and realise that people may be foreigners or outsiders but still contribute to building an intercultural bridge, simultaneously giving and learning.

Motion is what makes both the simplest of tourists and the greatest of travellers leave their familiar territory. They seek emotions and spiritual meanings and they live, more or less intensely, in relationship with space and 'otherness'. The belief that a tourist is the 'bastard sibling' of a traveller is better understood as a myth that is being torn apart by changes. Research needs to contribute to the understanding of this change and try to reframe both characters in a new way. A further consideration of the relationship between tourism and culture would certainly lead us to give due importance to the intercultural role of the tourist, a tourist increasingly respectful of the Other and curious about the Other's culture. Tourists have a privileged role as cultural go-betweens, who can strive, as foreigners, to participate, to interact and to integrate with local communities, while at the same time helping to protect the distinct features of their place and culture. This delicate balance has been referred to as sustainable development within tourism. The challenge arising from ease of travel in today's world, often accompanied by a tendency to standardisation, means that governments, companies, institutions and researchers need to be contributing to sustainable tourism development. While tourists might need to be educated, every tourist can surely find their place. The change of attitudes and behaviours in favour of intercultural dialogue would be a true legacy from the traveller and writer, Nicolas Bouvier.

Acknowledgements

Financial support for this research was provided by the Fundação para a Ciência e a Tecnologia, III Quadro Comunitário de Apoio, and the Centre of Studies on Migrations and Intercultural Relations. The authors wish to thank Tim Wallis for his comments on the initial version of the paper.

References

Bouvier, N. 1963. *L'Usage du monde*. Genève: Droz.

Bouvier, N. 1967. *Japon*. Lausanne: Éditions Rencontre.

Bouvier, N. 1975. *Chronique japonaise*. Lausanne: L'Âge d'Homme.

Bouvier, N. 1981. *Le Poisson-Scorpion*. Vevey: Bertil Galland.

Bouvier, N. 1987 [1981]. *The Scorpion-Fish* (translated by R. Marsack). Manchester: Carcanet.

Bouvier, N. 2001. *L'Œil du voyageur*. Paris: Hoëbeke.

Bouvier, N. 2004 [1992]. Routes et déroutes. Entretiens, in *Œuvres*, edited by N. Bouvier, Paris: Gallimard, 1249–1388.

Bouvier, N. 2007 [1963]. *The Way of the World* (translated by R. Marsack). London: Eland.

Bouvier, N. and Plattner, P. 1993. *Le Hibou et la Baleine*. Genève–Carouge: Zoé.

Cohen, E. 1979. A Phenomenology of Tourist Experiences. *Sociology*, 13 (2), 179–201.

Collins, R. 2004. *Interaction Ritual Chains*. New Jersey: Princeton University Press.

Deleuze, G. and Guattari, F. 2004. *A Thousand Plateaus: Capitalism and Schizophrenia* (translated by B. Massumi). London: Continuum.

Hambursin, O. 1997. Voyage et exercice de disparition: les dangers du Poisson-Scorpion de Nicolas Bouvier. *Lettres Romanes*, 51(3–4), 275–87.

Le Hibou et la Baleine (dir. Patricia Plattner, 1993).

MacCannell, D. 1976. *The Tourist: A New Theory of the Leisure Class*. New York: Schocken Books.

Michaux, H. 1979. *Saisir.* Paris: Fata Morgana.

Nicolas Bouvier – 22 Hospital Street (dir. Christoph Kühn, 2005).

Nicolas Bouvier, le vent des mots (dir. Joël Calmettes and Olivier Bauer 2008[1999]).

Nomad's land: Sur les traces de Nicolas Bouvier (dir. Gaël Métroz, 2008).

Ridon, J.-X. 2002. Pour une poétique du voyage comme disparition, in *Autour de Nicolas Bouvier. Résonances,* edited by C. Albert, N. Laporte, and J.-Y. Pouilloux, Genève: Zoé, 120–35.

UNWTO 2001. *Tourism Satellite Account: Recommended Methodological Framework* Available at: http://www.oecdbookshop.org/ [accessed: 15 January 2011].

Urbain, J.-D. 2002[1991]. *L'Idiot du voyage.* Paris: Payot.

Urry, J. 1990. *The Tourist Gaze: Leisure and Travel in Contemporary Societies.* London: Sage.

Usure du monde: Hommage à Nicolas Bouvier (dir. Frédéric Lecloux, 2008).

Chapter 7

Representations of Tourism in Twentieth-Century Opera

David Botterill

Introduction

Opera is often claimed to be the most complete art form because it combines the emotional power of music with dramatic performance, shaped by creative directors into a production utilising the theatrical arts of lighting, costume design and stage sets to effect a three dimensional, visual and aural experience. Action on the stage is accompanied by musicians in the pit, often on an equivalent scale to a symphony orchestra. The immediacy of the singers' voices as they soar above the orchestral accompaniment heightens characterisation and shapes the narrative just as much as the roles provided by the libretto, plot and production. The chilling chords that accompany a *verismo*[1] villain or the plaintive cries of a *bel canto*[2] soprano heroine communicate directly with the raw emotions of the audience. Narrative in opera is formed by a combination of the libretto, production and performance and is primarily 'experienced' in a comprehensive assault on the senses.

I am therefore very conscious that it is selling opera narrative somewhat short to only 'write' about it in this chapter. Indeed this is but one of many particularly difficult problems in providing an adequate account of the representation of tourism in twentieth-century opera. To do the art form justice it would be necessary to see, at least once, productions of the 38 operas selected for the research study. Given the variations between productions and between the performances of different singers, to see them just once might be considered inadequate. Even if it were practically possible then it is highly unlikely, since the cost of operatic productions severely limits the repertoire of operas in production in the world at any one time. Indeed, for this reason, many of the operas included here have only ever received a single production run and some have yet to be seen in their entirety. Enthusiasm for opera is highly dependent, therefore, on audio recordings and increasingly upon professional

---

1   'Realism' taken from literature and specifically applied to the brutal and earthy dramas of late-nineteenth century and early-twentieth century Italian opera (Holden 2001: 1101)

2   Literally 'beautiful singing', bel canto is a term generally applied to a vocal style originating in eighteenth-century Italy that emphasises an impeccable legato, well focussed timbre, and graceful phrasing.

quality film recordings of productions. Where they exist, these surrogates for performance experience are also important research data in this opera project. I have found that reading opera narratives in depth requires multiple 'listenings', or viewings, before the strands or themes of narrative assert themselves fully.

Opera involves collaboration between many intellectuals in the creative process of origination, production and performance. In common with many other performing arts, one of the criteria in the 'success' of an opera is measured in its ability to communicate with an audience. An opera must both provide points of connection with an audience in a contemporary sense and contain echoes of enduring human experience. Considering Dove's (1998) *Flight*, for example, the setting of this comic opera in an airport terminal presents a contemporary twenty-first century audience with a familiar space onto which they can project their own airport experiences, when interpreting the characterisations of the singer actors as they depict holiday makers, airline and airport staff. On its own, however, this is insufficient. The enduring communicative power of the opera is conveyed as the characters' stories emerge. The audience is drawn into the characters' struggles to confront their own human frailties, the 'lottery' of life opportunities and the powers of institutional authority and forces of nature that collude to enable and constrain their life's aspirations. As in many forms of art, the audience or viewer experiences their own lives reflected back to them; together with the characters they can laugh at their folly, cry at their despair, love, hate, and gain solace from their fortitude. In this chapter I attempt to address the following questions: first, how do the creative architects of opera make sense of tourism? Second, what do they see in tourism that is both reflective specifically of the twentieth-century era and yet enduringly human, providing a point of connection with the audience? Third, how might the creative output of these artists and intellectuals conform to, or challenge, the collective understandings of the tourism academy?

The Opera Project

I began the project by searching from page 1 of the 1038 pages of Holden (2001)[3] for operas written in the twentieth century that might be seen as 'representations' of tourism. My expectations were modest. The guide is organised alphabetically by the composers' surnames and to my utter amazement I found my first opera in the 'A' entries on page 4! It was Adams's (1991) *The Death of Klinghoffer*, an opera based on the 1985 event in the Mediterranean of the hijacking of the cruise ship the Achille Lauro by Palestinian terrorists and the eventual murder of Leon Klinghoffer, a paralysed American Jewish passenger. I immediately halted my survey of Holden and immersed myself in this monumental work for several

---

3   Holden's (2001) authoritative guide is a compendium of 122 contributing authors. I draw heavily on their descriptions of the operas in my chapter and I make this collective acknowledgement of their contribution to my chapter.

months, overwhelmed by the power of the narrative first experienced through audio CD and subsequently through Penny Woolcock's fine Channel 4 Productions film of the opera on DVD. Researching the biblical and historical background to the opera, I was very surprised to read of the controversial storm that raged in America in 1991, following the early performances in New York and San Francesco (Fink 2005). So fierce was the attack by the New York Times' critic, that Adams himself became subject to a CIA interview each time he flew in and out of the US and, despite the success of productions in Helsinki in 2004 and Auckland and Edinburgh in 2005, the opera disappeared from the stage in the US for 28 years until it received a semi-staged performance at the Julliard Opera Centre in January 2009, conducted by the composer himself. My personal circumstances did not permit my attendance but, despite this, the opera had already become much more than a major artwork to me. Broadcast news of the Middle East conflict suddenly meant so much more, chance meetings with Palestinian delegates at a conference in the Netherlands took on extra significance and conversations with friends of the Jewish faith had a new focus. I began to get a sense of what my opera project might offer to tourism studies. For me, at least, Adams' opera connected my study of tourism to wider political events of the twentieth century, notably the subsequent terrorist acts in New York, Madrid and London, aimed at travel infrastructure.

Subsequently, the Holden guide led me to several other relevant works, most notably Britten's (1973) *Death in Venice*, based on Mann's novella and adapted for opera by Piper, and Dove's (1998) *Flight*, a performance of which I was able to attend at the Peacock Theatre in September 2008. The three operas, mentioned above and discovered through entries A, B, and D of Holden (2001), are currently at the heart of my opera project and I continue to be inspired by them. Despite my musical illiteracy I sometimes attempt to scan the orchestra score while I listen to recordings, study the librettos in detail, read cultural criticism about the operas and the other works of their composers and actively search for forthcoming productions as I am simultaneously also beginning to write about them as a part of my critical realist tourism project (Botterill 2008, 2011). I have now completed my three year survey of Holden and this chapter presents the initial results. The output is presented at the end of the chapter as an anthology; an alphabetic list, by composer, of the 38 opera titles, with the librettist also indicated where known. It is important to note the limitations of such an analysis of opera narrative, based as it is on secondary descriptive accounts, limited experience of performances and a reliance on sound recordings.

A Realist Challenge to the Ontology of Tourism 'But that opera is not about tourism…'

If the term 'tourism' is used in absolutist or foundationalist sense, it may be true to say that none of the 38 operas, included in my anthology of twentieth-century operas, is 'about tourism'. However, if the term is considered instead to be contingent and refutable, then it is reasonable to accept that operatic representations may provide us with some evidence of what enables and constrains tourism; what, as critical realists might say, makes tourism possible? Tourism exists as an assemblage of so many things; it depends on a particular ontological assemblage and ordering. Critical realists speak of an 'intransitive' domain (that which may exist, independently of our thoughts about it), which is a particular ordering of natural, material, social and human elements that exists independently of one's accumulated experiences of tourism and one's understanding of the phenomenon as it is represented in tourism studies. In contrast to this 'intransitive' domain of tourism, representations of tourism (concepts, categories and the language used to describe them) fall within what critical realists call the 'transitive' domain. Within opera, language does not only imply words, of course, but also a visual performance and an aural language, incorporating music and song. In a critical realist frame opera narratives are, therefore, transitive representations of tourism that may confirm, contrast or compete with other such representations, for example those relating to scientific discourse in the tourism academy or popular, commonsensical accounts of tourism.

Working in the transitive domain, it is my reading of an opera narrative as a representation of tourism that defines it as being 'to do' with tourism. The 38 operas identified in my anthology, all of them monumental artistic works, position certain artefacts of tourism directly in the narrative of operatic form. The material 'stuff' of tourism, for example, provides the setting for many of the operas, so revealing a liminal, subversive social order within archetypical tourist spaces; cruise ships feature in nine operas, hotels in five, airports and airliners, crashed or in flight, feature in four, the beach and the seaside resort take centre stage in seven. Mobile spaces capture human life in transient and fluid form, thus inviting an exploration of human behaviour in two operas set in trains, one in a car and those, already mentioned, set in cruise ships and aeroplanes. The symbolism of the mountain (one opera), the metaphor of the postcard (one opera) and the hedonism of the spa (two operas) provide fertile settings in which to engage the audience with the familiar, while also seducing, delighting or horrifying them with new or unexpected narratives (comic, tragic or even absurd) through character development, plot and, of course, music.

The analysis of operatic narratives offered here is related to two, competing representations of the ontology of tourism and thus both confirms and challenges the tourism studies canon; the 'dominant' narratives of tourism, on the one hand, and (what might be called) the 'counter' narratives to the ontological claims made in tourism studies, on the other. In addition, there is one narrative line that does not fit these categories, as will be discussed later. My analysis addresses the tendencies within tourism studies that are confirmed by another, distinct twentieth-century intellectual community; opera composers and librettists, and the original authors of works of literature adapted for opera. In addition, I am interested in how these intellectuals shape a counter narrative that has been accidentally missed, or deliberately ignored, by the tourism studies community and I begin to question why this might be so. I treat the counter narrative as a challenge to the practical adequacy of the ontological claims of contemporary tourism studies, thus enabling an exploration of what my analysis of operatic representations of tourism tells us about the trajectory of tourism studies. I am interested in how the ontology of tourism is both ordered and disordered or, to put it another way, which representations of tourism ontology are better (or, as critical realists would say, more practically adequate) accounts of the intransitive ontology of tourism; the enduring tendencies, the powers of objects and the generative mechanisms that enable and constrain tourism. Within a 'realist' perspective, I am seeking to make rational judgements between different transitive accounts of tourism knowledge of what tourism is; its ontological form.

Narratives of Tourism in the 38 Operas

In most of the 38 operas listed composers have worked with a librettist, often a poet or author, however, in nine of the operas the composer was also responsible for the libretto, either solely or in collaboration. Librettos were sometimes based on the original works of highly talented authors, such as Forster, Gogol, Herbert, Mann, Maupassant, Moravia, Saint-Exupéry, and Strindberg, sometimes drawing on biblical passages or classical Greek and Roman texts, and sometimes originating in response to a contemporary event. In any case, literary styles in the 38 operas are wide-ranging, including absurdist, allegorical, romantic, satirical, social realist and surrealist. The analysis of opera narratives proposed here will begin with those that conform to the dominant narratives found within tourism studies: Exploration, Wandering, Opulence and Spectacle. Table 7.1 provides a summary of the operas referred to in this section.

Table 7.1   Dominant narratives

Exploration	Wandering	Opulence/Spectacle
The Voyage	*The Man who Strides the Wind*	*Hotel Eden*
Marco Polo	*Outis [Nobody]*	*Show Boat*
Atlas	*Ein Transpiel [A Dream Play]*	*Im Weissen Rössl [At the White Horse Inn]*
Volo di Notte [Night Flight]	*Il Viaggio [The Journey]*	*Jackie O*
	Dead Souls	*La Station Thermale [The Spa]*

Exploration, Wandering, Opulence and Spectacle

Exploration

The idea of 'Exploration' is prevalent in many of the concepts and theories associated with tourist behaviour and tourism development (e.g. see Cohen 1979 and Butler 1980). The lives of the explorers Columbus (Glass 1991), Marco Polo (Tal 1966) and Alexandra David-Néel (Monk 1988) are celebrated in three late twentieth-century operas. In addition, following de Saint-Exupéry, Dallapicco's (1939) opera *Volo di Notte [Night Flight]* depicts the exploits of pioneer aviators who experimented with night flying in providing postal services in South America.

The heroic discoverer of new lands and riches is a powerful spectre in the iconography of contemporary, so called, independent tourism but, as Glass' librettist, Hwang, reminds us in The Voyage, the inevitable clash of cultures and dislocation caused by exploration are omnipresent. Commissioned to commemorate the five hundred year anniversary of the arrival of Columbus in America, the libretto offers not just an account of geographical heroics but also an exploration of voyage in the mind. The Acts depict three explorations; in Act 1 a spaceship lands on the earth in prehistoric times, in Act 2 Columbus recounts his relationship with Isabella as he languishes on his vessel en route to America, and in Act 3 earth twins discover the crystals left by the space travellers from Act 1, announce the discovery of a new planet and begin another voyage. The opera ends in an Epilogue in which Columbus is visited by the ghost of Isabella as he lies on his death bed. She is unrepentant of her exploitation of his discoveries. He rejects her and floats towards the stars. The intertwining of Columbus' personal life with his public exploits provides audiences with a human point of connection to the storyline, aided by the deliberate ploy of confusing the time line. The effect of the Act 1 / Act 3 interplay is to dislocate the action from the fifteenth century and to position the narrative in a kind of 'anytime', including the here and now. The exchange between Columbus and Isabella in the Epilogue poses the audience with a contemporary question: what is a just relationship between discovery and exploitation?; a question that is all too often ignored in contemporary tourism studies, as the academy joins the tourism industry in the race to the newest destination, the translation of that destination into marketable products and the creation of the most profitable enterprises.

In Marco Polo, the travels of the famous thirteenth-century explorer are used as a metaphor for notions of journey in geographical, spiritual and musical senses. The inner world, opened up by Glass (1991) in the case of Columbus' private relationships, is investigated further by Tal (1966), since in his opera the character Marco Polo is actually split into two characters; Marco the 'man of action' and Polo who travels the inner world of memory. Exploration is clearly much more than simply a geo-physical concept in Tal's (2001) opera narrative. In her opera, Atlas, Monk (1988) draws upon the real life story of the French explorer, Alexandra David-Néel. The opera is in three parts each depicting a different chronological age of the explorer; 13, 23, and 60. The overall theme of the opera is the 'quest', the rite of passage enacted in both a physical and spiritual sense. By Part 2 the composer takes over the role of the 23 year old explorer and selects companions for 'Night Travels' through a variety of communities and landscapes in search of herself. Thus the explorer narrative transcends movement through a physical landscape in an acknowledgement of the reflective impact of the journey upon the construction of the self and the 'other', a process that also finds an expression in some contemporary travel writing.

Wandering

The wanderer character appears in five of the operas. In an opera influenced by Chatwin, Volans's (1993) *The Man who Strides the Wind* explores the life of the French symbolist poet, Arthur Rimbault. Acts 2 and 3 recount his wanderings in the Ethiopian wilderness. It is difficult to make a direct connection between Rimbaud and trends in contemporary tourism but the wanderer figure is clearly influential as a stereotype in studies of tourist behaviour. Berio and del Corno (1996) recall that the wanderer ideal goes back to ancient Greek myth; and *Outis [Nobody]* is developed from the myth of Odysseus, the homeless wanderer. Presented in a number of action cycles, the fifth cycle incorporates a seemingly idyllic cruise ship threatened by potential annihilation in a storm.

In Reimann's (1965) *Ein Transpiel [A Dream Play]* Agnes, the daughter of the god Indra, is sent to earth to discover the cause of mankind's grief. During the journey, her attempts to comfort those she meets are set in, amongst other places, a 'beach of shame', a mysterious seaside resort and the 'beautiful bay'. The metaphor of the journey as a form of therapeutic recovery has long haunted Western notions of the holiday; while the holiday escape is not often described as an escape from grief it might easily take the form of an escape to a longed for 'other' existence in a dream-like paradisiacal world of beaches, resorts and bays. Pursuit of the sea also provides the 'quest' in Vacchi's (1998) *Il Viaggio [The Journey]*. On their wedding day Rico promises his wife Zaira that he will take her to the sea. Many years later, they set out on a journey by foot. Locations along the way unleash unexpected memories. At last they reach the sea but it is shrouded in fog and they become separated. When they eventually find one another they remain locked in an embrace as the unseen sea sounds around them.

The somewhat sinister, outsider status associated with the wanderer who somehow also attracts kudos finds its parallel in a contemporary commoditised form of tourism that provides a new status for participants, perhaps a new form of cultural capital. Stepping outside mainstream life patterns, the wanderers of contemporary tourism engage in the following: the 'gap year', the career break, the 'rite of passage' to adulthood via an extended working trip round the world, the alternative lifestyle through travelling 'independently' and the temporary migration or long stay vacation, sometimes drifting figuratively in a yacht, sometimes drifting metaphorically from place to place. In Schedrin's (1977)

Dead Souls the accumulated cultural capital takes on a somewhat sinister form. Based on Gogol's (1842) unfinished novel, the wanderer is a traveller, Chichikov. Chichikov journeys through Russia, accumulating the dead souls of serfs whose names are still registered with their masters and who, therefore, are still alive in a bureaucratic sense. Thus, he gains imaginary wealth, though his motives for doing so are unclear. The image of the wanderer in *Dead Souls* is uncomfortably close to the conspicuous consumption of some 'wandering' tourists.

Opulence and Spectacle

Seven works from the list of 38 operas represent the more spectacular and opulent image of tourism. Four of these take a musical theatre form, with desires of the holiday fantasy being integral parts of the narrative. Juxtaposition of the words in the title – *Hotel Eden* – of Mollicone's (1989) feminist musical theatre piece set in a Palm Beach Hotel captures an imaginary, paradisiacal world that he and Fein exploit in an ironic and allegorical exploration of strong women. In Kern's (1927) musical, *Show Boat*, the action takes place on a Mississippi show boat and the characters visit the 1893 Chicago World's Fair, both settings providing spectacular backdrops against which the drama enfolds. Written during the Great Depression of the late 1920s, Benatzky's (1930) operetta *Im Weissen Rössl [At the White Horse Inn]* is set in the Austrian Tyrol and includes lavish scenes of tourists arriving by lake steamer, a rainstorm, the arrival of Kaiser Franz Joseph in the resort, as well as yodellers, clog dancers and cow hands.

Associations between the rich and famous and the promotion of tourism places are taken up in Daugherty's (1997) opera, *Jackie O*. The libretto concentrates on the tortured triangular relationship between Jackie Kennedy, Aristotle Onassis and Maria Callas, set against a backdrop of 'scenes' from the 1960s lifestyles of the rich and famous, including the yacht Christina and the island of Skorpios. Opulence takes a surrealist turn in Weill's (1927), *Royal Palace*. Recognised as one of the comparatively few surrealist operas, *Royal Palace* is set in a luxurious hotel on the Italian lakes. The main character is a woman, Dejanira, named after the homicidal wife of Hercules. Three men compete for her love; her husband, yesterday's lover and tomorrow's admirer. She rejects them all and, transformed into a mermaid, slips into the lake. The opulent setting of a lake side hotel offers the seemingly impossible plot a plausible location for a bodily transfiguration. A spa location is the setting for an opera based upon Goldoni's (1707–93) play, *I Bagnio d'Abano [The Baths of Abano], while* three acts chronicle the 'morning', 'afternoon' and 'evening' at the spa in Vacchi's (1993) opera, *La Station Thermale [The Spa]*. In a wry but humane commentary on life, the libretto celebrates the human body and its kaleidoscopic search for pleasure. Patrons fall in and out of love, while an opera diva, who has come to the spa to solve her vocal problems, is cured and recovers her confidence and hope for the future.

The analysis being presented in this chapter now continues by considering the counter narratives; by 'counter' I mean narratives that speak of reversals and omissions in the dominant narratives of tourism ontology held within the academy: Transgression, Inversion and Vulnerability. Table 7.2 provides a summary of the operas referred to in this section.

Table 7.2   Counter narratives

Transgression	Inversion	Vulnerability
Osud [Fate]	*Death in Venice*	*Flight*
Bless the Bride	*The Death of Klinghoffer*	*60e Parallèle [60th Parallel]*
Powder Her Face	*The Ice Break*	*Osud [Fate]*
Jonny Spielt Auf [Jonny Plays On]	*60e Parallèle [60th Parallel]*	*Les Oiseaux de Passage [Birds of Passage]*
Flight	*European Tourism*	*Neues vom Tage [News of the Day]*
The Gamblers	*Mona Lisa*	
Mario ed il Mago [Mario and the Magician]	*Albergo Empedocle*	
	Les Oiseaux de Passage [Birds of Passage]	
	Hotel Eden	

Transgression, Inversion, and Vulnerability

Transgression

Three operas use tourism spaces as sites of illicit relationships and sexual encounters. At the beginning of Janáček's (1907) *Osud [Fate]* his librettist Bartošová sets a meeting between a composer and his ex-mistress in a spa town with life displayed as backdrop, including the departure of a group of school children on an excursion. The principal characters are there to decide what to do as their liaison has produced a child. In *Bless The Bride* (Ellis 1947), the fictional resort of Euville-sur-mer is the venue for an elopement just before the outbreak of the Franco-Prussian war. Ades' (1995) opera, *Powder Her Face*, is set entirely in a hotel room and depicts, in a series of flashbacks, the life of Margaret Sweeny, later the Duchess of Argyll, whose divorce from the Duke in 1963 scandalised British society. In one of the greatest operatic 'hits' of the twentieth century, Krenek's (1926) *Jonny Speilt Auf [Johnny Plays On]* depicts a kaleidoscopic impression of European culture as the main characters engage in a series of sexual relationships in venues including the Alps, Paris and other unidentified cities. The drama includes the theft of a violin in a hotel, a car chase, more scenes in the Alps including a singing glacier (!) and a finale at a railway station where a locomotive crushes the womanising, 'villain-type' character, Daniello, before the rest of the cast board the same train to take them to America.

Sexual transgressions are also transacted explicitly in Dove's (1998) *Flight* as a comedic, farce-like, stage action. A couple read a sex manual while waiting for their flight in the apparent hope of an invigorating holiday. The doors of an elevator open in the departure lounge to reveal an airline steward and hostess as they enjoy a passionate burst of 'rumpy pumpy' facilitated by their overlapping flight schedules. The airline staff's enthusiasm means they are temporarily oblivious to the audience of travellers. Upon their discovery by the other characters the libretto is as follows:

Controller	Disgusting
Bill/Tina	Record lusting
Older woman	How does she do that with her arm?
Minkswoman	To think that sort of thing is done in uniform!
Controller	Such bad form
Tina	But then again, it may just be the holiday spirit.

(de Angelis 1997)

An electric storm closes the airport and the characters all bunk down in the airport terminal. When Tom reaches out to caress his wife, his touch unwittingly finds the airline steward and in the darkness they have a homosexual encounter that is discovered by their female partners the next morning because the men have inadvertently dressed in each other's trousers.

Two more operas demonstrate different transgressions. In Shostakovich's (1942) *The Gamblers*, the action takes place in a provincial hotel; Gogol's play tells the story of the visit of a gambler, Ikharyov, who sets up a complex but professional scam to win at cards. His fellow players are impressed by his 'professionalism', which involves bribing a hotel servant and his own valet to supply 'fixed' packs of cards, and pretend to join him. They gang up on him, however, and conspire to leave him with a worthless IOU. In a more sinister twist, Orefice plays out an allegory to Fascism in his opera *Mario ed il Mago [Mario and the Magician]*, based on Mann's (1930) novella *Mario and the Magician*. A magician, Cipolla, descends on an Italian seaside resort to give a show. He hypnotises the crowd except for Mario. In his attempts to win over the youth of the town to Fascism, Mario thinks that Cipolla has gone too far and shoots him.

The language of seduction and conquest suggest dark subterranean forces at work in an apparently innocent setting.

These transgressions all convey a murky under-belly of tourism spaces and of tourist behaviour. The tourist locations and their everyday activities are selected to act as a cover for what is really going on, either in, for example, the personal lives of the composer and his ex-mistress (Fate) or the political climate surrounding Fascism. The hotel is presented as a refuge for someone who has transgressed public outrage and as the location for the shady under-world of gambling. There is nothing deceptive here; the spa, the resort and the hotel are explicit sites of transgression, just as the mad-cap whirl of the tourist trip through central Europe becomes a vehicle for sexual excesses, jealousy and moral comeuppance in *Jonny Speilt Auf [Johnny Plays On]*.

Inversion

For the most part, the touristic narratives depicted above are transgressions against a moral order. This section considers the operatic narratives that deal with the inversion of the 'normal' ontological ordering of tourism. Shame, outrage and excess are replaced by confusion, power, ambivalence and tragedy. There are a surprising number of operas in this category; almost a third of those found in my survey represent aspects of an inversion of the normalised narrative of tourism studies.

Ontological order is overturned in Britten's (1973) *Death in Venice* through the cover up by the authorities of a cholera outbreak in the city. The subterfuge of their actions and the horror of disease appears in sharp contrast to the *serenissima*[4] that is tourist Venice. In Adams' (1991) *The Death of Klinghoffer* normal life on board a cruise ship is suspended as it is overtaken both literally and figuratively by a hijacking. Power relations are inverted; the captain becomes the captive. Passports, normally the vehicle to tourist freedom, become the mark of the enemy as British, American and Israeli passengers are singled out for rough treatment. The beauty of the deep blue Mediterranean Sea takes on a sinister hue and the captain sings of his situation: 'one can almost smell the air of a prison down below'.

Inversions of tourism ontological order are also a common element in other narratives; for example, Tippett's (1976) *The Ice Break*. The opening scene of Tippett's opera, whose central question is 'whether or not we (humanity) can be reborn from the stereotypes within which we live', is set in an airport lounge. A mother (Nadia) and son (Yuri) who have emigrated to the US are awaiting the arrival of the father and husband, Lev, who has spent 20 years in prison, labour camps and internal exile after being labelled a Soviet dissident. Also arriving at the airport is a champion of the 'Black' movement, Olympian. He arrives, much to the pleasure of his adoring fans, and rewards them with a rendition of his creed to black power. Gayle, the girlfriend of Lev's son Yuri delivers her creed of white liberalism and falls to her knees in front of Olympian. Yuri is incensed.

---

4   Serenissima, a name of the Republic of Venice, meaning the very serene.

An altercation between him and Olympian turns into a stand-off between the white and black occupants of the airport lounge. In subsequent acts several characters are killed in a race riot and Nadia dies. Lev asks why he has come to this new country just to see his wife's death and his son's hatred. The opera ends with a reconciliation between Lev and Yuri.

The life stories of passengers stranded in an airport by a blizzard in Manoury's (1997) *60e Parallèle [60th Parallel]* expose an unexpected set of events. Amongst the passengers are Wim, a war criminal, who is being pursued by Rudi with the intention to take Wim back to Paris to face a war tribunal. Rudy confronts Wim. Wim kills Rudi and escapes. The music here provides the inversion as the themes of the prelude, taken from the storm outside the airport, continue to shape the music that accompanies the travellers' narratives inside the airport. The disclosure of the nature of their relationship and the ensuing events between Wim and Rudi are expressions of the 'inner' storm, brewing and then raging, amongst a group of passengers. The allegorical form is also used by Josef Berg in his opera, *European Tourism*, to invert 'normal' consciousness and meaning. The opera is based around the cynicism of the composer towards the ritual of war and the idea of sacrifice for one's country, comparing and contrasting, through sarcasm, black humour and irony, an invading army to an invasion of tourists.

As in *Death in Venice*, the iconic image of a place is inverted in von Schilling's (1915) opera, *Mona Lisa*. The opera is sandwiched between a prologue and an epilogue, in which a modern tourist and his young wife are shown Mona Lisa's house in Paris and are told her story. Two acts of the opera depict a horrific imaginary account of the infidelity of Leonardo's model, resulting in the murder by suffocation of her lover by her husband and his similar murder of her, after he has raped her on the trap door covering the vaults where her lover is imprisoned. An inversion of the presumed innocence of tourists and the 'friendliness of locals' is also depicted in Peragallo's (1954) *La Gita in Campagna [The Trip in the Country]*. A bourgeois couple take a ride out into the country but their car breaks down and they encounter a group of peasants who have lost nearly everything during the war. They are helped by one woman but in the ensuing encounter with her family Mario's academic interest in the peasants is severely tested and by the time they drive away they have been robbed, even of most of their clothing.

Such inversions of the material and social ontology of tourism, exhibited above, contrast with a more ambivalent inversion of tourist spaces and social processes conveyed by the narratives in the next set of operas. Rather than the explicit disorder implied above, the narrative lines in these operas hint at ambiguity in ontological relationships. Vacchi's (1998) opera, *Albergo Empedocle*, based on a story by Forster, takes the straightforward story of a young English man who embarks on a trip to Italy with his prospective in-laws but then undergoes a mystical experience. In Vacchi's (1998) opera, *Les Oiseaux de Passage [Birds of Passage]*, the setting is a cafe somewhere on the border between the ex-Soviet East and the affluent West; emigrants fleeing from economic and ideological collapse give voice to their rootless and fragile aspirations for the future. Relationships spring up and are dissolved as people move into the unknown. There are nuances of the transitory, the fleeting, the passing-through of the 'mobile' human being in these operas; narratives that speak to contemporary experiences of (tourist) mobility. A metaphysical transcendence accompanies the physical spaces and journeys of the characters, symbolised in *Les Oiseaux de Passage [Birds of Passage]* by the release of a gull at the end of the opera.

In Mollicone's (1989) musical theatre piece, *Hotel Eden*, with text by the Hollywood scriptwriter Fein, three stories from the biblical book of Genesis are re-imagined in a Palm Beach hotel setting. Acts 1 and 2 take the stories as starting points (Adam and Eve, and Noah and his ark) before developing the story line. Act 3 is loosely based on the relationship between Sarah, Abraham and Hagar and the birth of Isaac. The opera deals with the underlying themes of marriage and the redefinition of the relationship between married couples. In addition to the principal characters, three angels appear at various times; in Act 1, as a cleaning girl, a bellhop and a waitress, in Act 2, as a repairman who does not work, a chef who tells the guest to send out for a 'chinese' and an MC preoccupied with her finger nails, and in Act 3, as a doctor and two nurses. The easy interchange of roles, from angel to bellhop to recalcitrant chef to nurse, suggests a playful inversion of common sense form and function that highlights the otherworldliness of *Hotel Eden*.

Vulnerability

Scholars in tourism studies so often try to concretise tourism; to 'fix' yet another category of tourist, to impose some order upon tourism in the form of a concept or model. These efforts of the academy, combined with the powerful interests of government and industry (probably inadvertently) collude to immunise tourism against the power of nature and the vulnerability of the human condition. The operas in this section represent a very different narrative to this dominant narrative of exploration, one in which the robustness claimed for tourism is shown to be a deception, if not entirely a delusion.

Nature's destructive powers that indiscriminately threaten human life and expose the inadequacies of the technologies necessary for tourism are evident in Dove's (1998) *Flight* (an electric storm), Manoury's (1997) *60e Parallèle [60th Parallel]* (a blizzard) and Berio's (1996) *Outis [Nobody]* (a storm). *Outis [Nobody]*, as mentioned previously, develops the Greek myths of Odysseus and draws on the idea of a homeless wanderer. The drama comprises a number of action cycles, the fifth cycle incorporating a seemingly idyllic cruise ship threatened by potential annihilation in a storm. In several of the 38 operas the storm, in its many forms, dramatically slashes through the gauze of tourism's solidity. The multiple effects of an earthquake and tsunami in Japan (in 2011) have recently provided evidence of the impacts natural disaster and technological failure may have upon the ontological order of tourism.

The vulnerability of tourists to political and criminal assault is seen in *The Death of Klinghoffer* and *La Gita in Campagna [The Trip in the Country]* respectively while, of course, in *Death in Venice* the devastating effects of a cholera infection emphasise the persistent fragility of human health. The political and ideological forces behind emigration, often the basis for subsequent reversed patterns of tourism flows, are represented in the *Les Oiseaux de Passage [Birds of Passage]*. A further human vulnerability, to the power of the media, is represented in Hindmith's (1929) *Neues vom Tage [News of the Day]*; a domestic dispute becomes a narrative of vulnerability. Turned into 'news', the press promote a young couple into celebrity status by demanding continual cycles of disagreement, divorce and reconciliation.

Absent Narrative: Love and Hope

Love and hope in Vacchi's (1993) *La Station Thermale [The Spa]* provide a link to my final observation on opera narratives and tourism. In many of the 38 operas, the characters live out narratives of tourism in the pursuit of love and the hope of a better future. Within the academy of tourism studies it is highly unusual to find any dialogue about these enduring elements of human existence (for an exception see Singh, 2002 on love). In terms of this chapter, this gulf between the operatic representations of tourism and the academy's representations can only be described as an absence and it is difficult to know how to respond to the observation. Are we dealing here with the differences between the subject matter of the social sciences and the humanities? Are love and hope simply ruled out of the scope of social scientific enquiry? Does the tourism academy simply 'bracket out' human emotion? I return to this matter in my conclusions below, regarding the trajectory of tourism studies, but it is worth noting here that, at least for a small community of tourism scholars, a dialogue about 'hope' is beginning to surface (Ateljevic et al. 2007).

Conclusions

In conclusion I return to the questions posed for my opera project: How do the creative architects of opera make sense of tourism? What do they see in tourism that is both reflective of the twentieth-century era for tourism and yet enduringly human? And, how might the creative output of these artists and intellectuals conform to, or challenge, the collective ontological claims of the tourism academy? In this chapter these questions have been addressed through a consideration of the representations of tourism in twentieth-century opera. The narratives of Exploration, Wandering, Opulence and Spectacle confirm aspects of the dominant narratives to be found in tourism studies, for example, in Tribe and Xiao's (2010) recent editorial article on the *Developments in Tourism Social Science*. However, I believe that the more important contribution of my opera project comes from the identification of relevant counter narratives; those of Transgression, Inversion, and

Vulnerability. In both cases a more rigorous analysis of the tourism studies canon is needed before definite parallels can be drawn. However, even in the present 'surface' survey, the exploration of operatic art provides an important challenge to the current trajectory of tourism studies.

This challenge is best represented by another opera, Britten's (1973) *Death in Venice*. The widowed author Aschenbach, suffering from writers block, is urged to take a trip to Venice by a mysterious traveller. In Venice he falls in love with a young boy, Tadzio, who is staying at the resort with his Polish family. Throughout the opera, the oppositional forces of Apollo (Tadzio) and Dionysius (variously the traveller, a gondolier, the hotel manager, a railway porter and a hairdresser) play out a compelling contest for Aschenbach's creativity as he struggles with his feelings for Tadzio. A cholera outbreak in Venice results in an exodus of tourists, but the warning came too late for Aschenbach and the aging author dies in his deckchair looking out to sea. What I am suggesting here is an analogy between the plight of Aschenbach and the trajectory of tourism studies. Mann's novella and Piper's libretto explore the various dichotomies (between art and life, reason and the senses, health and sickness, order and corruption) and represent the oppositional forces by reference to Apollo and Dionysius. Throughout the opera, Aschenbach struggles to confront the Dionysian spirit, so evident on his trip to Venice and so necessary for his escape from a self-imposed intellectual entrapment. Consequently he fails to recapture his creative vitality and, seemingly, chooses to die.

I consider that there is too much of Apollo and too little of the Dionysian in the ontological ordering of contemporary tourism studies. Too much attention is paid to life, reason, health and order and not enough is given to the Dionysian presence. Furthermore, there is a risk that, without a balanced, dynamic tension between these forces, tourism studies may be seduced towards an untimely ending, like the character, Aschenbach. The pursuit of truth, order and beauty in tourism studies is nothing, if it is not held in sharp relief with deception, chaos and ugliness. There are some encouraging signs of a Dionysian surge at the fringes of tourism studies (e.g. see Carr and Poria 2010). The Research Committee of the International Sociological Association meeting in Norway (2010) took tourism and violence as its theme, while an edited collection on tourism and war is in preparation (Butler and Wantanee, forthcoming). In my own collaboration with the criminologist Trevor Jones, I have been studying tourism and crime (Botterill and Jones 2010). There has, of course, also been a wide-ranging exploration of dark tourism, but not always with the serious intent of challenging the ontological claims of tourism studies. All of the above, however, present vital directions for tourism studies, if a fate similar to that of Aschenbach is to be avoided.

References

Ateljevic, I. Morgan, N. and Pritchard, A. 2007. Editor's introduction: Promoting an Academy of Hope in Tourism Enquiry, in *The Critical Turn in Tourism Studies: Innovative Research Methodologies*, edited by I. Ateljevic, A. Pritchard and N. Morgan. Oxford: Elsevier, 1–8.

Botterill, D. and Jones, T. (eds.) 2010. *Tourism and Crime: Key Themes*. Oxford: Goodfellow Publishers Limited.

Botterill, D. 2008. A Musical Interlude: Sensing Critically about Tourism and Hospitality Through the Medium of Opera, a Workshop on John Adams' The Death of Klinghoffer, in *The Proceedings of the 17th Annual CHME Research Conference*, Glasgow, 14th–16th May. Strathclyde University: Glasgow, 716–23.

Botterill, D. 2011. Towards a Realist Social Ontology of the Holiday: Seduction, Denial and Delusion in the Narratives of Tourism in 20th century Opera, in the *Proceedings of the Canadian Leisure Studies Association Conference*, Ontario, 18th–22nd May.

Butler, R.W. and Wantanee, S. forthcoming. *Tourism and War: A Complex Relationship*. Abingdon, Oxon: Routledge.

Butler, R.W. 1980. The Concept of Tourism Area Cycle of Evolution: Implications for Management of Resources. *Canadian Geographer*, 24, 5–12.

Carr, N. and Poria, Y. 2010. *Sea and the Sexual During People's Leisure and Tourism Experiences*. Newcastle-upon-Tyne: Cambridge Scholars Publishers.

Cohen, E. 1979. A Phenomenology of Tourist Experience. *Sociology*, 13(2), 179–201.

de Angelis, A. 1997. *Flight (libretto)*. London: Edition Peters.

Fink, R. 2005. Klinghoffer in Brooklyn Heights, *Cambridge Opera Journal*, 17(2), 173–213.

Holden, A. (ed.) 2001. *The New Penguin Opera Guide*. London: Penguin.

Singh, S. 2002. Love, Anthropology and Tourism, *Annals of Tourism Research*, 29(1), 261–4.

Tribe, J. and Xiao, H. 2011. Developments in Tourism Social Science, *Annals of Tourism Research*, 38(1), 7–26.

Opera Anthology

Adams, J. 1991. *The Death of Klinghoffer*. Goodman, A.

Ades, T. 1995. *Powder Her Face*. Hensher, P.

Argento, D. 1971. *Postcard from Morocco*. Donahue, J.

Barbieri, F. 1990. *Albergo Empedocle* (based on story by Forster, E.M.).

Benatzky, R. 1930. *Im Weissen Rössl [At the White Horse Inn]*. Müller, H. and Charell, E.

Berg, J. 1927. *European Tourism*. Berg, J.

Berio, L. and del Corno, D. 1996. *Outis [Nobody]*.

Britten, B. 1973. *Death in Venice*. Piper, M. (adaptation of Mann 1912).

Catán, D. 1996. *Florencia en el Amazonas [Florence in Amazonia]*. Fuentes-Berain, M.

Coleman, C. 1978. *On the Twentieth Century*. Comden, B. and Green, A.

Dallapicco, L. 1939. *Volo di Notte [Night Flight]*. Dallapicco, L. (after de Saint-Exupère 1931)

Daugherty, M. 1997. *Jackie O*. Koestenbaum, W.

Dove, J. 1998. *Flight*. de Angelis, A.

Ellis, V. 1947. *Bless the Bride*. Herbert, A.P.

Friml, R. 1925. *Rose-Marie*. Harbach, O. and Hammerstein, O.

Glass, P. 1991. *The Voyage*. Hwang, D.H.

Hindmith, P. 1929 [1953]. *Neues vom Tage [News of the Day]*. Schiffer, M.

Janáček, L. 1907. *Osud [Fate]*. Bartošová, F.

Kern, J. 1927. *Show Boat*. Hammerstein II, O.

Krenek, E. 1926. *Jonny Spielt Auf [Jonny Plays On]*. Krenek, E.

Manoury, P. 1997. *60e Parallèle [60th Parallel]*. Deutsch, M.

Mollicone, H. 1989. *Hotel Eden*. Fein, J.

Monk, M. 1988. *Atlas*. Monk, M.

Orefice, A. 1989. *Mario ed il Mago [Mario and the Magician]*. Orefice, A. (after Mann 1930).

Peragallo. M. 1954. *La Gita in Campagna [The Trip in the Country]*. Peragallo. M. (after Moravia 1944).

Porter, C. 1964. *Anything Goes*. Bolton, G. and Woodhouse, P.G.

Riemann, A. 1965. *Ein Traumspiel [A Dream Play]*. Henius (after Strindberg 1901).

von Schillings, M. 1915. *Mona Lisa*. Dovsky, B.

Schedrin, R. 1977. *Dead Souls*. Schedrin, R. (after Gogol 1842).

Shostakovich, D. 1942. *The Gamblers*. (after Gogol 1842).

Tal, J. 1966. *Marco Polo*. Griffiths, P.

Tippett, M. 1976. *The Ice Break*. Tippett, M.

Vacchi, F. 1989. *Il Viaggio [The Journey]*. Guerra, T.

Vacchi, F. 1993. *La Station Thermale [The Spa]*. Tanant, M. (after Goldoni's play).

Vacchi, F. 1998. *Les Oiseaux de Passage [Birds of Passage]*. Tanant, M.

Volans, K. 1993. *The Man who Strides the Wind*. Volans, K. and Clarke, C. (after idea by Chatwin, B.)

Weill, K. 1927. *Royal Palace*. Goll, Y.

Williams, G. 1961. *En Famille [A Family]*. Williams, G. (after Maupassant).

PART II

Place Narratives in Travel and Tourism

Chapter 8

Narrative Cartography in the Eighteenth Century: Defoe's Exploration of Great Britain in the *Tour*

Emmanuelle Peraldo

> I have, as near as I could, caused a Measure to be taken of this mighty, I cannot say uniform, Body; and for the Satisfaction of the Curious, I have here given as accurate a Description of it, as I can do in so narrow a Compass, as this of a Letter, or as I could do without drawing a Plan, or Map of the Place.
>
> (Defoe 1724–26, Vol. 2: 66)

Introduction

In this quotation from the *Tour thro' the whole Island of Great-Britain* Defoe (1724–26) tells his readers that he is attempting to be as faithful as possible to reality through his narration, but he acknowledges at the same time that he can never be as accurate as he would be if he were drawing a plan or a map. The binary structure of the sentence ('as I can do/as I could do') sets Defoe's narration in opposition to the cartographic technique, and yet in the *Tour* Defoe does actually use the map – real or narrative – for his travel account. The *Tour* is a domestic travel narrative, written in the form of thirteen letters that each describe a region of Great Britain, and Defoe uses different tools in order to think and represent the British space. A few years before the *Tour*, he had published *Robinson Crusoe,* an imaginary travel narrative located on an island Defoe had never been to; he was more a travel writer than a traveller! But in the *Tour* the relationship between the referential and the imaginary is more complex, since the journey takes place in the Great Britain that Defoe knew very well, working as an agent for Robert Harley. This chapter will illustrate how Defoe, a life-long student of geography, managed to narrate British space through cartography, chorography[1] and fiction and will discuss the interconnection between the geographic and literary tools that

---

1 Chorography, from the Ancient Greek Choros (country) is the representation of the distinctive character of specific places.

he brought to his travel account. The approach will be geocritical[2], in that it will propose a geographical examination of Defoe's literature, a methodology of literary analysis that gives an important place to geographical space. After analysing the *Tour* as a map, to see if Defoe may actually be considered a geographer or, as Parker (1995: 395) puts it, as 'a mere dabbler in the field of geography', the chapter will focus on the interconnectedness between geography and literature and on the literariness of the *Tour*, before seeing how it may be suggested that the use of these different tools for his narrative cartography turned Defoe into the architect of modern Britain.

The *Tour* as Map: The Referentiality of the *Tour*

Defoe's circuits begin in zones that are close to London and then go further and further away until they reach Scotland in letters 11 to 13, showing his interest in studying the different regions in their relationship with London and classifying them accordingly. Concentric circles define the limits of the zones to be studied in each letter. Each region thus delimited, Defoe then observes it as if it were under a microscope, rather like Hooke (1665), a member of the Royal Society, who observed tiny structures. By observing the country bit by bit, Defoe writes a chorographic history of Great Britain; the *Tour* can be considered as a sample of the regional-historical genre, alongside the texts of John Aubrey (1626–97) and Robert Plot (1640–96).

As the *Tour* is a domestic, rather than an exotic journey marked by a quest for the unknown 'other', and it is really more a survey, the aim of which is to offer a pedagogical and objective outlook on Great Britain in order to promote trade and commerce and to encourage progress. In order to carry out surveys like this the Royal Society had a number of rules concerning the acquisition of knowledge by experimental investigations, which were published in the famous *Philosophical Transactions*. One of the main principles of the Royal Society was the objectivity of the accounts and thus the exclusion of any bias or prejudice. In the *Tour* Defoe offers an account of all regions of Great Britain without exception, that is to say, in the context of the beginning of the eighteenth century, including Scotland, which inspired a lot of anxiety and distrust for English travellers. In his inquiry Defoe says he wants to stand against prejudiced, false and partial ideas on Scotland: '[h]itherto all the descriptions of Scotland, which have been published in our Day, have been written by Natives of that Country, and that with such an Air of the most scandalous Partiality, that it has been far from pleasing the Gentry or Nobility of Scotland themselves' (Defoe 1724–26, Vol. 2: 147). His natural history of that region, that chorography, will show the reality of Scotland:

---

2   Geocriticism is based on three theoretical premises: the connection between time and space, transgression and reference (see Westphal 2005, 2007).

As I shall not make a Paradise of Scotland, so I assure you I shall not make a Wilderness of it. I shall endeavour to shew you what it really is, what it might be, and what, perhaps, it would much sooner have been, if some People's Engagements were made good to them, which were lustily promised a little before the late Union.

(ibid.: 148)

Research methods and advice for travellers were also prescribed; as Vickers (1996: 132) shows in her book titled *Defoe and the New Sciences:* 'in the Royal Society's pursuit of knowledge, the traveller played an important role from the start'. Watt (1957) has underlined the link between Defoe's and Sprat's writing: 'certainly Defoe's prose style exemplifies the celebrated programme of Bishop Sprat' (ibid.: 102), where he also quotes Sprat's (1667) *History of the Royal Society* where travel writing style is offered: '... a close, naked, natural way of speaking; positive expressions; clear senses; a native easiness; bringing all things as near the mathematical plainness as they can; and preferring the language of artisans, countrymen and merchants before that of wits and scholars' (Sprat 1667 in Watt 1957: 68). Defoe was clearly inspired by the Royal Society, but also by Bacon and his scientific programme into which he had been initiated in Morton's dissenting school. Mayer (1997) says that '[i]n the Advancement *of Learning*, [Bacon] declared history the basis of all learning because it was the discourse that did the work of memory and served as the repository of *matters of fact*' (1997: 26, my emphasis). Defoe expresses that Baconian heritage when he claims that: 'I satisfy my self with transcribing the *Matter of Fact*, and then leave it as I find it' (Defoe 1724–26, Vol. 1: 108, my emphasis), and that intention is also repeated later: 'now after all these plausible Stories, the *Matter of Fact* is this, and no more (...)' (Defoe 1724–26, Vol. 1: 184, my emphasis).

Like many of his other texts, Defoe's *Tour* is full of lists, tables, figures and very accurate descriptions; it has even been considered 'a mere storebin of data' (Bowers 1993: 148). The traveller-writer is afraid of the void, rather like cartographers of the time, who filled in the blanks of their maps with images of ferocious beasts or fish. The survey of Great Britain is exhaustive, as can be seen in the abundance of toponyms in the text, but also in the tables, sketches or maps inserted in the text, for example on the map of the siege of Colchester (see Figure 8.1 below) inserted in the first letter of the first volume (Defoe 1724–26, Vol. 1: 68–9).

This map is made of text and figurative elements that seem to be dominated by the shadows of the fortifications, hence emphasising the prints of human activity and history on space. It works as a chronotope, celebrating the fusion of time and space, of history and geography. This view of the influence of geography on history, and vice versa, is echoed in many of Defoe's other texts, such as those on the plague, where as Bell (1994: v) notes, Defoe states clearly that the reorganisation of space by the authorities to circumscribe the epidemics influenced the history of that 'tragedy of the poor' by imposing a quarantine policy in the parishes that were most hit by the Pestilence. Defoe also inserts sketches, like the one shown

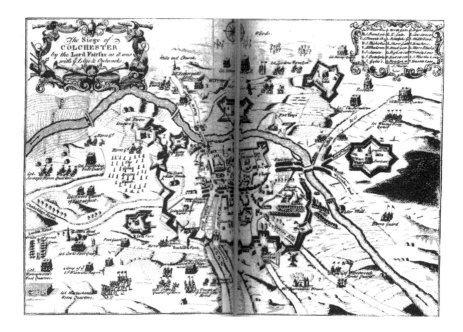

Figure 8.1   Map of the siege of Colchester (Source: Defoe 1724–26, Vol. 1: 68–9, reproduced with permission)

in Figure 8.2 to describe the square wells in the church of St Paul's. Defoe first describes the place verbally: 'they have small iron bars placed cross the angles for the men to set their feet on, in the manner here represented' (Defoe 1724–26, Vol. 3: 37). But as if the narrative description was not enough to visualise the place, he also adds a sketch. In the second letter of the first volume (Defoe 1724–26, Vol. 1: 233) there is a sketch of the 'form' of farms and here again the sketch contains text in the form of letters and a caption (see Figure 8.3).

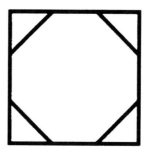

Figure 8.2   Sketch of a square well in St. Paul's Church (Source: Defoe 1724–26, Vol. 3: 37, reproduced with permission)

The Form of the several Farms would be laid out thus.

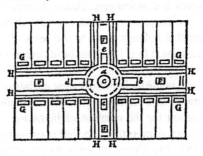

Figure 8.3   Sketch of the 'form' of farms (Source: Defoe 1724–26, Vol. 1: 233, reproduced with permission)

When Defoe considers his written descriptions to be insufficient on their own, these figurative elements borrowed from cartography or geography help him to provide a visual and aesthetic representation of his ideas and, at the same time, contain and present a narrative themselves. As Wordsworth (1898: 125) said in his poem *Simon Lee, The Old Huntsman*, there is 'a tale in every thing':

> O Reader! had you in your mind
> Such stores as silent thought can bring,
> O gentle Reader! you would find
> A tale in every thing.
> What more I have to say is short,
> And you must kindly take it:
> It is no tale; but, should you think,
> Perhaps a tale you'll make it.

Defoe's use of cartography is part of a larger representational strategy, as it brings authority and authenticity to his text, and he goes even further by using narration in order to map England. Not only does Defoe display an expert's ability to put into practice the procedures of map reading and construction, but he also creates narrative maps.

The *Tour* as Art: The Literariness of the *Tour*

> When treating natural settings, travellers toward the end of the century often seem more like poets than geographers or philosophers.
>
> (Batten 1978: 119)

Many things in the *Tour* do not only belong to the field of geography or tourism studies. In his use of words and of imagery, Defoe elevates his text to the rank of literature. For example, he frequently uses the word 'adventure' to describe his travels, which is a word that belongs more to the lexis of the novel than to the vocabulary of the referential text [e.g. 'I cannot omit here a small adventure, which was very surprising to me on this journey' (Defoe 1724–26, Vol. 1: 240)]. Many adventure stories were born while their authors were gazing at maps and charts. The idea of a 'terra incognita' or of a territory to explore stirs the imagination, hence creating the perfect situation for the creation of literature. As map critic Harley (1992: 231) says: 'maps are too important to be left to cartographers alone'. Indeed, according to Philips (1997: 14) Alpers, an art historian, argues that there are 'no intrinsic differences between maps and other forms of descriptive picture, despite commonly held assumptions that maps (not pictures) are authoritative and truthful'.

Defoe's Great Britain is often presented as a body, an organism, in his narrative: 'I have, as near I could, caused a measure to be taken of this mighty, I cannot say uniform, body' (Defoe 1724–26, Vol. 2: 66). From the very title onwards, we can see that Defoe considers the country as a whole, as a body made of different organs: England, Wales and Scotland. Defoe weaves this body metaphor all through his travel account; as he says, he goes through mouths (embouchures) and necks (peninsulas), and one city can shake hands with another:

> From Liskard, in our Course west, we are necessarily carry'd to the Sea Coast, because of the River Fowey, or Fowath, which empties it self into the Sea, at a very large *Mouth*.
>
> (Defoe 1724–26, Vol 1: 263)

> … the Peninsula, or Neck of Land between.
>
> (Defoe 1724–26, Vol 1: 263).

> Westminster is in a fair Way to shake Hands with Chelsea
>
> (Defoe 1724–26, Vol. 2: 66)

In order to differentiate the regions of Great Britain, Defoe represents Scotland as the epitome of feminine sensibility through the use of a synecdoche, that of the figure: '[t]he Union has seemed to secure *her* Peace, and to increase her commerce : but I cannot say she has raised her *figure* in the world at all since that time, I mean as a *body*' (Defoe 1724–26, Vol. 3: 11, my emphases). The metaphor of the body stands for Defoe's corporeal conception of society and it contributes to his geographical image of Britain as a system. Every city or village is part and parcel of that body and if one of them is sick, the whole body suffers, hence the insistence on the concept of decay in the *Tour*. Bowers (1993: 169) stresses the strength of the tie that unites the parts of the whole in Defoe's work:

The *Tour* envisions the geography of Great-Britain as a coherent and dynamic system. The island emerges in the *Tour* as a kind of organism. It is a body, vast and growing (the *Tour*, Defoe says, cannot be a 'finished account, as no cloaths can be made to fit a growing child'). But it is a cohesive body and made especially so by bridges, rivers, canals ...

Even though the body seems to be a functional unit, Defoe uses another metaphor, that of the monster, to represent London and the disproportion between the capital city and other places in Great Britain: '...what a Monster must London be' (Defoe 1724–26, Vol. 2: 134). Inevitably, some regions die in that hypertrophied body, and Defoe, as a good scientist, autopsies the remains of some cities:

Winchelsea, a Town, if it deserves the Name of a Town, which is rather the *Skeleton* of an *ancient* City than a real Town, where the *ancient* Gates stand near three Miles from one another over the Fields, and where the Ruins are so *bury'd*, that they have made good Corn Fields of the Streets ...

(Defoe 1724–26, Vol. 1: 168; my emphases).

The metaphor of the body can be read on the horizontal level of the travel itinerary; space and the individual are strongly connected, hence giving the possibility of a geocritical approach to the text, since it mixes geographical and literary tools. But the metaphor may also be read on the vertical level as a journey within the self, a 'rise' in the psyche of the traveller who discovers his own geography ('I-land', the geography of the self) while exploring his native country, his island. There is a potential link here with the concept of psychogeography, as described by Coverley, that is to say, 'the study of the specific effects of the geographical environment, consciously organised or not, on the emotions and behaviour of the individual' (Debord 1958 in Coverley 2006: 10), but this link is perhaps better epitomised in Defoe's (1665) *Journal of the Plague Year*, in which the geographical defamiliarisation of the urban space of London by the Plague has a direct impact on the emotions of the individual. In the *Tour*, the emphasis is really more on the acute awareness of place and space, staged in a narrative map.

Rogers's (1998) study of the *Tour* is entitled *The Text of Great-Britain*, hence laying emphasis on the link between geography and text where the task of the geographer is to describe the world (geo) through writing (graphy). Both maps and other forms of geographical writing can be read as 'cultural texts' (Harley 1992). Cartography, just as much as adventure stories or travel narratives, is geographical discourse and space is a metaphor for text. Ricoeur (1983) wrote that history and fiction talk about time by means of the narrative, operating a 'mise en intrigue'. In the same way, geography and fiction talk about space by means of the image/ picture, operating a 'mise en scène'. They are two tools to represent space through a poetics of the picture/image. Moreover, when the writer/traveller of the *Tour* goes through cities or follows roads, he mentions the toponyms, the geographical places, but he also narrates an anecdote or a historical event that took place in that very place : '[w]here Armies have marched, private travellers may certainly pass' (Defoe 1724–26, Vol. 3: 255). It is interesting to note that we say 'take place' to mean 'happen', hence underlining the intrinsic connectedness between time and space in what Bakhtin (1973) called the chronotope. The *Tour* is a topographic history, the history of a traveller following a route that enables him to narrate events he thinks interesting in order to account for modern Britain. The many toponyms of the *Tour* are more than mere spatial clues; they indicate the stages of the journey, giving it a chronology. Narrative is everywhere, in all aspects of the *Tour*, wherever there is reference to places. Defoe manages to create a narrative map, or rather he uses cartographic technique to build a narrative that is both a great geographical, travel and historical document.

Narrative/Thematic Cartography and Ideology in the *Tour*

'Thematic cartography' enables Defoe to 'transform physically and psychologically the landscape of Britain into a blueprint for economic development' (Parker 1995: 395). Again, this imaginative reworking of the British space by Defoe can be seen as belonging to the realm of psychogeography, in its subversive manipulation of space in order to promote a particular point of view with authority. There is a clear parallel between the narrative structure of Defoe's account and the geographic structures he is describing; between the space occupied by a narrative passage (on a city, for instance) in the *narration* and the space occupied in the *nation*. It may be said that Defoe writes to scale and that his writing becomes the microcosmic representation of the British nation. As a consequence, the narrative map of Britain drawn in the *Tour* becomes a forceful ideological weapon. The more space Defoe gives to a city in his narration, the more power it is considered to have; politically, economically, geographically and historically. Cities that Defoe considers insignificant are referred to only as names: '[t]he Towns of Rye, Winchelsea and Hastings, have little in them to deserve more than a bare Mention' (Defoe 1724–26, Vol. 1: 162). While the name of London occurs many times in the *Tour*, Rye, Winchelsea and Hastings are simply insignificant, tiny dots, barely visible on a map. Mentioning their names is, however, essential in order to emphasise the zone of influence and huge size of London, although Defoe wonders whether even smaller places, like Bramber for example, deserve even a mention on his narrative map: 'Bramber, (a little Ruin of an old Castle excepted) hardly deserves the Name of a Town' (Defoe 1724–26, Vol. 1: 168).

Maps never just reflect reality; they always go beyond that. As Jacob (1992: 32) points out, the map is a metaphor used to describe the human relationships, the power differentials and the hierarchy among a social group. In the same way as Robinson Crusoe needs to create a mental map of his island in order to control it, the traveller in the *Tour* appropriates the British landscape by creating a narrative map, through the use of geographic, cartographic and chorographic techniques. He appropriates space in order to promote the image of the nation and assist in the development of trade and commerce. He turns geography into art, in order to serve this wider purpose, as Bowers (1993: 577) says:

> Defoe's Tour continues a controversial enterprise initiated by William Camden's *Britannia* (1586, first edited in English 1610) and the works of early English chorographers and cartographers.. . These works were seen as a threat to royal power ... because their representation of England tended to marginalize the monarch. By focusing on the land, chorographic representations implicitly removed the monarch from the centre of English nationhood. Defoe's *Tour* enabled ordinary Britons to see their nation as a dynamic geographic body.

Because of its scientific rigour, Defoe's map acquired at the time a respectability and an authority that he needed to make his point, and because of its aesthetic qualities, it attracted a larger public following than the long descriptions of chorographers like Camden in *Britannia* (1586), Harrison in *Description of Britain* (1577), Blithe in *The English Improver* (1649) or Macky in *Journey Though England* (1714–23). Defoe's defamiliarisation of British space, carried out in a scientific-artistic way by fusing mapped space with personal experience and mixing literary metaphors with a monumental collection of data, gives as Coverley (2006: 38) says, an insight into 'the ways the most familiar geographies may be disrupted'.

Conclusion

> My husband was a perfect stranger to the country and had not yet so much as a geographical knowledge of the situation of the several places; and I, that till I wrote this, I didn't know what the word geographical signified.
>
> (Flanders in Defoe 1722: 256)

At the end of her narrative included above, Moll Flanders shows the little knowledge she has in the field of geography, at least before *writing* her account, hence emphasising the intrinsic connectedness between knowing geography and writing it, between geography and human life, between space and the individual. As for Defoe, he often writes about his doubts in choosing between two geographical notions and uses many epanorthoses[3] (as in 'Cities *or* Towns' (Defoe 1724–26, Vol. 3: 51), 'a Plan, *or* Map of the Places' (Defoe 1724–26, Vol. 2: 66) or 'a circuit *or Tour thro' England* would be very imperfect' (Defoe 1724–26, Vol. 2: 204), the latter being in the actual title of his travel narrative. More than evidence for his poor skills in geography, these stylistic figures of speech are part of a rhetorical manipulation by Defoe designed to circumscribe the referential discourse, just as he delimits regions through his use of chorography and cartography. By using

---

3 An epanorthosis is a stylistic figure consisting in replacing emphatically a word by another.

literary and geographical techniques, Defoe created a hybrid kind of geographical travel literature. It was precisely through his geographical imagination, through that imaginative reworking of space, that Defoe managed to give the most graphic contemporary account of the state of Great Britain in the first part of the eighteenth century. Defoe's greatest artistic achievement lay in his inauguration of a geopoetical tradition, creating a link and interaction between geographical space and literary creativity.

References

Alpers, S. 1983. *The Art of Describing*. Chicago: University of Chicago Press.

Bakhtin, M. 1979 [1973] *Questions of Literature and Aesthetics*, Moscow: Russian: Progress.

Batten, C.L. 1978. *Pleasurable Instruction: Form and Convention in Eighteenth-Century Travel Literature*. Berkeley: University of California Press.

Bell, W.G. 1994. *The Great Plague in London*. London: Bracken Book.

Blithe, W. 1649. *The English Improver. London: Eighteenth Century Collections Online. Gale Group*. Available at: http://galenet.galegroup.com/servlet/ECCO [accessed: 07 June 2011].

Bowers, T. N. 1993. Great-Britain Imagined: Nation, Citizen and Class in Defoe's Tour thro' the Whole Island of Great-Britain. *Prose Studies*, 16 (3), 148–77.

Camden, W. 1722 [1582]. *Britannia: or a chorographical description of Great Britain and Ireland, together with the adjacent islands. Written in Latin by William Camden, .. and translated into English, with additions and improvements. The second edition. Revised, digested, and published, with large additions, by Edmund Gibson, .. London: Eighteenth Century Collections Online. Gale Group*. Available at: http://galenet.galegroup.com/servlet/ECCO [accessed: 07 June 2011].

Coverley, M. 2006. *Psychogeography*. London: Pockets Essentials.

Darby, H.C. 1953. On the Relations of Geography and History. *Transactions and Papers (Institute of British Geographers)*, 19, 1–11.

Debarbieux, B. 1995. Le lieu, le territoire et trois figures de rhétorique. *L'Espace géographique*, 24(2), 97–112.

Debord, G. 1958 [2007]. Introduction to a Critique of Urban Geography, in *Situationist International Anthology*, edited by K. Knabb. Berkley: Bureau of Public Secrets.

Defoe, D. 1994 [1719]. *Robinson Crusoe*. Harmondsworth: Penguin Popular Classics.

Defoe, D. 2001 [1724–26]. A Tour thro' the Whole Island of Great Britain, in *Writings on Travel, Discovery and History by Daniel Defoe* (Vols. 1, 2, and 3), edited by W.R. Owens and P.N. Furbank. London: Pickering & Chatto.

Defoe, D. 1973 [1722]. The Fortunes and Misfortunes of the Famous Moll Flanders, in *Moll Flanders: an Authoritative Text Backgrounds and Sources Criticism*, edited by E. Kelly. New York: Norton.

Defoe, D. 1817[1665] *Journal of the Plague Year.* Michigan: Michigan University Press.

Harley, J.B. 1992. Deconstructing the Map, in *Writing Worlds: Discourse, Text and Metaphor,* edited by T.J. Barnes and J.S. Duncan. London: Routledge, 231–47.

Harrison, W. 1577. *The Description of Britain. Eighteenth Century Collections Online. Gale Group.* Available at: http://galenet.galegroup.com/servlet/ECCO [accessed: 07 June 2011].

Helgerson, R. 1986. The Land Speaks: Cartography, and Subversion in Renaissance England. *Representations*, 16, 50–85.

Hooke, R. 2005 [1665] *Micrographia: or Some Physiological Descriptions of Miniature Bodies Made by Magnifying Glasses.* Available at: http://www.gutenberg.org/files/15491/15491-h/15491-h.htm [accessed: 27 May 2011].

Jacob, C. 1992. *L'Empire des cartes: approche théorique de la cartographie à travers l'histoire.* Paris: Bibliothèque Albin Michel.

Macky, J.1724. *A Journey Through England. In Familiar Letters from a Gentlemam [sic] Here, to his Friend Abroad. Vol. II. The second edition with large additions Vol. 2. London. Eighteenth Century Collections Online Gale Group.* Available at: http://galenet.galegroup.com/servlet/ECCO [accessed: 07 June 2011].

Mayer, R. 1997. *History and the Early English Novel: Matters of Fact from Bacon to Defoe.* Cambridge: Cambridge University Press.

Orain, O. 2009. *De plain-pied dans le monde. Ecriture et réalisme de la géographie française au vingtième siècle.* Paris: L'Harmattan.

Parker, C. 1995. 'A True Survey of the Ground': Defoe's Tour and the Rise of Thematic Cartography. *Philological Quarterly*, 74(4), 395–414.

Peraldo, E. 2010. *Daniel Defoe et l'écriture de l'histoire.* Paris: Honoré Champion.

Philips, R. 1997. *Mapping Men and Empire. A Geography of Adventure.* London: Routledge.

Royal Society 1665–1934. *Philosophical Transactions of the Royal Society.* Available at: http://gallica.bnf.fr/scripts/catalog.php?IdentPerio=NP00396|NP 00397|NP00398 [accessed: 25 August 2010].

Ricoeur, P. 1983. *Temps et récit. 1. L'intrigue et le récit historique.* Paris: Le Seuil.

Ricoeur, P. 1984. *Temps et récit. 2. La configuration dans le récit de fiction.* Paris: Le Seuil.

Ricoeur, P. 1985. *Temps et récit. 3. Le temps raconté.* Paris: Le Seuil.

Rogers, P. 1988. *The Text of Great-Britain; Theme and Design in Defoe's Tour.* 1998. Newark: University of Delaware Press.

Shusterman, R. (ed.) 2000. *Cartes, paysages, territoires.* Bordeaux: Presses Universitaires de Bordeaux.

Sorrenson, R. 1996. Towards a History of the Royal Society in the Eighteenth Century. *Notes and records of the Royal Society of London*, 50(1), 29–46.

Sprat, T. 1959 [1667]. *History of the Royal Society.* Washington: Washington University Press.

Varey, S. 1990. *Space and the Eighteenth-Century English Novel*. Cambridge: Cambridge University Press.

Vickers, I. 1996. *Defoe and the New Sciences*. Cambridge: Cambridge University Press.

Watt, I. 1987 [1957]. *The Rise of the Novel: Studies in Defoe, Richardson and Fielding*. London: The Hogarth Press.

Westphal, B. 2005. *Pour une Approche géocritique des textes. Esquisse. Vox Poetica.* Avalable at http://www.vox-poetica.org/sflgc/biblio/gcr.htm. [accessed: 27 May 2011].

Westphal, B. 2007. *La géocritique. Réel, fiction, espace*. Paris: Les Editions de Minuit.

Withers, C.W.J. 1999. Reporting, Mapping, Trusting. Making Geographical Knowledge in the Late Seventeenth Century. *Isis*, 90(3), 497–521.

Wordsworth, W. 1898 [1798]. Simon Lee, the Old Huntsman, in *Lyrical Ballads*. London: Duckworth.

Chapter 9

Posting Over Seas: The Travelling Tales of Anthony Trollope

Angharad Saunders

Introduction

The relationship between travel and writing is far from simple. Travel is a form of cultural encounter; it is an immediate and embodied immersion in difference. Travel writing, in contrast, is a space of reflection and a form of cultural translation (Duncan and Gregory 1999). Consequently, there is a tension between the travel itself and its mediation, for experience can never be easily translated. There is slippage and incongruence as words and things, forms and norms escape translation and encounter resistance. The result is always the narration of an 'imagined geography' (Said 1978); a geography that is determined more by the place of reception than by the place of inspiration.

If this is so it behoves us to attend to the relationship between an author and their audience, for it is a relationship that cannot escape leaving traces of itself on the narration of place. Writing is not a solipsistic undertaking; rather, authors conceive their work in the world and seek to locate it within this world (Said 1983). Consequently, an intended audience, or an implied reader haunts the process of writing and works in the text to ensure its successful reception within the world (Iser 1974). The role of the implied reader becomes particularly powerful within the context of travel writing, for any representation of the 'other' will always be constrained by the horizon of expectation: the cultural norms, values and reference points of the audience (Gadamer 1975).

Any narration of place, therefore, is a negotiation between an author's self-identity and the expectations of their audience. An author is not able to write freely about their travels; what they write must resonate with their intended audience. This chapter explores this relationship within the context of Anthony Trollope's first novel, *The Macdermots of Ballycloran*, which was published in 1847. While not, ostensibly, a work of travel writing it was a novel that drew from Trollope's travels around Ireland in the 1840s. This chapter argues that travel became a complicating factor in the relationship Trollope had with his audience, for the more he travelled within Ireland the more he came to lose sight of who his audience was and what they expected from him.

Novels are not commonly seen as travel narratives; however, for much of the eighteenth and early nineteenth centuries the distinction between the novel and the travel narrative was far from stable or certain (Adams 1983, Bohls 2009). Tours, adventures and journeys of self-discovery were common narrative forms among early 'novelists' like Daniel Defoe, Henry Fielding and Jonathan Swift, and it was the novel that developed the art and convention of creating detailed presentations of the environment (Watts 1957). While the later nineteenth century saw an emerging distinction between texts that took travel as a plot device (novels) and those that took travel as the narrative (travel writing) (Korte 2000), it was a time when travel and its role in creating geographical knowledge remained a significant spur to creativity. Consequently, it is difficult to dismiss the novel at this time as a dislocated creation; rather, there is a need to explore how it, like the travel narrative, engages with and issues from an author's being within the world.

By Victorian standards Trollope was a prolific traveller whose geographical encounters stretched from Australasia, through Africa and the West Indies to North America. Trollope was also very astute and rarely missed an opportunity to turn these travels to his commercial advantage, popularising them in the form of travel narratives and also using them as material for his fiction. It was his early travels in Ireland that were to be so central to the creation of *The Macdermots of Ballycloran*. Yet Trollope was far from a conventional traveller, for he travelled not as a tourist, but as a Surveyor's Clerk for the General Post Office. Moreover, as a civil servant, Trollope did not just travel to and around Ireland, he resided there. Trollope arrived in Ireland in 1841 and did not return to live in England for any length of time until 1859. He became part of Ireland's Anglo-Irish population, and while Corkery (1931) condemns the writing that emerged from this population as little more than travellers' tales – stories written about Ireland, by the English for the English – Trollope's dwelling in place complicated his narration of it.

To 'dwell', as Ingold (2000) observes, is to construct and establish roots, both material and metaphorical, within place. Ireland was where Trollope met his wife, where he brought up his children and where he became a successful civil servant and writer, and therefore he put down deep roots, making his status somewhat ambivalent, for what was 'home' and what was 'away', was he an insider or an outsider, a native or a foreigner, a resident or a visitor? In literary terms this ambivalence was challenging for it raised questions over the location and expectations of Trollope's audience and of his ability to chime with this audience.

It is this ambivalence that makes *The Macdermots of Ballycloran* so interesting, for its narration of place does not easily conform to the conventions of Anglo-Irish writing or the expectations of an English audience at this time (Corkery 1931, Trumpener 1997). Rather, it is as though Trollope uses his travels around Ireland and his dwelling within place to offer a somewhat alternative vision of Ireland, wherein popular stereotypes of the nation are simultaneously employed and challenged as Trollope tries to balance his own self-identity with the expectations of his audience. Consequently, this chapter explores how the narratives of place Trollope creates within *The Macdermots* draw from his travels around the country and in so doing complicate conventional Anglo-Irish depictions of Ireland. While *The Macdermots* was never a successful novel, suggesting that Trollope misjudged his 'audience', it serves to focus discussion on the challenges travel poses to the author / audience relationship.

Trollope's Ireland: A Colonial Tale

The Macdermots of Ballycloran was published in 1847 and told the story of the Macdermot family. Larry Macdermot, his son Thady and his daughter Feemy once belonged to the Catholic gentry, but over the years the family had become more and more impoverished and indebted. Their plight was worsened by the arrival of the Protestant excise officer Ussher, whose seduction of Feemy led Thady, in a moment of madness, to murder him. Thady's attempts to elude the police and his subsequent trial and execution for murder led to the eventual demise of the family and the estate.

As Mullen (1990) observes, this was far from a pleasant tale, written as it was on the cusp of change. Famine was taking hold of the country and this, combined with poverty, religious differences and political tension, revealed an Ireland on the brink of catastrophe. As a surveyor's clerk Trollope encountered some of the worst of this distress, for his first eight years in the country were spent making '*continual journeys through its southern, western and midland portions*'. These were some of the most underdeveloped and least prosperous areas of the country and were to be worst hit by the potato famine (Mokyr 1983). It was during these journeys and his residence first in Banaghar on the banks of the River Shannon, and later at Clonmel that Trollope was 'thrown much among Irishmen of every class. I have seen them in their comparative prosperity and their too positive adversity' (Trollope 1849: 532).

Trollope's travels allow him to know. They give him a spatial knowledge that is unmatched by many of his contemporaries, and as such, he establishes for himself, and his writing, a position of authority, 'No Englishman has, I believe, had a wider opportunity than I have had of watching the changes which have taken place in Ireland during the last ten years' (Trollope 1850: 201). It is unsurprising, therefore, that Trollope is often seen as a representative of British power within Ireland and his fiction construed as little more than an extension of the administrative will to know, colonise and commodify Ireland (Corbett 2000, Deane 1994). In this light it is, perhaps, far from odd that Trollope develops such a dark theme within *The Macdermots*, for there is a need to establish Ireland's difference and discontinuity with the known, in order to justify his own role and intervention in Irish life and affairs.

Consequently, as Deane (1994) argues, one of the most persistent themes within Anglo-Irish writing is of Ireland as an anachronistic nation, whose romantic and archaic culture is in need of modernisation. The deployment of this theme serves to emphasise Ireland's difference and underdevelopment vis-á-vis Britain, and this simultaneously sanctions and endorses English intervention in the country. As Corbett (2000) observes, we only need look to the first page of *The Macdermots* for this to be reinforced. The novel opens with the depiction of the old Ballycloran estate near the village of Drumsna, in Country Leitrim:

> After proceeding a mile or so..I began to perceive evident signs on the part of the road of retrograding into lane-ism; the county had evidently deserted it.. Presently the fragments of bridge presented themselves, but they too were utterly fallen away from their palmy days, and now afforded but indifferent stepping-stones..These..I luckily traversed and was rewarded by finding a broken down entrance to..a demesne. But ah! How impoverished, if one might judge from outward appearances..The usual story, I thought, of Connaught gentlemen; an extravagant landlord, reckless tenants, debt, embarrassment, despair and ruins.
>
> (1991: 1–2)

In opening his narrative with a sweeping panorama of people and place, Trollope is deploying one of the most established traits of travel writing, the all-encompassing and authorial vision. It suggests a pervasive and penetrating knowledge; the author has perfect vision, knows the history and future of a place and has the power to reveal its darkest secrets (Hillis Miller 1969). At the same time, the encompassing panorama announces Trollope's arrival; he uses it to set the scene and this, as Pratt (2008) observes, is a conventional way of establishing the rules of contact. It allows Trollope to assert his control over the narrative, to identify his audience as English and reassure them that the social relationships on which the story will pivot will conform to their understanding of Ireland as 'other'.

The sweeping panorama presents to us an abandoned and archaic landscape, one that has been left to run wild. Here, Corbett (2000) argues, Trollope is drawing an implicit comparison with an English rural idyll. England is the ideal of an ordered and productive landscape and, in contrast, Ireland is left wanting. Its landscape is not just different, but is degenerate and degenerating. This is a reoccurring motif within Anglo-Irish writing and owes its origin, Foster (1989) argues, to the tensions between (often absent) landowners and their tenants. At a time of land-hunger, increasing population and the endless sub-division of farmed land, the traditions of land ownership were seen as far from conducive to the nation's rural economy. Thus, in characterising Ballycloran's decline as part of Ireland's 'usual story', Trollope intimates that its desolation is to be expected. As a result, the opening of *The Macdermots* hints not at a new tale, but rather, at one that is conventional and expected by an English readership.

Trollope's Ireland: An Alternative Tale

It is misleading, however, to accept without question that Trollope can only encounter Ireland through a colonial mentality, given his English origins. Narratives of place, as Gregory (1995) observes, are complex and often accommodate multiple and contradictory subject positions. If we probe *The Macdermots of Ballycloran* in more subtle ways the colonial voice begins to break down and there emerges, instead, a voice that is more humble and reflective. There is, Buzard (2005) argues, a tendency to see the majority of Victorian fiction as complicit in a process of 'othering', yet such a view closes down and over-simplifies the nuances of the novel, which is inescapably autoethnographic, not in the way that Pratt (2008) uses the term but, rather, in that it provides the author with a way of negotiating and thinking through their own identity.

Trollope's move to Ireland in 1841 was very much motivated by a desire to start afresh. In London he was unhappy and uncertain of himself:

> ... nobody thought I was right to go..To become clerk to an Irish surveyor, in Connaught, with a salary of £100 a year, at twenty-six years of age! I did not think it right even myself, – except that anything was right which would take me away from the General Post and from London.
>
> (Trollope 1980: 61–2)

Trollope was despised by his superiors in London, he lived beyond his means, had few friends and was beset by feelings of inadequacy and dissatisfaction (Trollope 1980). Consequently, his relocation to Ireland was a process of self-discovery; it is telling that Edwards (1991) refers to Ireland as Trollope's 'frontier'. Although this hints at a colonial mentality the intimation is that Ireland is a space where Trollope can find and reinvent himself, and while Trollope never came to consider himself Irish, he likewise never considered himself an alien or a foreigner (Trollope 1849). Trollope's travels around the country were part of his process of self-discovery:

> It was altogether a very jolly life that I led in Ireland. I was always moving about, and soon found myself to be in pecuniary circumstances which were more opulent in comparison with those of my past life. The Irish people did not murder me..I soon found them to be good-humoured, clever – the working classes very much more intelligent than those of England – economical and hospitable.
>
> (Trollope 1980: 65)

This offers a somewhat different vision of Ireland to that supposedly prevalent within England at this time (Curtis 1997) but it reflects, perhaps, the origins of Trollope's success. Unlike his contemporaries, who found their success in English contexts and spaces and for whom any depiction of Ireland was very much a depiction by an outsider, Ireland 'made Trollope' (Corbett 2000, Edwards 1983, 1991). Ireland was a country Trollope came to know in intimate geographic detail, it was where he met his wife, where he bought up his children, where he made himself indispensible to the postal administration (Trollope 1980) and, most importantly, where he succeeded as an author. Thus, while Trollope's English audience was important to the nature of his narrative, so too was his positionality within Irish society.

Returning to *The Macdermots*, a sense of this is evident in the novel's focus on the fortunes of a Catholic family. At the time Trollope was writing, Catholicism was seen in a very perfidious light by the English. Fears of popery and the power of Rome had been sufficient to curtail Catholic rights throughout the eighteenth century, while in the nineteenth century Irish Catholicism was being conflated with nationalist elements antithetical to the Union (Foster 2001). Yet, Ireland was a predominantly Catholic country and Protestant society was limited outside of Dublin, more so because of the preponderance of absentee Protestant landowners (Hill 1997, Foster 2001). Consequently, Trollope was part of a minority religious grouping in a society that was, as he quickly discovered, deeply divided along religious lines, for 'Soon after I reached Banaghar in 1841, I dined one evening with a Roman Catholic. I was informed the next day by a Protestant gentleman who had been very hospitable to me that I must choose my party' (Trollope 1980: 72).

Yet, Trollope was to disregard this advice and develop close friendships with men like the Mayor of Clonmel, Charles Bianconi, an ardent nationalist and Catholic (Glendenning 1993). Moreover, his travels around Ireland as a Surveyor's Clerk moved him out of the relative security of a middle-class urban lifestyle and brought him into contact with the extreme poverty that was swelling within the ranks of the Irish Catholic peasantry (Trollope 1980). Thus, where Anglo-Irish writing often depicted Catholicism in a negative light, Trollope came to display a more sensitive knowledge and understanding of Catholicism than many of his Protestant contemporaries (Edwards 1991). This emerges quite clearly in *The Macdermots*, where Father John McGrath, the local Catholic priest and confidant to Thady Macdermot, becomes one of the novel's heroes. Father McGrath had:

> been at college at St Omer, and afterwards at Paris, and had officiated as a curé there; he had consequently seen more of French manners and society than usually falls to the lot of Irish theological students..He possessed also very considerable talents, and much more than ordinary acquirements, great natural bonhomie, and perpetual good temper. He was a thorough French scholar, and had read the better portion of their modern literature.
>
> (Trollope 1991: 26)

Since the founding of St Patrick's College in Maynooth in 1795 few Catholic priests had received their training or travelled outside of Ireland (Foster 2001). Thus, far from reinforcing the popular caricature of the Irish priesthood as cloistered, insular and ignorant (de Nie 2004, Curtis 1997) Trollope began to complicate it. Trollope apparently despised racial stereotypes in fiction, believing them to reduce and mask the richness of social life (Escott 1913, Tracey 1982). Furthermore, he refused to slight that which was different. As he wrote of Father McGrath:

> I have drawn as thoroughly good and fine a man as I know how to depict..I have lived much with the clergy men of your church, and have endeavoured to draw them in their colours as I saw them. But, because they were priests of a church

which was not my church, I have never drawn one as bad, or hypocritical or unfaithful.

(Trollope 1983a: 645–6)

Trollope's residency in, and travels around, Ireland, afforded him social knowledges that moved him beyond simplistic stereotypes. Instead, he was able to offer the reader a vision of the Catholic clergy as an educated, enlightened and rational influence.

On its own, this does not suggest too great a disjuncture between Trollope and an English audience, but confusion begins to arise as the relationship between McGrath and Thady Macdermot develops. It is McGrath who Thady Macdermot turns himself into, and it is through McGrath that Thady receives some absolution for his crime. Although angry 'with the young man..at his folly in attempting to fly from justice' (1991: 281) McGrath regards the murder not as a premeditated act, but as an impulsive defence of his sister and his nation from English violence and dishonour. While it is one thing to challenge Irish stereotypes it is something else to depict them as disparaging of the English. It suggests that Trollope is not just narrating, but is getting inside, the Irish consciousness (Edwards 1991). He is losing some of his outsider status, and it is his travels around Ireland, Tracey (1982) believes, that are responsible for the development of an insider's deep and detailed knowledge of, and communion with, place. At the same time, Trollope's travels distance and detach him from England, making him, perhaps, more dispassionate about her relationship to Ireland. The result is uncertainty about whether Trollope is writing to smooth his way into Irish society or, alternatively, to educate an English audience.

This sense of ambivalence becomes even more pronounced if attention is paid to Trollope's metaphorical, as well as his spatial, travels. Trollope was an assiduous Irish scholar, and on his arrival in Ireland he renewed his acquaintance with his old schoolfellow, Sir William Gregory of Coole Park in County Galway. The house was not far from Trollope's first posting in Banaghar and it was here that he met Irish writers like Charles Lever and began, Escott (1913) claims, to study Ireland's literary canon. Any encounter we have with a narrative of place will always frame our own experience of that place (Tavares and Brosseau 2006), and in Trollope's case this led him to depict Ireland through the conventions and tropes of Ireland's native authors (Tracey 1982). The overriding convention, or tonality, was one of simmering tension and, as Tracey (1982) rightly acknowledges, Trollope's Irish fiction, in sharp contrast to his English fiction, is brutal and violent. In *The Macdermot's* alone there is murder, execution, torture, fighting and treasonable activities. This tonality was articulated through the trope of landownership, which captured the tensions between the landlord and the tenant class. Without wishing to reiterate Tracey's (1982) arguments, Trollope used this relationship, not to legitimise the existing pattern of landownership and exonerate Anglo-Irish landlords, but to critique it.

Irish landownership was characterised by a network of landowners who rented out their land to tenants. In the early nineteenth century, though, this was complicated by a rural populace that was too large to be accommodated on Ireland's available land. The result was land-hunger, instability of tenure and a process of rack-renting whereby the demand for land enabled landlords to push up rents and sub-divide land to maximise their incomes (Hoppen 1998, Trollope 1850). In a series of letters to *The Examiner* on the causes of the Irish Famine, Trollope was extremely critical of this system of landownership, believing it to have been causal to the famine, and it was this critique he first developed in *The Macdermots*. In this novel Lord Birmingham is:

> ... a kind, a good man, a most charitable man! Look at his name on all the lists of gifts for unfortunates..'Tis true he lives in England, was rarely in his life in Ireland..Could he be blamed for this? Could he live in two countries at once? or would the world have been benefited had he left the Parliament and the Cabinet, to whitewash Irish cabins..This would have been his own excuse. Yet shall no one be blamed for the misery which belonged to him?
>
> (Trollope 1991: 82–3)

In replicating Irish literary conventions and critiquing the system of land tenure instigated by the English, Trollope was participating in Ireland's production of its own narrative of space. The land and the soil, Deane (1994) argues, were tropes through which the Irish produced Ireland for the Irish. It was a theme that enabled them to articulate Ireland in a culturally specific, rather than a culturally generic, or English, manner. This was not, however, the only way in which Trollope moved across the frontier, as Edwards (1991) termed it, and entered the Irish consciousness. In contextualising Thady's murder of Ussher, Trollope presents Thady as a victim of political circumstances. As an excise officer Ussher was hunting 'Ribbonmen', who were accused of distilling illegal liquor. At this time the Ribbon Society was an agrarian group established to resist exploitation by the landowning classes and Thady's brief association with this group was enough for his murder of Ussher to be seen as a political act, rather than the act of defence that it was.

Trollope's intimation was that Ireland was herself a victim of circumstances. Ireland, with its agrarian violence and social tensions was viewed with suspicion and distrust by the English, and in this context any act of violence, particularly in rural areas, was seen as violence against the Union. Consequently, Trollope presented Thady as having little chance of a fair trial, for Ireland would always be judged by outsiders, not insiders. In recognising and narrating both this injustice and that of the land, Trollope displayed his affinity with Irish politics and his debt to Irish literature. His metaphorical travels through Ireland had allowed him to jettison caricatures of the nation and its people, and narrate them instead in a more nuanced and sensitive light.

Since the appearance of Sir Walter Scott's *Waverley* in 1814, novels with Celtic themes were proving popular among Victorian readers according to Trumpener

(1997), yet on the basis of *The Macdermots* it is doubtful that Trollope would agree. While the novel did not go unnoticed among English reviewers, they shared a belief that Trollope had lost sight of his horizon of expectation. As *Shilling Magazine* commented, 'We wish that the author had thought proper to modify his narrative, in some parts, for the roughness does not add one title to the full development of the story' (1847: 566). Meanwhile, *The Athenaeum* advised Trollope to turn away from an Irish context for it was synonymous with terror, tragedy and misery which was unpalatable and uninviting to many readers (1847: 517). This was something Trollope's publisher was to reiterate, noting 'that readers do not like novels on Irish subjects so well as on others. Thus you will perceive, it is impossible for me to give any encouragement to you to proceed with novel writing' (Trollope 1983: 17–18).

In seeking a London publisher and in recognising that in Ireland 'no one knew that I had written a novel' (Trollope 1980: 75), Trollope was writing not for the Irish, but for the English. Yet, in emulating Irish literary tropes, Trollope had created a novel that was far from agreeable, for it offered a somewhat unconventional, unromantic, but in Trollope's view, authentic vision of England's Celtic periphery (Trollope 1980: 80). It was a novel in which he abandoned any sense of happy-ending idealism, experimenting instead with the anti-hero, the flawed personality and a very dark and gritty realism. The result was a work of fiction that Sadleir, one of Trollope's earliest biographers, regarded as a political tract before it was a novel and an Irish novel before it was an English one. Ireland, Sadleir argued, 'having by friendliness, sport and open air saved Trollope from himself, all but choked the very genius that she had vitalised by her insane absorption in her own wrongs and thwarted hopes' (Sadleir 1927: 142–3).

It was, of course, pleasantness and happiness that English readers wanted and expected (Flint 2001), and their absence within *The Macdermots* was troubling. It was as though Trollope had poured into the novel too much of himself and his belief that Ireland was continually misrepresented by the British (Trollope 1849). Trollope had yet to learn in his fiction how to moderate his sense of self-discovery and its distillation. It was something he came to realise in later years, advising George Eliot not to 'fire too much over the heads of your readers. You have to write to tens of thousands, and not to single thousands' (Trollope 1983a: 670). Yet, in 1847 it was the message and not its narration that motivated Trollope, 'As to the plot itself, I do not know that I ever made one so good, or, at any rate, one so susceptible of pathos. I am aware that I broke down in telling, not having yet studied the art' (Trollope 1980: 70–71).

Conclusions

The Macdermots is not a piece of travel writing in the conventional sense, for it positions itself, before all else, as a novel. Yet, it is a novel that cannot escape the fact of Trollope's travels or his engagement with the narratives of place. While

Trollope does not substitute his own travels as the plot, the people and places he encounters during his journeys around Ireland haunt the novel's plot, character and narration. The novel's focus on an impoverished Catholic family whose life is spiralling out of control, the predatory English in the form of Ussher, the sensible and rationale influence of Father McGrath and the overlaying of all this with a tonality of despair and tension, point towards Trollope's growing familiarity with Irish cultural and political life.

It is not, however, merely the form of *The Macdermots* that bears the indelible imprint of Trollope's travels. Trollope's journeys shaped his own sense of self; they were, in many respects, voyages of discovery. He crossed frontiers and in so doing began to re-assess, re-mould and reinvent his own identity. Although he never relinquished his 'Englishness', his travels blunted it, for while they brought him into contact with difference, his residency in place divested this difference of its abstractness and romanticism. As a result, *The Macdermots* looked not upon the difference of Ireland, but upon the *causes* of this difference, and thus the novel was problematic for its readers as it offered a narrative of place that was far from expected. Novels, particularly those produced in cultures with firm moral codes, can rarely afford to offer a narrative of place that is unexpected, for to be unexpected implies a misjudging of the audience. The tale an author tells relies upon an audience to bring it into being, to adopt it, to support it, to read it. Yet, this audience is far from given; rather, authors rely upon response-inviting structures, which work within the novel to ensure it resonates with a particular place and its people. This, of course, is not an infallible outcome, for the implied reader is a creature of the author, emerging from authorial experience and understanding like the novel itself.

Ireland was Trollope's refuge, a place where he could remake and prove himself. It was a place for which he developed a great sympathy, since like him it had been mistreated by the English. Yet, in trying to convey the intensity of place and experience, *The Macdermots* emerged as an impassioned and impetuous response to Ireland. The novel attempted to narrate place in all its 'authenticity'; it sought to move beyond the superficialities and conventions of Ireland as narrative, to offer a form of knowledge that, in its intimacy, its 'realness' and its 'accuracy', would transform English perceptions of Ireland. In challenging conventions, however, Trollope created a narrative whose locality and particularity hindered its translation across space. *The Macdermots* indulged rather than articulated self-experience; it opted for a narrative that was introspective rather than extrospective, specific rather than general. Its difference was too extreme, with the result that it alienated rather than enlightened its intended English audience.

References

Adams, P. 1983. *Travel Literature and the Evolution of the Novel.* Lexington: University of Kentucky Press

Anon, 1847. New Books, *Douglas Jerrold's Shilling Magazine*, Vol. 5, 564–6.

Anon, 15th May 1847. New Novels, *The Athenaeum*, 517.

Bohls, E. 2009. Age of Peregrination: Travel Writing and the Eighteenth-Century Novel, in *A Companion to the Eighteenth-Century English Novel and Culture*, edited by P. Backscheider and C. Ingrassia. Oxford: Blackwell, 97–116.

Buzard, J. 2005. *Disorientating Fiction: The Autoethnographic Work of Nineteenth-Century British Novels*. Woodstock: Princeton University Press.

Corkery, D. 1931. *Synge and the Anglo-Irish Literature: A Study*. London: Longman.

Corbett, M.J. 2000. *Allegories of Union in Irish and English Writing*. Cambridge: Cambridge University Press.

Curtis, L.P. 1997. *Apes and Angels: the Irishman in Victorian Caricature* (Revised edn.). London: Smithsonian Institute Press.

de Nie, W. 2004. *The Eternal Paddy: Irish Identity and the British Press, 1798–1882*. London: University of Wisconsin Press.

Deane, S. 1994. The Production of Cultural space in Irish Writing. *Boundary 2*, 21(3), 117–44.

Duncan, J. Gregory, D. 1999. Introduction, in *Writes of Passage: Reading Travel Writing*, edited by J. Duncan and D. Gregory. London: Routledge, 1–13.

Edwards, O.D. 1983. Anthony Trollope, the Irish writer. *Nineteenth-Century Fiction*, 38 (1), 1–42.

Edwards, O.D. 1991. Introduction, in *The Macdermots of Ballycloran*, by A. Trollope. Avon: Folio Society, vii–xlviii.

Escott, T.H.S. 1913. *Anthony Trollope: his Public Services, Private Friends, and Literary Originals*. London: John Lane.

Flint, K. 2001. The Victorian Novel and its Readers, in *The Victorian Novel*, edited by D. David. Cambridge: Cambridge University Press, 17–36.

Foster, R.F. 1989. *The Oxford History of Ireland*. Oxford: OUP.

Foster, R.F. 2001. *The Irish Story: Telling Tales and Making it up in Ireland*. London: Penguin.

Gadamer, H-G. 1975. *Truth and Method*. London: Sheed and Ward.

Glendenning, V. 1993. *Trollope*. London: Pimlico.

Gregory, D. 1995. Between the Book and the Lamp: Imaginative Geographies of Egypt, 1849–50, *Transactions of the Institute of British Geographers*, 20(1), 29–57.

Hill, J. 1997. *From Patriots to Unionists: Dublin Civic Politics and Irish Protestant Patriotism, 1660–1840*. Oxford: Oxford University Press.

Hillis Miller, J. 1969. *The Form of Victorian Fiction*, London: University of Notre Dame Press.

Hoppen, K.T. 1998. *The Mid-Victorian Generation, 1846–1886*. Oxford: Oxford University Press.

Ingold, T. 2000. *The Perception of the Environment: Essays on Livelihood, Dwelling and Skill*. London: Routledge.

Iser, W. 1974. *The Implied Reade; Patterns of Communication in Prose Fiction from Bunyan to Beckett*. Baltimore: John Hopkins University Press.

Korte, B. 2000. *English Travel Writing from Pilgrimages to Postcolonial Explorations*. Basingstoke: Palgrave.

Mokyr, J. 1983. *Why Ireland Starved: a Quantitative and Analytical History of the Irish Economy, 1800–1850*. London: Allen and Unwin.

Mullen, R. 1990. *Anthony Trollope: a Victorian in his World*. London: Duckworth.

Pratt, M.L. 2008. *Imperial Eyes: Travel Writing and Transculturation* (2nd edn), London: Routledge.

Sadleir, M. 1927. *Trollope: A Commentary*. London: Constable

Said, E.W. 1978. *Orientalism*. London: Penguin.

Said, E.W. 1983. *The World, the Text, and the Critic*. London: Harvard University Press.

Tavares, D. and Brosseau, M. 2006. The Representation of Mongolia in Contemporary Travel Writing: Imaginative Geographies of a Travellers' Frontier. *Social and Cultural Geography*, 7(2), 299–317.

Tracey, R. 1982: 'The Unnatural Ruin': Trollope and Nineteenth-Century Irish Fiction, *Nineteenth Century Fiction*, 37(3), 358–82.

Trollope, A. 1849. Irish Distress. *The Examiner*, 25th August 1849, 532–3.

Trollope, A. 1850. The Real State of Ireland. *The Examiner*, 30th March 1850, 201–2.

Trollope, A. 1980 [1883]. *An Autobiography*, edited by M. Sadleir and F. Page. Oxford: OUP.

Trollope, A. 1983. *The Letters of Anthony Trollope*, vol. 1, *1835–1870*, edited by N. John Hall. Stanford: Stanford University Press.

Trollope, A. 1983a. *The Letters of Anthony Trollope*, vol. II, *1871–1882*, edited by N. John Hall. Stanford: Stanford University Press.

Trollope, A. 1991 [1847]. *The Macdermots of Ballycloran*. London: Folio Society.

Trumpener, K. (1997). *Bardic Nationalism: The Romantic Novel and the British Empire*. Princeton: Princeton University Press.

Watts, I. 1957. *The Rise of the Novel*. London: Chatto and Windus.

Chapter 10

Walking the Kumano Pilgrimage Roads (Japan) and Writing Diaries: Narratives in Japanese Travel Culture

Sylvie Guichard-Anguis

Introduction

For hundreds of years, only a small elite of Japanese travellers and pilgrims could afford the comfort of a horse or a palanquin, while most went on foot. Their travel experiences were recorded in numerous literary works; walking and writing together produced some of the most famous volumes within the genre of Japanese travelogue (Guichard-Anguis and Moon 2008). New forms of transport revolutionised this tradition, with trains in particular being favoured by travellers who aimed at writing. The tradition is still alive, as the shelves of libraries today bear witness, but it now encompasses wider horizons, including places outside Japan. The so-called 'culture of travel' [*tabi no bunka*], within which this literature is still blossoming, started its development at a very early time, during the Edo period (1603–1868). Pilgrimages and journeys to hot springs were two types of travel authorised by the feudal administration during those centuries. Gradually, travels to famous shrines, temples or hot springs began to involve additional sightseeing trips to famous places and the discovery of the cities of that time with all their attractive features, such as theatres and famous shops to name just a few.

One area that was important in terms of the developments outlined above was the Kii peninsula, south of Osaka, with its three famous pilgrimage shrines of Kumano, dating back more than one thousand years (see Figure 10.1 below). The very long period of time during which the Kumano sacred places have attracted pilgrims offers the researcher the opportunity to analyse how such an association of writing while travelling evolved over time in one part of the country. A span of eight hundred years can be found between the earliest literary works on the Kumano pilgrimage and the ones published today. As the accounts speak about the same pilgrim roads and sacred places, it is interesting to explore the extent to which these narratives differ, as well as to consider what present day traveller-writers, who often rely on transport before reaching the starting point of their walk, have in common with their counterparts of the past who used to walk all the way from the old capital of Heian (today's Kyoto). In order to understand the context of the writings associated with the Kumano pilgrimage, this chapter will

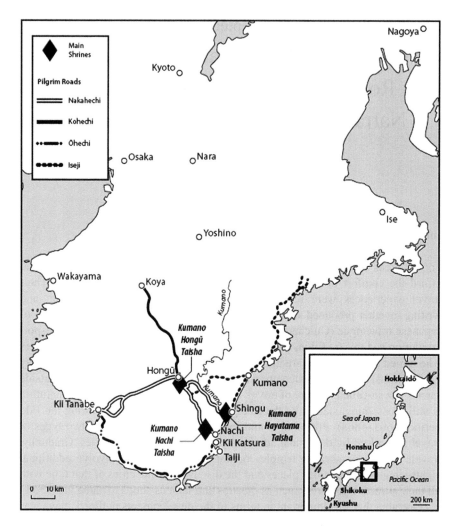

Figure 10.1   Pilgrim roads in the Kii mountain range (Source: author's own map)

begin by introducing the concept of Japanese travelogue as well as the places of worship and pilgrim roads in the Kii mountain range which were also inscribed on World Heritage list in 2004 (see UNESCO 2011), thereby giving a new impetus to their attraction. After this, the roads of pilgrimage and their natural environment will be examined to see how much is left of the routes of the Middle Ages in the early twenty-first century. It is important to underline the difference in social context between the early thirteenth and the early twenty-first centuries when attempting to assess whether the narratives written about (supposedly) the same walks actually have anything in common.

Japanese Travelogue: A Long-lived Tradition

Travelogue has a long history in Japan, as shown by the existence of one of the most famous early diaries; the *'Tosa Diary' [Tosa no nikki]* written in 935AD by Ki no Tsurayuki. The diary, written by a woman of his entourage, describes the return by the governor of Tosa (a province in Shikoku Island) to the old capital of Heian from Tosa. The number of travel diaries increased dramatically in the thirteenth century, as is illustrated by another very famous work, *'Travel to the Eastern Provinces' [Tokan kikō]*, written by an anonymous author around 1242. It records a journey from Heian to Kamakura in the autumn of that same year. In their 'Handbook for the Study of Classical Japanese Travel Diaries' published in 1975, Fukuda and Plutschow make a selection of 70 works dating from the Heian period (794–1185) to the Momoyama period (1573–1603). Among these works, one example concerns the pilgrimage to Kumano undertaken by the retired Emperor Gotoba in October 1201, written by Fujiwara Teika (Fukuda and Plutschow 1975). The Emperor left Heian on 5th October, and was back in the capital on 26th October, which indicates a surprisingly fast journey.

The narrating of historical travel is not confined to diaries but is also found in poetry, adorned by pillow-words [*uta-makura*], and is even included in works of drama and *Michiyuki,* a poetic genre dealing with literary travels, including imaginary ones. There is a long tradition of illustrations associated with the written literature on travel. Printed guidebooks that included a few illustrations became available as early as the mid-seventeenth century (Nenzi 2008). Later on, in the nineteenth century, most of the Japanese population became familiar with famous places inside the archipelago through coloured woodblock *ukiyoe* (Satō and Fujiwara 2000). The close link between travel writing and illustrations is still evident, for example in children's illustrated books. A great part of the fame of the very popular illustrator Anno Mistumasa (1926–), who has been awarded many prestigious prizes around the world, depends on the series of *'Journey Illustrated Books' [Tabi no ehon]*. Narratives may also become illustrations, as exemplified in a small museum called *'The Historical Museum on the Kumano Roads'* located in Kii Mihara (Wakayama prefecture). Here, several panels illustrate Fujiwara Teika's diary on a day-by-day basis (see Figure 10.2 below) with humour and a keen sense of realism. Teika is shown, freezing cold, on the night of 15th October, and then, arriving with tears in his eyes at his long cherished goal, the Great Shrine [*Taisha*] of Hongu Kumano, on the following day.

Some of the most famous and popular works of Japanese literature are associated with travel; for instance, the *'Narrow Road to the Deep North' [Oku no hosomichi]* by Matsuo Bashō (1644–94). Besides their literary merits, these works offer detailed documentation of the history of travel inside Japan. Matsuda's insight

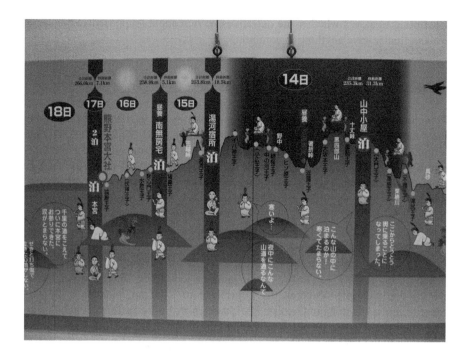

Figure 10.2   Teika's diary (1201) (Source: author's own photograph)

into the history of hot springs, shown in his *'Water cures during the Edo period'* *[Edo no onsen-gaku]*, is repeated in narrative form in several guidebooks issued between 1733 and 1845 (Matsuda 2007). Works written by foreigners (especially Portuguese) in the sixteenth century, and during the Edo period (1603–1868) by other Europeans, also give very valuable information about the Japan of bygone times. Among them, *The History of Japan* by Engelbert Kaempfer, first published in 1727 in London, offers a detailed description of the road to Edo (which is not found in Japanese literature of the time), seen through the eyes of a foreigner endowed with an acute sense of observation. This German physician with the Dutch East-India Company (1651–1716) was also a scholar and remained in Japan from September 1690 to October 1692. Together with several other Dutch people, he was granted the honour of paying homage to the Shogun in his Edo castle (Tokyo today) on an annual basis, compelling him to undertake long journeys back and forth to the capital. On his first journey, he left Nagasaki on 13th February, 1691, reached Edo on 13th March and was back in Deshima on 7th May. He met *Bikuni* nuns from the Kumano region several times; the ones he met in Yokkaichi on his way to Edo he described as follows:

Even stranger and odder, however, was the begging of some young and delicate *bikuni*, or nuns, who attached themselves to travellers, sang songs with gentle tunes to entertain them, and stayed to divert them as long as desired... To distinguish them from other begging nuns, they are called *Kumano bikuni*, and they are always in pairs and only on this stretch of the highway. Every year they have to pay a certain percentage of their earnings to the Shrine of Ise.

(Bodart-Bailey 1999: 330–31)

The travelogue tradition is still very much alive today, as will be illustrated by reference to contemporary works on Kumano. I have even been asked to contribute to this literature myself (see Guichard-Anguis 2011). Travelogue as a literary genre tends to focus on emotions, which are at the core of the Japanese identity. Travel associated with that literature falls very easily into the broad notion of pilgrimage, as it encompasses wandering and the idea of nostalgia for the past. When the traveller-writers walk, they do it inside history, having a lot of literary references in mind, with a feeling for the passage of time and with a kind of sorrow. Travelogue is still mainly associated with the use of the world '*tabi*', which can be translated into English as 'moving' or 'journey'. This idea of *tabi* also carries the meaning 'road of life' and corresponds to the first Chinese character of the Japanese word for travel [*ryoko*]. It is used to stress the emotional aspect of the trip, generally a solitary one, as will be seen in the selection of contemporary narratives about Kumano discussed below. The more recent usage of the word '*ryoko*' tends to refer to travel in a group, on packaged tours and the like, as the person who travels in the '*ryoko*' style is not expected to write.

The Kii Mountain Range and Places of Worship

In order to understand the context of the narratives presented in this chapter, it is important to introduce the part of Japan about which these have been written. The Kii mountain range roughly corresponds to the southern part of the Kii peninsula. It is the largest peninsula in Japan, separated from the plain of Osaka and the basin of Nara by a huge tectonic event. As is suggested by its name, 17 passes over 1000 meters dot the region and 81 per cent of the slopes have slope angles over 30 per cent. In contrast with the regions surrounding the three largest urban centres of Tokyo, Nagoya and Osaka, and Kyoto a forested natural environment dominates the Kii mountain range. This characteristic gives a rather negative image to this part of the country, as there is a lack of large plains on which to develop urban/industrial activities or a good network of communications (although there has been some development of agricultural and forestry industries) and the area has also suffered rural population exodus. In spite of being devoid of the usual icons of Japanese modernity, and retaining the image of a rather remote area inside Japan, this region is still attracting Japanese visitors as a kind of 'elsewhere' inside their own country, forming a contrast to their normal environment.

The mountain range, characterised by abundant precipitation, deep forests, hot springs, an indented coastline and a lack of communication, has always been associated with the presence of gods. Various belief systems, including mountain asceticism, Shinto, Shugendo, Buddhism and a fusion between Buddhism and Shinto, gave birth to sacred places and religious landscapes. Leaving aside Yoshino and Ōmine in the north-east and the Kōyasan in the north-west of the Kii mountain range, this chapter focuses on three sacred places named *Kumano sanzan* [the three mountains of Kumano] (see Figure 10.1). The main buildings include three large Shinto sanctuaries [*taisha*], Kumano Hongū Taisha, Kumano Hayatama Taisha and Kumano Nachi Taisha, and two Buddhist temples, Seiganto-ji and Fudarakusan-ji. The three sacred places are comprised, not only of historic buildings, but also of natural environmental elements such as trees, primeval forests, rivers and waterfalls. Kumano Hongū Taisha is located deep in the Kumano mountains, along the river of the same name. Kumano Hayatama Taisha is situated forty kilometres to the south, near the mouth of the Kumano River, while Kumano Nachi Taisha can be found 20km to the west, a few kilometres from the Pacific coast, at 350m above sea level.

The Kumano pilgrimage route developed as long ago as the tenth century, along roads which came to connect these sacred places set among the mountains. During the eleventh and the twelfth centuries, several Emperors left the old capital, Heian (today's Kyoto), with a large escort to undertake this pilgrimage to the mountains. If the old form of pilgrimage lost some popularity later on, a new one took shape using those same roads and was very popular during the Edo period (1603–1868). The route of the 33-stage Western Provinces circuit [Saikoku *henro*] associated with the Buddhist deity Kannon still begins at the Seiganto-ji, a Buddhist temple close to the Kumano Nachi Taisha. The cultural assets associated with the sacred places have been recognised by the acknowledgment of the routes and sites as National Treasures, Important Cultural Properties, Historic Sites, Places of Scenic Beauties and Natural Monuments according to the Japanese Law for the Protection of Cultural Properties (Three Prefectures Council … 2005). The roads and sacred places, already benefiting from national designations by the Japanese Agency of Cultural Affairs, as mentioned earlier, were also inscribed on UNESCO's World Heritage List in 2004. If the promotional tourist campaigns recently instituted by the local authorities are considered, it seems that the spiritual powers of these sacred places are not thought to be sufficient to attract visitors to this part of Japan today. At the beginning of the twenty-first century other characteristics, such as the natural environment, nostalgic Japanese landscapes, well-being therapy, healthy walking, and the location of cultural assets among deep forests, have to be emphasised, since these are assumed to form a large share of the attraction to the mountains. We may wonder whether pilgrimage narratives have followed the same route of perceptual evolution.

Figure 10.3   Nakahechi (Source: author's own photograph)

Walking the Roads of Pilgrimage in Kumano

Considering the large span of years between the first narratives and contemporary ones, it is useful to consider what is left of the roads of pilgrimage at the opening of the twenty-first century. The Kumano Sankeimichi consists of the routes leading to the three Great Shrines of Kumano (Three Prefectures Council to Promote World Heritage Registration 2005). The main historical route starts from the present Kyoto and after reaching the present Osaka follows the Pacific Ocean shore to Tanabe where it forks into two, the Nakahechi (see Figure 10.3) and the Ōhechi. The Nakahechi directly leads through the mountains to Kumano Hongū Taisha and then forks again in order to reach each of the two other Great Shrines, near the Pacific seashore. The Kumano-gawa, the only river belonging to the World Heritage Site as a pilgrimage route is one of these branches. The Nakahechi remains the most popular road among walkers today. The Ōhechi roughly follows the coastline to the South until it reaches Kumano Nachi Taisha. The Iseji (see Figure 10.4 below) starts from Ise on the other side of the peninsula and, more or less following the coastline, leads to Kumano Hayatama Taisha. The Kohechi winds through the mountains of the peninsula from Kōyasan and connects it to Kumano Hongū Taisha.

According to Kuwahara (2002), the word *hechi* included in the names of those Kumano roads was first used in the case of the uneven roads along the indented coastline. Later on it came to be associated with the roads walked by the Shugendo

Figure 10.4   Iseji (Source: author's own photograph)

followers. The pilgrimage roads were also communication routes between places and a natural setting where asceticism according to Shugendo could be practised. The harsh natural environment, composed of mountains dotted with steep slopes, rocks, peaks, rivers, falls, deep forests and so on, contributed directly to the ascetic experience (for example, immersing oneself in the iced water under a water fall), as much as the spiritual (Nara. Mie. Wakayama-ken kyoiku iinkai 2005). The Kumano deities were recognised as manifestations of Amida, Yakushi and Kannon in premodern Japan; since they were worshipped in the Buddhist temples mentioned previously, the pilgrimage roads were supposed to lead to the paradises of those Buddhas or bodhisattvas (Moerman 2006).

The roads are approximately one metre in width and have different surfaces according to their location. The presence of inter-twined tree roots compel the walker to watch their step at all times, but sometimes pavements of very large stones, or even stairs made of smaller stones, provide relief on the slopes. The Iseji dates back at least to the tenth century as testified by the earliest historical document which alluded to the state of the road (Kinan bunkazai kenkyūkai 2007). It was partly paved during the Edo period, as it became a trunk road and traffic on it increased considerably at that time with the growing popularity of the 33-stage Western Provinces circuit [Saikoku *henro*]. The historic evolution of the different roads has followed varying patterns according to their specific locations. Compared to Ōhechi or Iseji, the Nakahechi still benefits from large stretches of genuine road (Three Prefectures Council to Promote World Heritage Registration 2005). At the opposite end of the spectrum, walking on the Iseji means finding authentic stretches only on the top of the mountains, between the small bays where tiny fishing harbours used to be located. Even some parts of the road on the mountain-top have been reconstructed, as at the Magome pass, for example. The very heavy annual rains, causing erosion and small landslides, that particularly characterise this side of the peninsula, used to prevent constant attention being paid to the road. In some places it even splits into two branches, which date back to the Edo and Meiji periods (1868–1912), as for example, on the slope to Mikisato from the Yakiyama pass. Other stretches of the roads, for instance, the Daimonshin coming from Tanabe on the Nakahechi, need to be redesigned as they have completely disappeared.

Some sections of the roads were also used for administrative purposes, controlling the fiefs among which the peninsula was divided during the Edo period. These were also used in general everyday life until the middle of the twentieth century; by farmers to reach their fields or the next village, or to go the nearest market, and by peddlers, merchants and other travellers. The presence here and there of ruined tea houses [*chaya*], where the walker could rest while enjoying green tea and snacks (Guichard-Anguis in press), speaks of the previous life on these roads. Until the mid- twentieth century, inns could be found in a few places, for example, before reaching Kōguchi from Kumano Nachi Taisha. The building of national roads where the pilgrimage road used to be may be the greatest factor in the disappearance of large stretches of the routes, as in the case of the Ōhechi. The opening of new roads and the arrival of cars completely changed the communication pattern in the Kii mountain range. Today, walking on the roads is not a very attractive proposition as only short 'authentic' stretches remain, connected by ordinary roads. On the other hand, the building of new roads away from the pilgrimage routes helped either to protect the latter, or sometimes to lead to their disappearance, as the remaining stretches were too remote to be used in daily life and to be maintained in the second part of the twentieth century. The Nakahechi belongs to this second type in most respects.

From the Meiji period (1868–1912) onwards forestry took its toll too, as it was undertaken on a completely different scale from that of the Edo period. The building of forestry roads helped forest workers go deeper into the mountains by car, sometimes using parts of the old pilgrimage roads. The perceptions of the pilgrimage roads by the elders of the remote Kumano mountain range villages tell us about their use during the twentieth century (Kyoto daigaku ... 2007). The elders spoke of forestry roads and everyday roads, seeming not to understand their historic value. Another consequence of the industrialisation of the forest industry in the twentieth century was tremendous change to the natural environment, with increasing domination by the Japanese cypress [*hinoki*] or cryptomeria [*sugi*] and the disappearance of evergreen broad-leaved trees. This was associated with the introduction of the chainsaw, which enabled timber to be cut very quickly, and trucks which could carry the timber along the forestry roads (Kumano no mori ... 2008). Subsequently, long negotiations with landowners were necessary in order to reinstate some stretches of the roads to their former width, as they had been planted with trees. Today, even if buffer zones exist along the protected pilgrimage roads, walkers need to be made aware that the surrounding forests have little to do with the ones of ancient times, even of the Edo period.

In present day Japan, there is an unprecedented boom in walking, which has little to do with pilgrimage. A new word, borrowed from English, was created to name this activity, *wuōkingu*, in spite of the existence of a Japanese word. Walking on ancient roads [*kaidō*], whether trunk roads, commercial roads or pilgrimage roads, has never been so popular (Miyata 2002). The Japanese media and local tourist bureaus have responded to this trend by introducing planned walking routes or annual events. The roads associated with the Kumano pilgrimage were called *kaidō* in Japanese, the usual word used for all historic roads and which corresponds to all the various functions they included. Towards the end of the twentieth century, local administrative bodies that wanted to promote this part of the Kii peninsula created a new word, *kōdō* [ancient road], in order to emphasise one of the functions of the roads and to underline their historic aspects. Today, this word is the one mainly used when the pilgrimage roads of the Kii mountain range are referred to.

From Fujiwara Teika to Present Diaries: Walking and Narrating the Kumano Roads

Before analyzing the ways in which changes in the natural and human environments are perceived through present day diaries it is important to study the historical narratives, beginning with the very first diaries on the Kumano pilgrimage. Fukuda and Plutschow analysed two pieces of writing (1975). The first of these, named *Ionushi*, is a section of a poetic travel diary, dating back to the end of the tenth century or the beginning of the eleventh century, collected by the Buddhist priest Zōki. The section known as the '*Kumano travelogue' [Kumano kikō']* depicts a pilgrimage from Heian to Kumano Hongū and then the return, partly by sea, on the other side of the peninsula in (what is now) the Mie-prefecture. It describes a pilgrimage route largely similar to the ones taken by several Emperors of the medieval period (Koyama 2000). The second narrative, written by Fujiwara Teika (1162–1241), will be considered in greater detail since references to this pilgrimage are still numerous today. These are even to be found on the roads themselves, with numerous signs testifying about his movements, or among the references in contemporary diaries, as will be discussed later. Teika, or Sadaie, was a *waka* poet, a critic, a calligrapher, a scribe and scholar and is regarded as one of the greatest Japanese *waka* poets of all times. *Waka* refers to Japanese language poetry, one of the major genres in Japanese literature.

The retired emperor, Gotoba (1180–1239), undertook 29 trips to Kumano (fewer than the 33 taken by the abdicated emperor, Goshirakawa (1127–92). As Moeman states: 'the Kumano pilgrimage was from the start a consciously constructed ritual of state' (Moeman 2005: 150). Fujiwara Teika took part in Gotoba's fourth one in October 1201 (Koyama 2000). A procession of several hundreds of people left Heian on 5th October, reached Hongū on 16th October, Shingu on 18th October and Nachi on 19th October, before going back to the capital on 26th October (Fukuda and Plutschow 1975). This represents a rather surprising speed of travel (22 days in total), considering that the Nakahechi from present Tanabe on the Pacific to Hongū is roughly 58km long according to present guidebooks. Teika wrote his famous diary *'The Visit of the Retired Emperor Gotoba to Kumano' [Gotoba-in Kumano Gokō Ki]* (1201) in classical Chinese, except for the *waka*. He did not seem to have enjoyed the trip very much as he keeps complaining about the state of his health, as illustrated by the exhibit in the small museum described above (see Figure 10.2).

As a historian of the Middle Ages involved in the preparation of scientific documentation which led to the World Heritage designation by UNESCO, Koyama (2000, 2004) has walked the roads of Kumano and depicted them in his two books. Both volumes contain a third part, named *'Walking Kumano kōdō'* (2000) and *'Walking the Roads of Pilgrimage'* (2004). He explains that he walked here for the first time in 1977, invited by a medieval travelogue specialist. He complained about the state of the roads at that time, with overgrown bushes and path collapses preventing them from walking and delaying their journey so that they had to walk the last few kilometres in the dark. He believes there are two kinds of walkers; some walk for fitness and some are attracted by the history. He confesses that he belongs to the second type, as is testified by his keen observation. He seems more interested than anything else in the authenticity, or lack of authenticity, of the roads and in tracing their historic development.

As examples of present day travelogue, the recent narratives by a retired editor, Hosoya Masako (2003), an ordinary employee, Yamamura Shigeki (2002, 2003), and a travel writer, Takagi Michiko (2010), will be discussed. One of the main differences between these writers and the pilgrims of earlier periods lies in the fact that contemporary authors do not normally walk the road from beginning to end at one time, but divide the walk into sections which they complete all through the year, starting on each occasion where they left off the previous time. In addition, contemporary writers include information about the trains and buses that they take in order to reach their destination; reaching the bus stop on time seems to be an obsession for some of them, especially Yamamura. Finally, they depict their own relationship with the roads and the local places in the Kii mountain range, rather than treating the actual journey as a spiritual quest.

Hosoya (2003) is definitely walking alone and, in speaking about the Nakahechi, feels the present 'awful quietness' [*hidoku shizuka da*] of the road, noticing that ruins of *chaya*, or houses, can be found here and there. She concentrates on what she is discovering while walking. Endowed with a keen sense of observation, she notices that the forests date back only to the latter half of the twentieth century and is well aware that the landscape of older times was quite different. Being familiar with many documents written about the roads and their origin in legends and history, she seems to walk side by side with Teika, always making references to his deeds. She meets many local people, involved in one way or the other in the life of the area and in the pilgrimage itself. Her book of carefully planned and documented walks is a relevant introduction, not only to the walks on the Nakahechi, but also to the region *per se*. She notes the timings of her walks from start to finish in different stages, without forgetting the time devoted to meals.

Yamamura (2002, 2003) shares this concern for timing with her and appears more obsessed with bus timetables than with the sacred aspects of the pilgrimage. Reaching his target on time seems more important than anything else; apparently, he had a terrible experience on one occasion, left alone without any means to get back to a city. Saving money seems another concern for him too and this deeply influences the decisions he makes on the road. He does not stay in local inns and, generally speaking, has little contact with local people due to his pattern of walking, which is to start from the Osaka prefecture where he lives and just walk a few hours a day before getting back home. Fishing being his hobby, he is already familiar with some parts of the Kii peninsula, unlike Hosoya who first visited from Tokyo before settling in the mountain range. Yamamura notes the state of the road very carefully as he is walking it, making reference to varied documents from local administrative bodies, implying that he carefully plans his walks in advance.

Takagi wrote her narrative very recently, in 2010, and does not seem to be walking alone, or at least remains silent on this matter, in contrast to the other two authors referred to above. She does not describe some stretches of the road and the reader may wonder, therefore, if she has really walked them. As an example, in speaking of the Nakahechi her description of the route between Chikatsuyu and Hongū seems very short but she includes two photos of herself taken with local people and also specifically mentions local festivals and cultural events. There is some doubt as to whether walking is the main aim of her visit as it does not seem to be the focus of her narrative. She seems to be more interested in introducing some of the local places to the reader rather than in describing her walks.

Conclusions

Apart from the physical relief, today's natural environment in the Kii mountain range has little to do with that observed by famous figures of antiquity. The landscape of the Kii mountain range offers a great majority of Japanese people a contrast to their everyday life within large urban areas. Time passes in a different way among these mountains and walkers seem to concentrate on contemplating another Japan, quite separate from their daily surroundings. This 'other country' speaks of a time gone by, before the Japanese way of life was so deeply influenced by modernisation and internationalisation; it alludes to issues of personal identity and self-awareness. The brief introduction to the travelogue literature regarding the Kumano pilgrimage roads included in this chapter provides some insight into the ways in which memory is constructed in Japanese culture. Landscapes have dramatically changed since the historic records were written, and memory is built on literary references rather than on the presence of authentic landscapes. Many of today's walkers choose to travel in the steps of ancient pilgrims rather than seeking to live entirely within contemporary Japanese culture.

References

Bodart-Bailey, B.M. 1999. *Kaempfer's Japan Tokugawa Culture Observed by Engelbert Kaempfer*. Honolulu: University of Hawai'i Press.

Fukuda, H. and H.E. Plutschow. 1975. *Nihon kikō bungaku benran [A Handbook for the Study of Classical Japanese Travel Diaries]*. Tokyo: Mushashino-shoin.

Guichard-Anguis, S. and Moon O. (eds). 2008. *Japanese Tourism and the Culture of Travel*. London and New York: Routledge.

Guichard-Anguis, S. 2011. *Watakushi no Kumano kōdō kikō [My Own Journey Story on the Pilgrimage Roads of Kumano]*, Mahora, 67, 38–41.

Guichard-Anguis, S. 2011. Diffusion d'une culture alimentaire régionale et restauration : Kii Tanabe (Japon) [Enlarging a local Food Culture and Catering: Kii Tanabe (Japan)], *NOROIS*, n°219 2011/2, p. 23–39

Hosoya, M. 2003. *Kumano kōdō michikusa hitori aruki [The Pilgrimage Roads of Kumano The Diary of a Lonely Wanderer]*. Tokyo: Shinhyoron.

Kinan bunkazai kenkyūkai. 2007. *Tanabe-shi Sekai isan Kumano sankeimichi [City of Tanabe The roads of pilgrimage of Kumano as World Heritage]*. Tanabe: Tanabe-shi kyoiku iinkai.

Kumano no mori netto wāku ichiigashi no kai. 2008. *Myonichi naki mori [A Forest without day after]*. Tokyo: Shinhyoron.

Koyama, Y. 2004. *Yoshino. Koya. Kumano o yuku Reijō to sankei no michi [To go to Yoshino. Koya. Kumano Sacred Places and Pilgrimage Roads]*. Tokyo: Asahi shimbumsha.

Koyama, Y. 2004. *Kumano kōdō [The Old Roads of Kumano]*. Tokyo: Iwanami.

Kuwahara I., 2002. Kumano Kaidō no « heji » shikō [Personal thoughts on the notion of Heji and the historic roads of Kumano], *Wakayama Chiri*, 22, 1–12.

Kyoto daigaku bungakubu shakaigaku kenkyū shitsu and Kansai gakuin daigaku shakai gakubu. 2007. *Chiiki manabu Dai 13 shū Mie-ken Kumano chiiki kara [Learning through the local From Kumano the prefecture of Mie, Vol. 13]*, Kyoto: Kyoto daigaku bungakubu shakaigaku kenkyū shitsu.

Matsuda, T. 2007. *Edo no onsen-gaku [Water cures during the Edo period]*. Tokyo: Shinchosha.

Miyata T. 2002. *Kaidō de yomitoku Nihonshi [The History of Japan through reading which explain roads]*. Tokyo, Seishun shuppansha.

Moerman, D.M. 2006. *Localizing Paradise: Kumano Pilgrimage and the Religious Landscapes of Premodern Japan*. Cambridge, Massachusetts: Harvard University Asia Center.

Nara. Mie. *Wakayama-ken kyoiku iinkai.* 2005. Kii sanchi no reijō to sankeidō [Sacred places and roads of pilgrimage in the Kii mountain range], *Bunka zai,* 1, 26–39.

Nenzi, L. 2008. *Excursions in Identity.* Honolulu: University of Hawai'i Press.

Satō, Y. and Fujiwara, C. 2000. *Ukiyoe ni miru Edo no tabi [Travel during the Edo period through Prints].* Tokyo: Kashutsu shobōshinsha.

Takagi, M. 2010. *Kumano Kōdō Saisei no chi no miryoku o sagasu [The Old roads of Kumano Looking for the Attraction of a Land of Rebirth].* Tokyo: Kakaugawa shoten.

Three Prefectures Council to Promote World Heritage Registration. 2005. *Sacred Sites and Pilgrimage Routes in the Kii Mountain Range.* Tsu, Nara, Wakayama: Three Prefectures Council to Promote World Heritage Registration.

UNESCO 2011. World Heritage List: *Sacred Sites and Pilgrimage Routes in the Kii Mountain Range,* Available at: http://whc.unesco.org/en/list/1142 [accessed: 5 June 2011].

Yamamura, S. 2002. *Arisan no Kumano kikō I. Kii-ji Nakahechi o iku [Travel Story on Kumano by an Ant I. The road Kii Nakahechi].* Kyoto: Nakanishiya.

Yamamura S. 2003. *Arisan no Kumano kikō II. Shin Ōhechi o iku [Travel Story on Kumano by an Ant II. The New Ōhechi Road].* Kyoto: Nakanishiya.

Chapter 11

Narratives and Counter-narratives: Contesting a Tourist Site in Jerusalem

Chaim Noy

Introduction: The (Critical) Narrative Study of Tourism

In recent years there has been a vibrant and growing body of research in tourism studies that may be described as the 'Narrative Study of Tourism', approaching the study of contemporary forms and practices of tourism from the perspective of narrative scholarship. The close relations that exist between the two are not surprising, since in many ways contemporary forms of tourism rest on the wide shoulders of the Romantic and modern travel narrative – the experience, accounts, and literature of travel – which are both representative and constitutive of the western-colonial mind. To put it differently, contemporary travel is very much about narratives; about consuming and producing them, about narrative identity and narrative entitlement.

The narrative approach in tourism studies encompasses a variety of issues and topics, including the construction of images of collective identities, of destinations, sites, and places. It also examines the charged personal narratives of tourists, through which individual and collective experiences of travel are conveyed and tourists' identities are performed. Structural approaches have always highlighted a 'correlation' between *stories*, which evolve progressively (or at least seem to do so), and *travel*, which likewise progresses through time as it progresses through space. From this perspective, the narrative form is ideal for the organisation and representation of experiences, since it blends temporality, events and perspective/ subjectivity. While works, such as the many inspired by Labov's (1972) original study, have tended to emphasise temporal sequences, Bakhtin (1981), specifically through the notion of chronotope, de Certeau (1984) and others have highlighted the spatial dimensions of narrative and the interconnection between temporal and spatial dimensions.

It would be wrong, however, to view the Narrative Study of Tourism merely in terms of structures of social organisation and activity, for this might restrict our comprehension of how narratives are employed politically and manipulatively by agents working in, and shaping, the spheres of tourism. The critical Narrative Study of Tourism emphasises how stories, above and beyond their functions of describing and organising the social world, are also power structures; vehicles for the implementation and performance of social hierarchies, exclusions and

Otherness. A critical perspective brings to the fore the immense performative (or enunciatory) power of narratives in the tourism industry and raises a set of questions regarding the constitution of social agency. The shift from structural and functional centred approaches to more critical approaches involves not only a change in the interpretation and analysis of narrative contents and themes, but also a shift in focus towards the question of who has the rights and resources to recount narratives publicly, and who or what is implicated by them; who has a well-ordered and aesthetic narrative to tell and who has a traumatic (non-)narrative, punctuated by silences and stuttering.

In this chapter I present findings of a research project that addresses innovative and subversive narratives in tourism. The research does not merely seek to analyse counter or non-hegemonic narratives, but crucially to examine the 'narrative-tellers'; the individuals, or organisations and institutions (usually small-scale), that project these subversive narratives in, and into, the spheres of contemporary tourism. I employ the terms 'hegemonic' and 'counter-hegemonic', borrowed from Gramsci's (1971) well-known conceptualisation, to examine and illuminate the ideological role that narratives play at a specific tourist site, arguing that tourism should be construed as a highly ideological social sphere where political narratives, and the voices or meanings that they evoke and perform, are constantly in conflict (Noy 2008a, 2011). My main interest lies in identifying *and* amplifying subversive stories and in recognising the social agents that project them provocatively on to the public stages of tourism. The most influential players on the stages of international tourism are, of course, normally global conglomerates, rather than local, subversive actors but, when subversive agents act within tourism, employing methods from the domain of tourism (guided tours, maps, souvenirs, and so on) to destabilise hegemony, they become interesting and relevant subjects for study, illuminating and rewarding the researcher both ethically and intellectually.

Experimental Art(Ists) in Ein Karem

Sala-Manca is a Jerusalem-based group of experimental artists founded in 2000 by Lea Mauas and Diego Rotman. The group creates in various fields, including performance, video, installation and new media. In its own words, the group examines the 'poetics of translation, with textual, urban and net contexts and with the tensions between low-tech and high-tech aesthetics, as well as social and political issues' (Sala-Manca Group 2010). Thanks to a personal acquaintance with Lea Mauas and Diego Rotman, I have been able to follow the group's activities and evolution almost from its inception. I have attended many of the group's projects, exhibitions, and experimental presentations in Jerusalem, and have been inspired and affected by their sometimes provocative and often thought-provoking artistic productions, usually performed in public urban spaces around the city, even though at times I have felt at a loss to understand the artistic message of particular avant-garde activities and performances. I have been attracted to, and even fascinated

Figure 11.1   Ein Karem from the southwest (Source: author's own photograph)

by, Sala-Manca's activities, precisely because they felt avant-garde, and thus not very coherent. As I regard myself as an intellectual, I have found this particularly challenging. As a Jerusalemite, I have deeply appreciated Mauas' and Rotman's efforts to revive art and creativity in this city, which has several large museums but is nearly devoid of fringe-type artistic activity. The Group's activities involve interactions between art and everyday life and spaces, and between the seemingly coherent and apolitical nature of everyday life routines and the challenge posed to these routines by experimental art.

The narratives examined below, and the social agents that enacted them, were part of an artistic activity organised by the Sala-Manca Group over the course of three intense days (15–17 October 2009). The activity took place in the neighbourhood of Ein Karem (lit. Vineyard Spring), which is located in southwest Jerusalem, near but outside the densely built-up area of the city. Ein Karem (see Figure 11.1) is a beautifully picturesque area with a spring, surrounded by churches, monasteries and residences that were built over the centuries. The following passage, taken from one of many websites catering to tourists, is typical of tourist brochures that describe it: 'In a peaceful valley between mountains and hills, surrounded by the beauty of natural groves, nestles one of Jerusalem's most picturesque neighbourhoods' (Go Israel 2010). According to some Christian traditions, it was the birth-place of John the Baptist and the home of his mother, Elizabeth, who was visited there by the Virgin Mary. Ein Karem was also a Palestinian village, one of the numerous Palestinian villages and towns that were deserted by their Arab inhabitants when the Israeli forces conquered them in the 1948 War, in what became known in Palestinian collective consciousness as the 'Nakba' ('Disaster'). Hence this 'most picturesque neighbourhood' is also a politically contested site, which embodies two very different sets of historical facts and events, memories and narratives. It is at the same time an object and subject of remembering but also of the denying of memories and words.

From the perspective of research into the politics of tourism in Israel and Palestine, Ein Karem raises interesting questions regarding the roles that tourism agents and narratives play in the current Israeli-Palestinian conflict. These have received some scholarly attention in studies examining the phenomenon of politically aware tourism in Hebron, in the Old City of Jerusalem, around the separation barrier and elsewhere (Bowman 1996, Brin 2006, Clark 2000, Feldman 2008, Noy 2011). This body of research concentrates on the conflict's hotspots. However, less attention has been paid to sites where the conflict has already been relegated to the status of recent history. These are mainly sites that were occupied by the Israeli forces not during the 1967 war, but earlier, in 1948–49. Brin and Noy (2010) term such sites 'non-flashpoints' sites, and suggest that 'if these places are remembered by Palestinians and are a focus of longing, more often than not their transformation into Jewish locales is regarded as *fait accompli*' (p. 21).

The Sala-Manca Group's three-day project in Ein Karem, appropriately titled 'What's Hidden behind the Pastoral?', sought to examine, expose and challenge hegemonic and accepted narratives of the neighbourhood/village. It involved over 30 artists and a large number of activities, exhibitions, and workshops that took place at and near the Group's workshop in Ein Karem, attended by more than 700 visitors. Many of the activities took place at the centre of the neighbourhood, near its main tourist attractions (for more information on Sala-Manca's project see Mamuta 2010). In what follows I shall focus on only one aspect of the project, namely the audio-tours of the neighbourhood. Throughout the three days, Sala-Manca invited visitors to tour the area with a map and a small MP3 player on which two guided tours of the area were recorded, which were delivered by two different guides, presenting different perspectives relating to Ein Karem. The tours offered a (re-)narrativisation of this popular tourist site, which did not duplicate hegemonic depictions and knowledge and were not presented from the perspective of the all-knowing narrator. Rather, the stories were situated, following the physical paths and routes in and of the site, evoking memories, concerns and emotions, and pursuing distinct ideological agendas and interests. By emplacing the stories and by mobilising them, both literally and metaphorically (that is, by supplying the visitors with mobile listening devices), the creators turned the stories into embodied and situated performances. They were not so much stories *about* places, events and histories, that is, narratives serving a referential function, but stories that took place *in* an emplaced and embodied sense, that is, situated performances.

By attending Sala-Manca's Pastoral project, and by participating in the recorded tours, visitors too were transformed into agents of social change, publicly pursuing contested paths, images and narratives.

'What's Hidden Behind the Pastoral?'

The MP3 players were handed out by two college students who sat at a small table near the road leading up to the famous Ein Karem spring. This was actually my first stop at Ein Karem and the first activity in which I took part during the days of the art project. The college students requested my ID card as a deposit, and gave me an MP3 player and earphones and a hand-drawn map of the neighbourhood, showing more than 20 listening stations and the routes of the tours.

It is significant that the two recorded tours were delivered by different institutional agents. The first tour I followed was given by Omar Agbaria, a Palestinian who works at a non-profit organisation called Zochrot (lit. 'Remembering'). This organisation is dedicated to remembering Palestinian life before 1948 and to raising awareness of the Nakba: the catastrophe suffered by the Palestinian people in the 1948 war (see Zochrot 2010). The second narration was given by Pnina Ein Mor, a Jewish-Israeli resident of Ein Karem, who has led the neighbourhood's struggles against the municipality and the real estate developers who repeatedly attempt to build large projects in the area.

Within the scope of this chapter, I will present two segments from each of the tours. It is notable that the two tours do not follow the same route, nor do they refer to the same attractions (buildings, landscapes, etc.). For instance, Agbaria's tour stops at and elaborates about the main cemetery, a Muslim site that is not mentioned in Ein Mor's tour; conversely, Ein Mor's tour pauses at the monastery of Les Soeurs de Notre-Dame de Sion for a scenic stop that is not included in the Zochrot tour. This discrepancy suggests, even prior to a textual-narrative analysis, that the diverging narratives in and of a given place are told about and by means of different physical resources and geographical points of reference.

Setting the Narrative

Neither of the audio narratives I followed began immediately with descriptions of houses, streets, and so on; that is, with the 'itinerary' itself. Instead, they started with introductory segments providing the narrative setting, with background information about both Ein Karem and the narrators. Thus, rather than offering an authoritative voice, telling the story of Ein Karem from a purportedly 'neutral' perspective (like the guided tours produced by the Jerusalem municipality, for example), the tours offered a personal perspective; 'personal' not so much in the romantic sense of providing an encounter with an individual, but in the sense that the narrators explicitly elaborated on who they were and what their goals were in conducting the tour. The opening segments of the two audio tours are reproduced below.[1]

Omar Agbaria's Introduction

Welcome. We will [now] begin the tour of the village of Ein Karem. Naturally, the tour will also tell of the Palestinian village of Ein Karem, which was abandoned in 1948. We will see some of its magnificent houses and beautiful neighborhoods. Ein Karem is the largest of the [Arab] villages in the Jerusalem area that were occupied in 1948.

Hello. We will shortly begin a tour of the village of Ein Karem – a Palestinian village until 1948. We will appreciate the splendid houses and beautiful neighborhoods of this village, which was the largest [Arabic] village in the Jerusalem area until the Nakba in 1948.

My name is Omar, Omar Agbaria. I work for the non-profit organization Zochrot as a coordinator of tours in Palestinian villages that were occupied in [nineteen] forty-eight. One of the villages that we have researched and produced a tour for is the village of Ein Karem. The aim of this tour is to inform the general audience, and particularly the Israeli audience, about life in the village before it was occupied in nineteen forty-eight. We also publish a booklet that includes information about the village: documents, pictures and of course testimonies by refugees who tell their story. The village was occupied in the middle of July ... [by Israeli forces that] evacuated all the inhabitants. The Palestinian inhabitants were obviously not allowed to return, and [Ein Karem] became an Israeli village and part of the city of Jerusalem. What is special, also in the eyes of the Palestinians, is that the village of Ein Karem has been left intact – as it was when it was [first] conquered in nineteen forty-eight – and today you can see it in almost the same condition. The houses are all inhabited by new residents. All of them Israeli Jews.

Pnina Ein Mor's Introduction

Hello. My name is Pnina Ein Mor. I have been living here since nineteen seventy-five. You could say that [living here] is really a dream I had as a girl in Bat Yam. This **forest**. I so envied the Jerusalemites. I didn't know the city; I knew it [only] from reading books, but even then I already decided that once I complete my obligatory [military] service, I'd come here. And indeed I came to

---

1 In the transcriptions, bold text indicates words that were stressed; italics indicate words that were spoken and/or pronounced in Arabic; three dots indicate an ellipsis; square brackets indicate words or comments added for clarification. I thank Michael Komem for his help with the translation from the Arabic.

Jerusalem, and later to Ein Kerem.[2] Every morning I thank God that I live here. These beautiful orchards; the changing seasons, each with it its fruits and colors; the paths between the houses.

However, I'm very very sad that the village is neglected, and I'm sorry for those pilgrims who come here, enjoy the natural beauty, but the neglect is unmistakable. And what I am most concerned with is the issue of conservation. That's why I was recruited in the past to act as chair of the [neighborhood] council, and I led a move, which was a national precedent back then, to draw an urban building plan initiated by the residents – which means that the residents can say what they want and not just resist other's plans. I hope you enjoy your trip today in the village, and that you will join us in the struggle to conserve it.

As mentioned earlier, these introductory segments convey the perspective from which the tours unfold; an embodied viewpoint rather than a 'neutral' one, told 'from above', as it were, which aims to share knowledge, recollections and experiences, as well as concerns about possible future threats that have not been admitted in hegemonic accounts. Though very different in content and themes, these introductory segments serve similar functions in both narratives. As self-presentation segments (Goffman 1959), they introduce the identities of the narrators, and lend authenticity and validity to the(ir) stories. In the case of Omar Agbaria's narration, this is evinced immediately by the language of his opening sentences. These are spoken in Arabic, even though, as Agbaria himself acknowledges, the tour is intended mainly for Hebrew-speaking Israelis who know little or no Arabic. Hence, the opening remarks in Arabic (which are, in fact, immediately repeated in Hebrew) serve an ideological goal; they evoke issues of linguistic ideology and the perceived indexical relations between the language spoken and the identity of the speaker (Noy 2008b). Starting the narration in Arabic establishes the identity and authority of the narrator and presents the entire text as a translation, an adaptation to Hebrew from Arabic, which is the authentic language, the 'language of the place'. It will be noted that Arabic is present not only in the opening lines, but in the numerous names of places and persons throughout the narrative. Further into the introductory segment Agbaria gives his institutional affiliation (Zochrot), and describes the organisation's ideological goals and the means by which they are pursued. Here, terms such as 'research', 'testimony by refugees', and 'documents and pictures' serve to establish discursively the authority of both the Zochrot organisation and of Agbaria himself as legitimate narrators of the Palestinian Nakba and of pre-Nakba Ein Karem.

---

2   Ein Mor sometimes pronounces the name of the neighborhood 'Ein Kerem', which is the official Israeli Hebrew name, and sometimes 'Ein Karem', which is the Arabic pronunciation and also the more common pronunciation, which I use throughout this chapter.

Establishing identity and authority is also one of the main concerns in the introductory segment narrated by Pnina Ein Mor. Immediately after giving her name, Ein Mor indicates that she is, and has been for a number of decades, a resident of the neighborhood ('I have been living here since 1975'). Her narrative, then, is presented as a story told not by an impersonal institutional agent but by a local resident, reflecting a first-hand experience of living in Ein Karem. It should be mentioned that Pnina Ein Mor is both a long-time activist *and* the owner of a local business that organises tours, workshops and events in Ein Karem. It is noteworthy that Ein Mor's story includes some conspicuous gaps. Noticeably, she states that her arrival in Ein Karem was a 'dream come true', but does not explain how her move from Bat Yam (then a relatively poor suburb, south of Tel-Aviv, with a rather poor reputation) to the up-market artist colony of Ein Karem was actually accomplished. Ein Mor's introductory segment establishes her identity as a local activist and presents her concerns about the conservation of the neighbourhood, or the 'village', as she sometimes calls it (a description that lends it an attractive air of a pastoral rural location rather than an urban one). In fact, conservation is a major motif of her narration and recurs throughout it; for example, her introductory segment ends with a direct appeal to the audience: 'I hope that you'll ... join us in the struggle for its conservation'. By stressing this theme, Ein Mor accomplishes two goals simultaneously; she attempts to recruit support for the preservation of Ein Karem and at the same time further establishes her authority, not merely as a local resident but as a local agent who is committed to the place and well acquainted with its treasures and features. Finally, in terms of language, if Agbaria's name indexes his identity as an Arab and helps establish his authority over the Zochrot narrative, Ein Mor's Hebrew name clearly does something comparable through its similarity to the name of the neighborhood (Ein Karem); both personal and district names include the word 'ein', which means 'spring' in both Hebrew and Arabic.

The introductory segments by Agbaria and Ein Mor serve not only the Goffmanesque function of self-presentation but also the function of narrative orientation sections (in the sense of Labov's [1972] classical typology of narrative functions-structure), by outlining the context within which the subsequent tour-narrative will evolve. Orientation sections are normally located in the beginning of narrative sequences, where they supply the setting of stories, presenting the time, the place and the characters involved. They are clearly functional, in the sense that they supply the informative baseline from which later events unfold, but it is illuminating to examine them also in terms of what information is *deemed relevant* by particular narrators on particular narrative occasions. In this sense they do not simply provide information so much as reflect selectivity and subjective perspective.

In Omar Agbaria's introduction the historically constitutive events, characters, and time-line are those that form part of the situated performance of the Palestinian Nakba narrative. As the expressed aim of the tour is 'to inform ... about life in the village before it was occupied in nineteen forty-eight', the narrative's time-frame is *not* primarily concerned with the present but rather with the *past*. Indeed, Agbaria's initial narrative clauses (for example, 'The village was occupied in the middle of July') describe what is actually the (traumatic) chronologic *end-point* of the story of Ein Karem as a Palestinian village. This kind of 'reverse' temporal structure, or chronotope, serves to establish the drama/trauma of the Nakba, and the fact that the site being toured is at the same time a reality and a place that no longer exists. The characters involved in the 1948 drama are the Palestinian inhabitants on the one hand and the Israeli forces on the other. Later, as the tour's narrative turns to pre-1948 village life, only everyday Palestinian life is described. But before this unfolds, the introduction ends quite dramatically with a statement about the present day condition: 'The houses are all inhabited by new residents, all of them Israeli Jews'. Listeners are normally aware that most of the present residents of Ein Karem are Jewish Israelis, yet by describing them as 'new residents' Agbaria and Zochrot achieve one of the goals (and express one of the axioms) of the Nakba narrative; the physical and symbolic (narrative) displacement of Palestinians by Israelis.

Read as an orientation section, Pnina Ein Mor's introduction establishes a different context of and for the tour's narrative, in terms of characters, events, and time-frame. In her introduction, and consistently throughout her tour, the time-frame with which she is concerned is that of the *future* and the drama spans the present and the (potentially negative) developments to come. Near the beginning of the section, when she explains what she yearned for as an adolescent in the town of Bat Yam, she mentions 'this **forest**'. Shortly after, she gives a more orderly and elaborate description of the 'natural beauty' of Ein Karem: 'These beautiful orchards; the changing seasons ... the paths between the houses'. For Ein Mor, the key issue is the exceptional natural beauty of Ein Karem, which includes Palestinian houses and paths. It is important to note that this *naturalisation* of the remains of Palestinian life and (material) culture is typical of Israeli narrative; such remains are de-politicised and to some extent also de-historicised by being treated as part of 'natural' landscape, along with the local flora and fauna. Both at this point and later in the narrative, Ein Mor indicates that the beauty and unique attractions of the neighbourhood are being neglected by the various municipal and national agents. More disturbingly and dramatically, they are threatened by large-scale development projects, such as planned hotels, restaurants, recreation areas and parking lots. The drama in Ein Mor's narration thus concerns the fragility of the neighbourhood (the endangered 'village') at the present time as well as the possibility of harmful events in the future.

Next stop: Mary's Spring

As mentioned earlier, most of the stops in the Zochrot tour are not part of Ein Mor's tour, and vice versa. Yet there were a few stops, which particularly piqued my curiosity as ethnographer-cum-visitor-cum-tourist, where both recorded tours

Figure 11.2   Mary's Spring at Ein Karem (Source: author's own photograph)

paused and provided explanations. Most of these were at the neighbourhood's prominent tourist attractions, such as Mary's Spring, where, according to tradition, the Virgin Mary met Elizabeth, the mother of the Baptist (see Figure 11.2).

Agbaria's 'Mary's Spring'

> This is the spring called Miryam Spring [in Hebrew], *Maryam* in Arabic, referring to the Holy [Virgin] Mary. On top of the spring was built a mosque.. This combination of a spring that is holy to the Christians, and a mosque, which is a Muslim house of prayer, reflects the composition of the village's population, which consisted of both Christians and Muslims. At least according to the story told by the inhabitants, the mosque was built in this location because they believed that the famous Muslim *Khalif* Umar ibn al-Khattab came here and prayed near the spring. Today, or course, the mosque is **sealed** and entry is prohibited to Muslims and others, as we can see. We also know that above the mosque there used to be another floor, which housed the boys' school of Ein Karem village. That floor still stood when the village was occupied in nineteen forty-eight, and it lasted for several years after that. However, it seems that [sometime] in the sixties, after [nineteen] sixty-seven, the floor was demolished.

Ein Mor's 'Mary's Spring'

Hello. We've reached Ein Karem Spring, or Miryam Spring, by its other name. And like in **any other** place in Ein Karem, here too there are **plenty** of stories. Once, this spring was considered at its time to be **the best** of the Jerusalem springs, and today you see the sign: drinking the water is forbidden. I regret [to say] that sewage from a cesspit located above the spring seeps into it, and the water of the best of the Jerusalem springs mingles with the sewage. In the past, [the spring] watered **the entire** amazing wadi beneath it. But even though sewage seeps into the spring, it can still be holy. Hence, to the many Christian pilgrims that come here, this is the water that Mary – Maria – blessed, and the pilgrims fill plastic bottles with the holy water. And if someone at home is ill, they let him drink it, and believe it or not, he recovers – for such is the power of faith. On the other hand, ten days before [the Jewish festival of] Passover, instead of the flocks of storks [that pass through Israel in that season] we see flocks of *hassidim*[3] who sing and dance and fill containers with this water, so that [during the Passover meal] we can have a *matza shmura* on our table.[4] So it doesn't really matter to whom it is holy.

Today the spring is threatened by the [planned] construction of a multistory hotel, with no parking space, near the spring and the spring's tunnel. And one of the things that we are **most** afraid of is that the Spring's aqueduct will be blocked by the construction work for the new hotel. That's it.

As I stood near Spring Road in front of Mary's Spring, and listened to the voices and stories being played into my ears, I found the experience to be rather disorienting, not to say schizophrenic. If I thought that, because both narrators agreed on the importance of the spring and therefore made a stop there, their stories would be similar, I could not have been further from the truth. The reason for the discrepancy is, of course ideological, having to do with the different goals of the two tours. From the perspective of narrative analysis, the significant divergence emerges, or may emerge, from the fact that neither narrative actually involves a straightforward description of the site (Mary's Spring), which is to say a description of the events and attributions that have made the small spring into a popular destination for Christian pilgrims. Instead, both narratives assume, quite correctly, that the site is familiar and therefore refer to it briefly, using it primarily as a trigger or anchor for other stories and accounts. In the case of Agbaria these

---

3 The *Hassidim* are members of Ultra-Orthodox Jewish sects. The narrator makes a play on words here, because the word 'Hassidim' is similar in sound to the Hebrew word for storks ('hasidot').

4 *Matza shmura* (lit. guarded matza) refers to unleavened bread, made of special wheat and under particularly strict supervision to ensure it is kosher for Passover.

are historical narratives while in the case of Ein Mor these narratives concern future prospects.

For Agbaria, the presence of a mosque above Mary's Spring is significant because it attests to the coexistence of Christians and Muslims in Ein Karem across the centuries. From a general perspective, it is a story of inter-faith tolerance; specifically, it illuminates the relationship between Christians and Muslims, against the background of the relationship between Christianity and Judaism on the one hand and between Islam and Judaism on the other. Zionism exalts the relations between Israel and various Christian sects and communities, mostly in the Unites States. These relations are also enacted in the ideological and political narratives of conventional tourism. Feldman (2008) recently showed that, when giving joint tours to Christian pilgrims in the Old City of Jerusalem, the pastor and the (Jewish) Israeli guide collaborate in describing the local Palestinian merchants and population in negative terms. In Agbaria's narrative, the present neglected state of the mosque (which is closed and sealed), and the destruction of the top floor, are contrasted with how things used to be when Muslims and Christians lived in the neighbourhood before 1948. The story's end, that is, how things are today, is epitomised by the sorry state of the mosque.

Consistent with her own narrative goals, Ein Mor too laments the neglected state of Ein Karem. Here, at Mary's Spring, this motif is manifested in the spring's contaminated water; she emphasises that the spring was once known as '**the best** of the Jerusalem springs', whereas today it is forbidden to drink the water. Thus, her narrative too contrasts how things were and how they are in the present. However, for her it is an *escalating narrative*; it does not stop at the present, but projects alarmingly into the future, warning, in the segment's coda, of what Ein Mor and the residents are '**most** afraid' of, namely future construction work. It is notable that Ein Mor is highly selective in choosing which *past* events to focus on. She does not elaborate on, or even mention, that the Spring was once part of the ebb and flow of Palestinian life (here the wording is opaque and schematic: 'at its time'). This omission is particularly interesting here, because above and beyond the general avoidance of the Palestinian past and the Nakba in Zionist narrative, an *escalating narrative* could easily have been told by Agbaria, with the escalation including the Israeli occupation and its impact on the character of the Palestinian village. In fact, one of the few things that both narratives do converge on is the once-acclaimed quality of the water at Mary's Spring! Ein Mor then turns to a description of the pilgrims who consume the holy water, thereby offering us a unique perspective; that of the *host's gaze* on her guests. In an unmistakably cynical tone, she says that faith, whether that of the Ultra-Orthodox Hassidic Jews or that of evangelical Christian pilgrims, is oblivious to the quality of the water and, by extension, to the quality of the Spring or the site as a whole ('Such is the power of faith', she ruminates). Her message, it seems, is twofold. In the first place, she implicitly differentiates the audience of her recorded tour (who can be assumed to be secular Israelis) from the religious and ignorant crowds of pilgrims. The subtext here is that the latter are blind believers who will not be of any help in efforts to conserve the Spring and the neighbourhood, whereas her audience (that is, the rational tourists and visitors) may be. Secondly, she asserts that if the tunnel of Mary's Spring is blocked no water will flow, no bottles will be filled and no rituals, Christian or Hassidic, will be performed. From this perspective, the concern for the maintenance of the Spring, and therefore the neighbourhood, should actually be everyone's, but the responsibility for enlightenment obviously rests on the shoulders of Ein Mor.

Conclusions

As the Sala-Manca Group realised when preparing the 'What Lies behind the Pastoral' project, narratives in tourism are immensely powerful in their ability to maintain, eradicate and transform the meanings of places; their histories, memories, feelings and so on. For this reason, one of the many situated activities that took place as part of the three-day project was the tours described in this chapter, which served to probe and examine the neighbourhood of Ein Karem (where Sala-Manca's work space is presently located). During these tours, the everyday tourist life of Ein Karem was seemingly uninterrupted. Crowds of visitors to an experimental art exhibition seamlessly intermingled with mass pilgrims and other visitors who poured out of huge air-conditioned buses. For a moment, a touristic mixture or even hybrid was sustained (performed), where essential questions were raised about the nature of tourism, about who has access to and authority over truth in tourism, about how artistic, touristic and pilgrim aesthetics co-relate, about how one site may be so many different things to different groups of people, and so on. All this was possible because Sala-Manca's experimental art is performative; it gets people to engage, to move around, to carry and create meanings in public spaces. The visitors, myself included, were embodying and thus performing what de Certeau (1984) called 'everyday tactics', which are subversive routes and paths.

The Sala-Manca group attempted to destabilise common hegemonic versions of Ein Karem by choosing the specific narrators that they did; by giving the microphone, metaphorically, but also quite literally, to past and present inhabitants. The spatial and mobile narratives of Agbaria and Ein Mor are both clearly counter-hegemonic. There is a substantial difference between the two place-narratives produced, in terms of the opposition they offer to hegemonic ideology and the difficulties they experience in narrating against hegemonic perceptions, but Sala-Manca did not state a preference for one narrative over the other. At the Pastoral project the narrators talked and the visitors walked, thereby allowing new meanings to evolve, be embodied and negotiated.

Acknowledgement

I am indebted to Lea Mauas, Diego Rotman, and Noa Guez of the Sala-Manca Collective for their time and assistance.

References

Bakhtin, M.M. 1981. *The Dialogic Imagination: Four Essays* (translated by C. Emerson and M. Holquist). Austin: University of Texas Press.

Bowman, G. 1996. *Passion, Power and Politics in a Palestinian Market, in The Tourist Image: Myths and Myth Making in Tourism*, edited by T. Selwyn. Chichester: John Wiley, 83–103.

Brin, E. 2006. Politically-oriented Tourism in Jerusalem. *Tourist Studies*, 6(3), 215–43.

Brin, E., and Noy, C. (2010). The Said and the Unsaid: Performative Guiding in a Jerusalem Neighborhood. *Tourist Studies*, 10(1), 19–33.

Certeau, M. d. 1984. *The Practice of Everyday Life* (translated by S. Rendall). Berkeley: University of California Press.

Clark, R. 2000. Self-presentation in a Contested City: Palestinian and Israeli Political Tourism in Hebron. *Anthropology Today*, 16(5), 12–18.

Feldman, J. 2008. Constructing a Shared Bible Land: Jewish Israeli Guiding Performances for Protestant pilgrims. *American Ethnologist*, 34(2), 351–74.

Goffman, E. 1959. *The Presentation of Self in Everyday Life*. Garden City, N.Y.: Doubleday.

Go Israel 2010. *Attractions: Ein Kerem*. Available at: http://www.goisrael.com/Tourism_Eng/Articles/Attractions/Ein+Kerem.htm [accessed: 18 December 2010].

Gramsci, A. 1971. *Selections from the Prison Notebooks of Antonio Gramsci* (translated by Q. Hoare and G.N. Smith). London: Lawrence & Wishart.

Labov, W. 1972. *Language in the Inner City: Studies in the Black English Vernacular*. Philadelphia: University of Pennsylvania Press.

Mamuta 2010. *Mamuta at the Daniela Passal Art and Media Center*. Available at http://mamuta.org/?page_id=confirmsubscription&u=74c6046f215523ff353d5650779a681f. [accessed: 4 November 2010].

Noy, C. 2008a. Pages as Stages: A Performance Approach to Visitor Books. *Annals of Tourism Research*, 35(2), 509–28.

Noy, C. 2008b. Writing Ideology: Hybrid Symbols in a Commemorative Visitor Book in Israel. *Journal of Linguistic Anthropology*, 18(1), 62–81.

Noy, C. 2011. The Political Ends of Tourism: Voices and Narratives of Silwan/the City of David in East Jerusalem, in *The Critical Turn in Tourism Studies: Creating an Academy of Hope* (2nd edn), edited by I. Ateljevic, N. Morgan and A. Pritchard. Amsterdam: Elsevier Publications.

Sala-Manca Group 2010. *Sala-Manca Group*. Available at: http://sala-manca.net/salamancagroup.htm [accessed: 4 November 2010].

Zochrot 2010. *Zochrot*. Available at http://www.zochrot.org/index.php?lang=english [accessed: 4 November 2010].

Chapter 12

Narratives of National versus 'Universal' Belonging of the Athenian Acropolis in Travel Guidebooks

Tijana Rakić

Introduction

Narratives about 'touristic' places can be found within a wide variety of secondary sources ranging from popular media such as travelogues, novels, poems, travel blogs, travel videos and stories posted on social networking sites to a range of materials produced for the purposes of tourism such as official destination websites, brochures and travel guidebooks. What makes these place narratives particularly interesting from the perspective of scholarly research is that these, among other cultural texts, social and cultural practices, individual experiences, stories and memories, can also be considered to play a role in the making of that place and its meanings.

While a number of existing studies have focused on people's narratives about their travel and tourism experiences (e.g. some of the essays in Robertson et al. 1994, Noy 2004a, 2004b, Benedix 2002, Bruner 2005, Elsrud 2001), fewer studies seemed to have focused on narratives of particular 'touristic' places within popular media, or indeed within tourism materials such as guidebooks (e.g. see Beck 2006). With its focus on narratives of the Athenian Acropolis in guidebooks, this chapter aims to contribute to this literature. In addition, as part of a wider research project surrounding the complex relationships between World Heritage, tourism and national identity at the Acropolis (see Rakić 2008), this chapter also aims to complement previous publications which focused on the meanings of the Acropolis as constructed and conveyed in postcards from 1886 until 2007 (Rakić and Travlou forthcoming) and within governmental promotional campaigns from 2002 until 2006 (Rakić and Chambers 2007). Through an analysis of Acropolis relevant content within guidebooks which were available in Athens city centre in 2006, this chapter explores the modes in which the narratives contained in these guidebooks construct or reinforce some of the meanings related to its status as a World Heritage site, a popular tourist attraction, and 'the ultimate symbol of Greek identity' (Yalouri 2001: 75).

Places, National Identities and World Heritage in Guidebooks

Places are 'meaningful locations' (Agnew 1987 in Creswell 2004) which, unless these are virtual places (Casey 1997), are actual physical locations imbued with meanings through a wide range of social and cultural practices, popular media and individual experiences. Therefore, places and their meanings are also fluid and changeable social, cultural and personal constructions in a continuous process of being made and re-made (e.g. see Relf 1976, Creswell 2004, Tuan 1977, Stokowski 2002). Tourism is only one of the dynamic forces through which places and their meanings are constructed (Crang 2004, Bærenholdt and Haldrup 2006) and tourism materials such as guidebooks, promotional campaigns, postcards and postage stamps, have also been acknowledged to play a role in the construction, or at the very least reinforcement, of both national identities and place meanings (e.g. see Bhattacharyya 1997, Koshar 1998, Pritchard and Morgan 2003, Raento 2009, Rakić 2008, Rakić and Travlou forthcoming, Rakić and Chambers 2007).

According to Therkelsen and Sørensen (2005) guidebooks have only been given sporadic attention in scholarly research. Some of the existing studies focused on histories of guidebooks (e.g. see Buzard 1993, Koshar 2000), some analysed travel guidebook content (e.g. see Gilbert 1999, Travlou 2002, Bhattacharyya 1997, Lew 1991, Siegenthaler 2002, Laderman 2002, Fei 2010), some focused on the usage of guidebooks by tourists (e.g. see Therkelsen and Sørensen 2005, Nishimura et al. 2007, Nishimura et al. 2006, Osti et al. 2009) and some also studied the relationships between the tourists and the contents of the guidebooks they used (e.g. see McGregor 2000). While authors who analyse guidebooks tend to suggest, either implicitly or explicitly, that guidebooks are scripting tourist behaviour (Therkelsen and Sørensen 2005), the behaviour and experiences of tourists are also likely to be informed not only through their individual travel guidebook readings but also through other sources as well as their own lifeworld (Therkelsen and Sørensen 2005, McGregor 2000). Interestingly, McGregor's study (2000), which examined the relationships between guidebooks and tourists in Tana Toraja, found that guidebooks nevertheless provided 'lenses' through which tourists viewed the world. Therefore, while it is important to acknowledge that tourists inevitably produce their own selective, subjective and, in some occasions also critical readings of guidebooks (Therkelsen and Sørensen 2005) and that not all tourists use guidebooks (McGregor 2000), given their widespread popularity guidebooks are instrumental in informing tourists' perceptions of cultures and meanings of places they visit. It is this role of guidebooks as informants (Travlou 2002) that can be seen to play a role in the construction, or reinforcement, of the meanings tourists attach to places and cultures, making them remarkably interesting 'data' for scholarly research.

Gilbert (1999), for example, analyses the content of guidebooks from the mid-nineteenth until the end of the twentieth century and traces the changes in the interpretations and representations of London. He also emphasises the importance of examining 'the construction of guidebooks' accounts of place, not least because of their influence on popular perceptions of places and on the practices of millions of tourists (ibid.: 283). In an earlier study, Koshar (1998) discusses the historical development of guidebooks in Germany and Europe from the mid-nineteenth century onwards, in which he also traces the representations of national identities, while Bhattcharyya (1997) in her analysis of a 1993 edition of the Lonely Planet for India, concludes that, among other things, this guidebook not only mediates tourist experiences but also serves to create particular images of India and its people. Therefore, while undoubtedly millions of tourists who read guidebooks bring their own subjectivities and lifeworlds into their selective readings and, sometimes critical, interpretations of their contents (e.g. see Therkelsen and Sørensen 2005), semiotic and/or content analyses of narratives and representations of places and cultures contained in guidebooks are nevertheless instrumental in revealing the mode in which both place meanings and national identities are constructed and conveyed.

Of particular relevance among existing analyses of guidebooks is Travlou's (2002) retrospective study of the symbolic representations of the city of Athens in guidebooks dating from the mid-nineteenth century to the end of the twentieth century. Her analysis reveals that in addition to creating the 'discourse of the other' (ibid.: 120) in which similar stereotypes of Greekness are noticeable over a long period of time, these guidebooks also tend to represent the city as if it consisted only of the tourism infrastructure and the main monuments, the best known of which is the Acropolis. What is interesting in the context of the analysis contained in the later sections of this chapter is that typical descriptions of the Acropolis in guidebooks from this period resonate with meanings which often go beyond its sense of Greekness. Fielding's (1965) guidebook for example states that 'Athens with its Acropolis is the birthplace and heart of Greek culture and Western civilisation, a must for all visitors', while *Let's Go Europe* (1991) states that the Acropolis is 'the oldest, most sacred monument of Western civilisation' (see Table 12.1 below).

The question is, is the Acropolis, the ultimate symbol of Greekness (Yalouri 2001), a symbol of the World Heritage idea (UNESCO 2006) and a World Heritage site since 1987, still represented in a similar way in the more recent guidebooks, and importantly, what is the role its World Heritage site status is given? Namely, on a conceptual level World Heritage sites, or heritage sites deemed to be of outstanding universal value, are expected to be perceived as being sites of 'outstanding value to humanity' and sites which 'belong to all the peoples of the world, irrespective of the territory on which they are located' (UNESCO 2011). Given that many of the World Heritage sites are perceived as belonging to the nation rather than humanity as a whole, the concept of World Heritage has also been seen as problematic and paradoxical (e.g. see Ashworth 1997 and Rakić and Chambers 2007). The power of guidebooks to inform the meanings millions of tourists attach to places, including meanings related to national versus 'universal' belonging and ownership of World Heritage sites, is therefore of particular significance in this context, not only because guidebooks contribute to tourists' perception of place meanings but also because these can be seen 'as a form of popular geography' (Gilbert 1999: 279).

Table 12.1   Descriptions of the Acropolis in guidebooks (1845–1997)

Guidebooks	Terms Used to Describe the Acropolis
Murray 1845: 70	The Acropolis is the first object which attracts the attention of the traveller.
Murray 1854: 70	On turning into the Acropolis, the Parthenon rises in all its majesty before you. The finest edifice on the finest site in the world.
Life 1963: 39	Yet in the modern city's midst, the Acropolis with its Parthenon still stands as a shining citadel of an ideal.
Fielding 1965: 1650	Athens with its Acropolis is the birthplace and heart of Greek culture and Western civilisation, a must for all visitors.
Frommer 1968: 463	To ride from the airport to Athens [...] and suddenly to see the Acropolis, high over-looking the city, is literally a thrill that comes once in a lifetime.
Let's Go Europe 1991: 397	The oldest, most sacred monument of Western civilisation.
Lonely Planet – Web Page 1997	The Acropolis, crowned by the Parthenon, stands sentinel over Athens, visible from almost everywhere in the city.

(Source: Travlou 2002: 118)

Interestingly, in the light of World Heritage narratives in guidebooks, a remarkable study which focused on European World Heritage sites in guidebooks revealed that:

> … surprisingly few places are labelled as World Heritage even in the most comprehensive books. While practical problems and lack of awareness may be one explanation for this, inherent difficulties of conceiving and presenting narratives of world heritage as opposed to national, regional or local heritage may be more significant.

(Beck 2006: 521)

Although Beck (2006), on the one hand, focused on guidebooks for a number of European nations rather than solely on guidebooks for Greece, Athens or the Acropolis, and her analysis did not include an in-depth exploration and interpretation of narratives of the Acropolis contained in these guidebooks, she nevertheless found that the World Heritage title of the Acropolis was present in only one of the seven guidebooks for Greece with publication dates ranging from

1997 to 2002. Travlou (2002), on the other hand, explored some of the typical descriptions of the Acropolis from the mid-nineteenth century to the end of the twentieth century in slightly greater depth. However, her analysis did not focus specifically on the Acropolis or the tensions which might have existed between its national and 'universal' significance and belonging. In this light, it is particularly relevant to see whether the 'universal' belonging of the Acropolis signified by its World Heritage status is surfacing in the more recent guidebook narratives. Is the Acropolis still represented as a 'must see' tourist attraction in Athens? Are there any narratives of national versus 'universal' belonging and ownership of the Acropolis, which might possibly be entrenched within the narratives contained in guidebooks and which went unnoticed in earlier analyses?

Collecting and Analysing Travel Guidebooks

The ten guidebooks used as data in this analysis include Acropolis, Athens and Greece themed guidebooks which were available in bookshops and souvenir shops in Athens city centre in 2006 (see Table 12.2 below), the year when my ethnographic fieldwork at the Acropolis commenced (see Rakić 2008). Therefore, these are inevitably only a selection of Acropolis, Athens and Greece themed guidebooks which circulated globally that year, although arguably many of these guidebooks were available in earlier editions before 2006 and most are still likely to be available in the same or a later edition.

As will become evident in the following section – similarly to some of the earlier guidebook analyses (e.g. see Bhattcharyya 1997, Travlou 2002) – I also rely on a semiotic approach in my exploration and interpretation of place narratives of the Acropolis contained in these guidebooks. While any semiotic analysis is inevitably subjective, given that researchers bring their own subjective selves to the process, in addition to undertaking this analysis in a rigorous manner by conducting several in-depth readings, I also revisited my interpretations of Acropolis relevant content contained in these guidebooks several times. In acknowledging and embracing the subjective nature of both semiotic analysis and popular readings of guidebooks (e.g. see discussions in Therkelsen and Sørensen 2005), as well as simultaneously remaining faithful to my constructivist philosophical position which recognises the possibility of different interpretations, in the analysis which follows I also include some of the relevant quotes from these guidebooks, in order to enable readers to produce their own interpretations of both the quoted text and my analysis of it.

Narratives of the Athenian Acropolis in Travel Guidebooks: A 2006 Snapshot

The first and only Acropolis specific guidebook included in this analysis (Andronicos 1980), firstly narrates the long history of the Acropolis as a place before giving any attention to particular monuments still present at the site. In his narration of the

Table 12.2   Guidebooks

No	Title	Year	Type	Place of Publication
1	*The Acropolis* (English edition translated from Greek)	1980; reprinted in 2006	Acropolis	Athens, Greece
2	*Athens: Art and History* (English edition translated from Greek)	1995; reprinted in 2005	Athens	Florence, Italy
3	*Athens: Between Legend and History* (English edition translated from Greek)	1995	Athens	Athens, Greece
4	*Athens: A Cultural and Literary History* (1st Edition)	2004	Athens	Oxford, UK
5	*Lonely Planet: Best of Athens – The Ultimate Pocket Guide and Map* (2nd Edition)	2004	Athens	London, UK
6	*AA Essential: Athens – All You Need to Know, the Top Places to Go, Where to Shop and Eat Out, and How to Get About*	1999; reprinted in 2004	Athens	Whitchurch, UK
7	*Time Out: Athens* (2nd Edition)	2005	Athens	London, UK
8	*Heritage Walks in Athens*	2004	Athens	Athens, Greece
9	*The Rough Guide to Greece* (11th Edition)	2006	Greece	New York, London, Delhi
10	*Lonely Planet: Greece* (7th Edition)	2006	Greece	London, UK

history of the Acropolis as a place Andronicos, a Professor of Archaeology, briefly goes over the main historical periods such as the prehistoric age, the archaic period, the classical period, the medieval and the modern period. An emphasis is given to the classical period as one for which the Acropolis of Athens is most renowned. The classical period of the Acropolis is mentioned even within the histories of its non-classical periods, such as the pre-classical periods. For example, within the history of the Acropolis in the prehistoric age the reader is told that:

> No one possibly could have dreamt [in the prehistoric age] that the roughly hewn stones supporting the masonry of their crude dwellings would some day become the foundation stones of an architecture second to none and of a story unique in the annals of history.
>
> (Andronicos 1980: 5, text in brackets added)

In other words, from the very beginnings of the text, the reader is guided towards the significance of the classical history of the Acropolis, while its other histories are represented as not as relevant as the classical.

Another point of history of the Acropolis as a place, which is given much emphasis, is its 'destruction' in the seventeenth and the nineteenth centuries, beginning with the Venetians and Morosini when explosions destroyed big parts of the temples and going on to Lord Elgin and battles between the Greeks and Turks. At this point, the reader is given the very first hint of the symbolic resonances of the Acropolis as a national symbol of Greece. The reader is told that:

> Athens finally reached its freedom on March 31st 1833, when the Turkish garrison handed the Acropolis over to the Greeks.
>
> (Andronicos 1980: 13)

By this, the text suggests that the Acropolis is not only a strategic geographical point of Attica, but it is also the core of the whole of Greece, without which neither Greece nor the Greeks could be free. What the reader is told about the archaeological restoration and preservation project within which one of the tasks was to remove the 'latter [post-classical] additions' (ibid.: 13–14, text in brackets added) at the Acropolis and which followed shortly after the handing over of the Acropolis to the Greeks are relatively few details about the projects and that:

> ... the work lasted for many years ... Many of the slabs from the Parthenon frieze which had escaped the eye of Lord Elgin and remained in the native land were found among the ruins.
>
> (Andronicos 1980: 14)

This again is an explicit reference to the symbolic significance of the Acropolis for the Greek nation and its national rather than 'universal' ownership and belonging. Lord Elgin is suggested to have taken some of the most remarkable slabs from the Parthenon frieze, from the place these naturally belonged to ('the native land' or Greece), leaving behind only the ones which had 'escaped his eye'. Simultaneously, while its 'universal' belonging does not seem to be directly alluded to, the support of UNESCO towards the conservation works at the Acropolis is mentioned in this guidebook.

In the second guidebook, titled *Athens: Art and History* (Vingopoulou and Casulli 2005) the first 30 pages (out of a total of 128) are mainly about the Acropolis. What this implies is that the Acropolis is the most important place in Athens. What is remarkable within the history of Athens narrated in this guidebook, is that although a particular emphasis is placed on the rapid growth of the 'European admiration' of the classical antiquities from the mid-seventeenth century onwards and the significance of the remnants of this 'exceptional civilisation' which left a mark 'on the entire ancient world and laid the foundations of the modern one' (ibid.: 3), the World Heritage site status signifying the very 'universal' value of the Acropolis is not mentioned once again. The World Heritage status of the Acropolis is omitted even though the Acropolis is described as 'the universal symbol of art and values that were born' (ibid.: 6) in the classical period. One interpretation of this might be that what is indirectly suggested is that although the Acropolis is a 'universally' important monument, in its essence it is also a monument which is more about a sense of Greekness than it is about a sense of 'universality'.

The narrative of the third guidebook titled *Athens: Between Legend and History* (Mavromataki 1995) is much the same in this respect as the two guidebooks referred to above. In the history of Athens particular emphasis has been placed on the 'priceless contribution' of the city 'to what is the heritage of the entire world' (ibid.: 4). Although its World Heritage status is not explicitly mentioned here, the fact that the Acropolis is perceived as the heritage of the entire world alludes to its 'universality'. However, the national ownership and belonging of the Acropolis is once again reiterated within the narrations of the history of destructions of the Acropolis, whereby for example 'under Turkish occupation, the Acropolis became a Turkish village and suffered untold damage' (ibid.: 22). The narrative of national ownership seems not to be constructed in the claims of damages of the Acropolis, many of which indeed happened in this period, but in the suggestion that by becoming a Turkish village the Acropolis suffered 'untold damage'. An interpretation which would add to the actual physical damages to the Acropolis during this period might be that the very sacredness of the Acropolis to the Greeks was seen as being damaged, violated and defiled by it being inhabited.

The fourth guidebook, written by a historian and a former British Ambassador to Athens and titled *Athens: A Cultural and Literary History* (Smith 2004) is an in-depth historical and cultural guidebook with elements of ethnographic style accounts about Athens and its people. Although this guidebook includes even the lesser known histories of both Athens and the Acropolis, the World Heritage site status of the Acropolis is not mentioned. Instead, the Acropolis is represented as: 1) the reason why Athens was chosen as the capital of Modern Greece; 2) the cultural capital of the nation; and 3) a sacred place for the Greeks, an integral part of Greek national identity and, at the same time, a popular tourist attraction. As Smith himself writes:

Athens was chosen as capital of the Greek state, although some thought it should not have been, because of this glorious past, symbolized by the Acropolis and its monuments.

(Smith 2004: 5)

The Acropolis and the Parthenon were rightly seen then as a symbolic capital of the new nation. They represented in stone the direct link between ancient and modern Greece, integral to the identity and "presence" of the new nation state.

(Smith 2004: 50)

By the end of the nineteenth century, the Acropolis was much as it is today: an "archaeological carcass stripped to the bone", cleaned down to the bare rock, the marble sculptures and fragments displayed in the Acropolis Museum, the whole site fenced off and guarded as both a sacred place and a tourist attraction.

(Smith 2004: 56)

Again, an interpretation of these texts is likely to be that the Acropolis is very much about a sense of Greekness and a means through which images of Greekness and of the Modern Greek nation state are constructed. The Acropolis is presented as 'integral' to this [Greek national] identity, rather than to any sense of 'universality' of the site, something which its World Heritage site status intends to convey. In addition, the reader is also told that the Acropolis is 'guarded as both a sacred place and a tourist attraction'; one interpretation of this part of the text might also be that the Acropolis is sacred to the Greeks while being, at the same time, an attraction to the non-Greeks/tourists (see also Rakić and Chambers 2007). A reference in the wording 'archaeological carcass stripped to the bone' is also being made both to Lord Elgin and the Parthenon Marbles taken to Britain as well as to the restoration project of the Acropolis in which many of the remains belonging to historical periods other than the classical were removed from the site (e.g. see Hamilakis 2007, among other authors). An additional interpretation of the wording 'archaeological carcass' might also be that the Acropolis is now less an archaeological wonder and more a symbolically charged monument symbolising all things Greek. In other words, it seems that the symbolic resonances of the Acropolis as being about Greek national identity have become slightly more important than its archaeological value.

The fifth guidebook titled *Lonely Planet: Best of Athens – The Ultimate Pocket Guide and Map* (Kyriakopoulos 2004) is very much a typical city guide including, among other topics, routes, restaurants, maps, and places to visit. Surprisingly, Lonely Planet does briefly mention the World Heritage site status of the Acropolis (ibid.: 9), although it seems to be included as yet another accolade of the site, with the significance of the World Heritage title excluded from the text. It is suggested to the reader that the Acropolis should be the very first place to visit in Athens as it is the city's 'crowning jewel' (ibid.: 8). In addition, the Acropolis is represented with a slightly romantic note as the opening text states:

> Even if you live in Athens, the sight of the Acropolis can still make your heart
> skip a beat.
>
> (Kyriakopoulos 2004: 9)

The Lonely Planet's city guidebook (ibid.) also includes a strong narrative of
national ownership of the Acropolis; for example, the caption of a photograph of
the Parthenon does not include the name of the building (i.e. Parthenon) but the
text 'The bits of the Parthenon Lord Elgin couldn't fit in his suitcase' (ibid.: 10).
This caption not only suggests that the Parthenon, and by extension the Acropolis
is seen as belonging to the Greek nation (and thus not to the world), but also
that Lord Elgin took parts of it which weren't rightfully his since those naturally
belonged to Greece.

The sixth guidebook in this analysis, the rather brief *AA Essential: Athens –
All You Need to Know, the Top Places to Go, Where to Shop and Eat Out, and
How to Get About* (Gerrard 2004) includes no mention of the World Heritage site
status of the Acropolis, nor does it make a clear distinction between the different
monuments at the site. It does however suggest that the Acropolis is the top 'must
see' attraction in Athens.

The seventh guidebook, *Time Out: Athens* (Sales 2005) includes a rather
detailed history of the Acropolis, Athens and Greece for such a small volume
guidebook. The Acropolis is presented as the number one place to visit in
Athens, but neither its World Heritage site status nor any references to national or
'universal' ownership and belonging are made throughout the text. However, what
is interesting in this guidebook is that it is the first guidebook in this analysis which
seems to vaguely 'justify' the deeds of Lord Elgin by saying: 'Elgin was not the
first to take treasures from the Acropolis, neither did the rock escape other forms of
vandalism' (Sales 2005: 82). Thus, this guidebook does not emphasise the national
ownership and belonging of the Acropolis, but neither does it make a clear case
for its 'universality'. This guidebook in fact seems to slightly shift the focus on the
Acropolis as a site which is very much related to the sense of Greekness to one in
which the Acropolis is more related to its status as a popular tourist attraction. In
addition, having 'justified' the deeds of Lord Elgin, this guidebook could also be
seen as attempting to slightly decontextualise the Acropolis as the most important
symbol of Greekness.

By contrast, in the eight guidebook *Heritage Walks in Athens* (Carras and
Skoumbourdi 2004) there is a strong emphasis on the Greek ownership of the
Acropolis, which is mainly described as very much a Greek and Athenian sacred
site. For example in the prologue, the then Mayor of the city of Athens, Ms Dora
Bakoyiannis, writes:

> *Our* monuments stand as continuous guardians of memory. It is not only the past
> of Greece but the roots of the Western World and the influence of the East that
> can be found in *our* museums.
>
> (Bakoyannis 2004: 5, italics added)

In this text, there is an explicit reference to *our* (meaning Greek) monuments, which are not only the 'past of Greece but which are also the roots of the Western World and the influence of the East'. An interpretation of this text would be that despite its 'universal dimension', the primary ownership and belonging of these monuments is Greek. Once again, similar to a number of other guidebooks, the Acropolis is represented as a 'must see' heritage site in Athens, while its World Heritage site status is omitted.

The ninth guidebook in this analysis *The Rough Guide to Greece* (Benison et al. 2006) is a guidebook for the whole of Greece. In it, although the Acropolis is once again represented as the number one 'must see' tourist attraction in Athens, and the opening lines of the text about the Acropolis briefly mention that the Acropolis is 'one of the archetypal images of Western culture' (ibid.: 117), there is once again no mention of its World Heritage site status, while significant space is used for the debate over the ownership of the Parthenon or 'Elgin' Marbles which are in the British Museum in London. For example, in the context of the new Acropolis Museum, the reader is told that:

> ... it is hoped, the Parthenon Marbles (those already in the Acropolis Museum, plus the restored Elgin Marbles ...) will finally be reunited in a fitted setting.
>
> (Benison et al. 2006: 147)

This is an explicit reference to the belief that the Acropolis is Greek and therefore the Parthenon or 'Elgin' Marbles which are still in London, should be returned to Greece, where they rightfully belong.

Finally, in the tenth and last guidebook in this analysis, *Lonely Planet: Greece* (Hellender et al. 2006) there is once again a strong reference to the 'rightful' ownership of the Parthenon or 'Elgin' Marbles by Greece. The reader is quite straightforwardly told that:

> The British Museum has continuously rejected calls to return the marbles, which were hacked off the Acropolis by Lord Elgin in 1801.
>
> (Hellender et al. 2006: 108)

Interestingly, the words used to describe the taking of the Parthenon Marbles by Lord Elgin in 1801 are 'hacked off' and the connotation here is that these natural, almost bodily parts of the Parthenon should not have been taken and furthermore that these belong to Greece rather than to the world. In addition to reference being made to the removal of the Parthenon Marbles by Lord Elgin, this text makes a very strong reference to the sense of force employed in this very violent event. As elsewhere, the Acropolis is once again listed as the number one place to visit in Athens and its World Heritage site status, although briefly mentioned in the context of the current restoration project at the Acropolis, is not commented on.

Conclusions

> The tourists ... before even gazing at the Athenian landscape, carry it inside them
> in the form of stereotypical images and myths. ... The Acropolis in particular
> seems to embrace most of the tourist interest and therefore most of the travel
> narrative about Athens.
>
> (Travlou 2002: 116)

Indeed, the Acropolis and its meanings seem to occupy significant amounts of space in the guidebooks included in this analysis. Many of these guidebooks included not only the various narratives about the Acropolis but also its images, both of which enable guidebook readers to imagine the place, even before their visit. The Acropolis was also described as the most important place in Athens.

The key theme of this analysis has been whether the narratives contained in these guidebooks were describing the Acropolis, a popular tourist attraction, as being more about a sense of Greekness or about the sense of 'universality' which its World Heritage site status seeks to convey. A particularly interesting theme to emerge was its attribute of sacredness. In many of the narratives, the Acropolis was essentially represented as sacred to the Greeks and an attraction to the tourists, something which also surfaced in other analyses of tourist materials (e.g. see Rakić and Chambers 2007). Stronger claims of national over 'universal' belonging of the Acropolis were also apparent in many of these guidebooks, regardless of whether those were published in Greece or abroad. Many of these guidebooks also contained the notion that the meanings of the Acropolis were more about its sense of Greekness than about its sense of 'universality', with its World Heritage site status being mentioned only in two[1] of the ten guidebooks. It seems therefore that in these guidebooks the meanings of the Acropolis were primarily marked by its attributes of being a 'Greek' site, a site which was sacred to the Greeks, a visit to which might possibly resemble a pilgrimage. For non-Greeks, the Acropolis was mainly represented as a tourist attraction known throughout the world, which belonged to Greece but which was also a place they were clearly encouraged to visit and admire.

References

Andronicos, M. 1980. *The Acropolis*. Athens: Ekdotike Athenon

Ashworth, G.J. 1997. Is There a World Heritage? *Urban Age*, 4(4), 12.

---

1   Both of these guidebooks were published by Lonely Planet, with one being solely authored by Kyriakopoulos and the other being a co-authored text where Kyriakopoulos was one of the seven authors, indicating an authorial and perhaps also an editorial link between the two publications.

Bakoyannis, D. 2005. Prologue, in *Heritage Walks in Athens*, edited by C. Carras & A. Skoumbourdi. Athens: Municipality of Athens Cultural Organisation, Hellenic Society and Oxy Publications, 5.

Bærenholdt, J.O. and Haldrup, M. 2006. Mobile Networks and Place Making in Cultural Tourism: Staging Viking Ships and Rock Music in Roskilde. *European Urban and Regional Studies*, 13(3), 209–24.

Beck, W. 2006. Narratives of World Heritage in Travel Guidebooks. *International Journal of Heritage Studies*, 12(6), 521–35.

Bendix, R. 2002. Capitalizing on Memories Past, Present, and Future: Observations on the Intertwining of Tourism and Narration. *Anthropological Theory*, 2(4), 469–87.

Benison, A., Chilton, L., Dubin, M., Edwards, N.M.E., Fisher, J., et al. 2006. *The Rough Guide to Greece*. New York, London and Delhi: Rough Guides.

Bhattacharyya, D.P. 1997. Mediating India: An Analysis of a Guidebook. *Annals of Tourism Research*, 24(2), 371–89.

Bruner, E.M. 2005. *The Role of Narrative in Tourism*. Conference paper presented at the On Voyage: New Directions in Tourism Theory Conference, Berkeley, October 7-8. Available at www.nyu.edu/classes/bkg/tourist/narrative.doc [accessed: 10 January 2010].

Buzard, J. 1993. *The Beaten Track: European Tourism, Literature, and the Ways to Culture, 1800–1918*. Oxford: Clarendon Press.

Carras, C. and Skoumbourdi, A. (eds) 2004. *Heritage Walks in Athens*. Athens: Municipality of Athens Cultural Organisation, Hellenic Society and Oxy Publications.

Casey, E.S. 1977. *The Fate of Place: A Philosophical History*. Berkley: University of California Press.

Cresswell, T. 2004. *Place: A Short Introduction*. Oxford: Blackwell.

Elsrud, T. 2001. Risk Creation When Travelling: Backpacker Adventure Narration. *Annals of Tourism Research*, 28(3), 591–617.

Fei, S. 2010. Ways of Looking: the Creation and Social Use of Urban Guidebooks in Sixteenth- and Seventeenth-century China. *Urban History*, 37(2), 226–48.

Gerrard, M. 2004. *AA Essential: Athens – All You Need to Know, the Top Places to Go, Where to Shop and Eat Out, and How to Get About*. Whitchurch: AA Publishing.

Gilbert, D. 1999. 'London in All its Glory-or How to Enjoy London': Guidebook Representations of Imperial London. *Journal of Historical Geography*, 25(3), 279–97.

Hamilakis, Y. 2007. *The Nation and its Ruins: Antiquity, Archaeology, and National Imagination in Greece*. Oxford: Oxford University Press.

Hellender, P., Armstrong, K., Hannigan, D., Kyriakopoulos, V., Raphael, M. and Stone, A. 2006. *Lonely Planet: Greece*. London: Lonely Planet Publications.

Koshar, R. 2000. *German Travel Cultures*. Oxford and New York: Berg.

Koshar, R. (1998). 'What Ought to Be Seen': Tourists' Guidebooks and National Identities in Modern Germany and Europe. *Journal of Contemporary History*, 33(3), 323–40.

Kyriakopoulos, V. 2004. *Lonely Planet: Best of Athens – The Ultimate Pocket Guide and Map London*: Lonely Planet.

Laderman, S. 2002. Shaping Memory of the Past: Discourse in Travel Guidebooks for Vietnam. *Mass Communication & Society*, 5(1), 87–110.

Lew, A.A. 1991. Place Representation in Tourist Guidebooks: An Example from Singapore. *Singapore Journal of Tropical Geography*, 12(2), 124–37.

Mavromataki, M. 1995. *Athens: Between Legend and History*. Athens: Haitalis.

McGregor, A. 2000. Dynamic Texts and Tourist Gaze: Death, Bones and Buffalo. *Annals of Tourism Research*, 27(1), 27–50.

Nishimura, S., King, B. and Waryszak, R. 2007. The Use of Travel Guidebooks by Packaged and Non-packaged Japanese Travellers: A Comparative Study. *Journal of Vacation Marketing*, 13(4), 291–310.

Nishimura, S., Waryszak, R. and King, B. 2006. Guidebook Use by Japanese Tourists: a Qualitative Study of Australia Inbound Travellers. *International Journal of Tourism Research*, 8(1), 13–26.

Noy, C. 2004a. Performing Identity: Touristic Narratives of Self-Change. *Text and Performance Quarterly*, 24(2), 115–38.

Noy, C. 2004b. This Trip Really Changed Me: Backpackers' Narratives of Self-Change, *Annals of Tourism Research*, 31(1), 78–102.

Osti, L., Lindsay, W. and King, B. 2009. Cultural Differences in Travel Guidebooks Information Search. *Journal of Vacation Marketing*, 15(1), 63–78.

Parsons, N.T. 2007. *Worth the Detour: A History of the Guidebook*. London: The History Press.

Pritchard, A. and Morgan, M. 2003. Mythic Geographies of Representation and Identity: Contemporary Postcards of Wales. *Journal of Tourism and Cultural Change*, 1(2), 111–30.

Raento, P. 2009. Tourism, Nation and the Postage Stamp. *Annals of Tourism Research*, 36(1), 124–48.

Rakić, T. 2008. *World Heritage, Tourism and National Identity: A Case Study of the Acropolis in Athens, Greece*. PhD Thesis. Edinburgh: Edinburgh Napier University.

Rakić, T. and Chambers, D. 2007. World Heritage: Exploring the Tension Between the National and the 'Universal'. *Journal of Heritage Tourism*, 2(3), 145–55.

Rakić, T. and Travlou, P. forthcoming. Constructing and Conveying a Sense of Place: the Athenian Acropolis in Postcards, in *Tourism and Postcards,* edited by J. Ploner and M. Robinson. Clevedon: Channel View Publications.

Relf, E. 1976. *Place and Placelessness*. London: Pion Limited.

Robertson, G., Mash, M., Tickner, L., Bird, J., Curtis, B. and Putnam, T. (eds) 1994. *Traveller's Tales: Narratives of Home and Displacement*. London: Routledge.

Sales, R. 2005. *TimeOut: Athens*. London: Time Out Guides.

Siegenthaler, P. 2002. Hiroshima and Nagasaki in Japanese Guidebooks. *Annals of Tourism Research*, 29(4), 1111–37.

Smith, M.L. 2004. *Athens: A Cultural and Literary History*. Oxford: Signal.

Stokowski, P.A. 2002. Languages of Place and Discourses of Power: Constructing New Senses of Place. *Journal of Leisure Research*, 34(4), 368–89.

Travlou, P. 2002. Go Athens: A Journey to the Centre of the City, in *Tourism: Between Place and Performance,* edited by S. Coleman and M. Crang. Oxford: Berghahn Books, 108–27.

UNESCO. 2011. *World Heritage*. Available at: http://whc.unesco.org/en/about/ [accessed: 06 May 2011].

UNESCO. 2006. *World Heritage List: Acropolis*. Available at: http://whc.unesco. org/en/list/404/ [accessed: 9 February 2006].

Vingopoulou, I., and Casulli, M. 2005. *Athens: Art and History*. Florence: Bonechi Publications.

Index